## WATER HISTORIES AND SPATIAL ARCHAEOLOGY

This book offers a new interpretation of the spatial–political–environmental dynamics of water and irrigation in long-term histories of arid regions. It compares ancient Southwest Arabia (3500 BC–AD 600) with the American West (2000 BC–AD 1950) in global context to illustrate similarities and differences among environmental, cultural, political, and religious dynamics of water. It combines archaeological exploration and field studies of farming in Yemen with social theory and spatial technologies, including satellite imagery, Global Positioning System (GPS), and Geographic Information Systems (GIS) mapping. In both ancient Yemen and the American West, agricultural production focused not where rain-fed agriculture was possible, but in hyper-arid areas where massive state-constructed irrigation schemes politically and ideologically validated state sovereignty. While shaped by profound differences and contingencies, ancient Yemen and the American West are mutually informative in clarifying human geographies of water that are important to understandings of America, Arabia, and contemporary conflicts between civilizations deemed East and West.

Michael J. Harrower is Assistant Professor of Archaeology in the Department of Near Eastern Studies, Johns Hopkins University and has over fifteen years of archaeological experience exploring the remote desert-highlands of Ethiopia, Jordan, Yemen, and Oman. He is a leading expert in spatial technologies, and is co-editor, with Douglas C. Comer, of *Mapping Archaeological Landscapes from Space* (2013).

# Water Histories and Spatial Archaeology

## Ancient Yemen and the American West

**MICHAEL J. HARROWER**

Johns Hopkins University

# CAMBRIDGE
UNIVERSITY PRESS

32 Avenue of the Americas, New York, NY 10013-2473, USA

Cambridge University Press is part of the University of Cambridge.

It furthers the University's mission by disseminating knowledge in the pursuit of education, learning and research at the highest international levels of excellence.

www.cambridge.org
Information on this title: www.cambridge.org/9781107134652

© Michael J. Harrower 2016

This publication is in copyright. Subject to statutory exception and to the provisions of relevant collective licensing agreements, no reproduction of any part may take place without the written permission of Cambridge University Press.

First published 2016

Printed in the United States of America by Sheridan Books, Inc

*A catalog record for this publication is available from the British Library*

*Library of Congress Cataloging in Publication Data*
Names: Harrower, Michael J.
Title: Water histories and spatial archaeology : ancient Yemen and the American West / Michael J. Harrower (Johns Hopkins University).
Description: Cambridge, United Kingdom : Cambridge University Press, 2016. | Includes bibliographical references and index.
Identifiers: LCCN 2015039554 | ISBN 9781107134652 (hardback)
Subjects: LCSH: Irrigation – Yemen (Republic) – History – To 1500. | Irrigation – West (U.S.) – History. | Water-supply – Yemen (Republic) – History – To 1500. | Water-supply – West (U.S.) – History. | Human geography – Yemen (Republic) – History – To 1500. | Human geography – West (U.S.) – History. | Spatial analysis (Statistics) in archaeology | Yemen (Republic) – Antiquities. | West (U.S.) – Antiquities. | East and West – History.
Classification: LCC S616.Y4 H37 2016 | DDC 333.91/309533–dc23
LC record available at http://lccn.loc.gov/2015039554

ISBN 978-1-107-13465-2 Hardback

Cambridge University Press has no responsibility for the persistence or accuracy of URLs for external or third-party internet websites referred to in this publication, and does not guarantee that any content on such websites is, or will remain, accurate or appropriate.

# Contents

| | |
|---|---|
| *List of Plates* | *page* vii |
| *List of Figures and Tables* | viii |
| *Acknowledgments* | ix |

1. Introduction: Comparing water histories of America and Arabia.................................................. 1
    *Water histories and Orientalism* 8
    *Water histories and the archetypes of America and Arabia* 11
    *Geopolitics of East and West: Commonalities and contemporary conflict* 22

2. Comparison and juxtaposition in archaeology: Water, agriculture, and state formation in space and time .............. 29
    *Spatial analysis and spatial theory in studies of water histories* 34
    *Water histories of ancient Yemen: Comparison and juxtaposition in space and time* 38
    *Water, space/time, and the beginnings of agriculture* 41
    *Water, space/time, and the rise of complex polities* 46
    *The future of comparison, juxtaposition, and spatial archaeology* 49

3. Water histories of ancient Yemen in global comparative perspective................................... 51
    *Irrigation, hunting, and gathering* 54
    *Water, irrigation, and pastoralism* 60
    *Water, irrigation, and incipient farming* 64

|     | Irrigation among chiefdoms, kingdoms, and states | 72 |
|---|---|---|
|     | Long-term water histories of ancient Yemen in comparative perspective | 82 |
| 4.  | Water and the beginnings of pastoralism and agriculture in Southwest Arabia.................... | 84 |
|     | The beginnings of Southwest Arabian pastoralism | 86 |
|     | Spatial dimensions of water flow and cattle grazing territories along Wadi Sana | 93 |
|     | The beginnings of Southwest Arabian irrigation | 97 |
|     | Spatial dimensions of water flow and irrigable areas along Wadi Sana | 104 |
|     | Agricultural origins, frontiers, and water in ancient Southwest Arabia | 109 |
| 5.  | Water histories of Southwest Arabian kingdoms (and the American West) ................. | 112 |
|     | The elaboration of agriculture and irrigation in Bronze Age Yemen | 116 |
|     | Intermediate-scale irrigation: A comparative perspective | 120 |
|     | Irrigation and the rise of Iron Age kingdoms | 125 |
|     | Spatial dimensions of water flow and ancient Southwest Arabian kingdoms | 134 |
|     | Irrigation, the Kingdom of Himyar, and the rise of highland power | 144 |
|     | Water, complex polities, and spatial heterogeneity in ancient Southwest Arabia | 150 |
| 6.  | Conclusion: Water histories, comparison, geopolitics, and spatial archaeology................. | 153 |
|     | Water histories, contrastive juxtaposition, and spatial archaeology | 154 |
|     | Water and ancient transitions to agriculture | 156 |
|     | Water and the rise of ancient complex polities | 158 |
|     | Xenophobia, water crises, and the War on Terror | 161 |

| Bibliography | 167 |
|---|---|
| Index | 207 |

# Plates

Color pages follow page 150

   I  Landsat satellite image of ancient irrigation at Ma'rib
  II  Map of the topography, hydrology, and ancient geography of Yemen
 III  GIS Model of ancient grazing areas along Wadi Sana, Hadramawt (Yemen)
 IV  Intermediate-Scale Floodwater (sayl) Irrigation along Wadi Daw'an, Hadramawt (Yemen)

# Figures and Tables

## Figures

| | | |
|---|---|---|
| 1.1 | The Great Dam at Ma'rib | *page* 2 |
| 1.2 | Average annual precipitation across the United States | 5 |
| 1.3 | Average annual precipitation across southern Arabia | 6 |
| 1.4 | The Hoover Dam | 14 |
| 1.5 | Monument of books written about President Abraham Lincoln | 15 |
| 1.6 | The tomb and sanctuary of *Mawla Matar* (Patron of Rain), Hadramawt (Yemen) | 17 |
| 2.1 | Bronze Age tower tomb overlooking Wadi Sana | 40 |
| 3.1 | Middle Wadi Sana irrigable areas | 70 |
| 4.1 | Fasad projectile point discovered along Wadi Sana | 88 |
| 4.2 | Water flow direction and flow accumulation modeling in GIS | 96 |
| 4.3 | Histogram of water flow accumulation for Wadi Sana, Hadramawt (Yemen) | 107 |
| 4.4 | Lane's Balance of water flow and sediment transport | 109 |
| 5.1 | Irrigation canals of Wadi Daw'an, Hadramawt (Yemen), and the ancient Hohokam, near Phoenix, Arizona | 122 |
| 5.2 | Histogram of maximum water flow accumulation within 5-km radius around a selection of major archaeological sites in Yemen | 135 |

## Tables

| | | |
|---|---|---|
| 4.1 | Wadi Sana watershed landform class definitions using for GIS Modeling | 91 |
| 5.1 | Major watersheds of Yemen and associated archaeological sites including ancient state capitals | 136 |

# Acknowledgments

First and foremost, I am greatly indebted to the people of Yemen for their gracious welcome and tremendous hospitality. The current crisis in Yemen is extremely distressing, with millions caught in the crossfire, including many without access to sufficient food and water; one hopes that peace will soon prevail. While this book deals predominantly with ancient rather than contemporary times, one of its central arguments – that the long-standing dichotomous categorization of civilizations into Eastern and Western types conceals underlying commonalities and perpetuates conflict – is among the most basic conceptual shifts in thinking about histories necessary to shape a more peaceful future.

I am grateful to a great many individuals and institutions that have contributed to research and writing of this book. Joy McCorriston, E.A. (Rick) Oches, and Abdalaziz Bin 'Aqil played a critical role as directors of the Roots of Agriculture in Southern Arabia (RASA) Research Project, which afforded my first fieldwork opportunities in Yemen. Numerous colleagues helped propel my interests in Yemen, including most notably Tony Wilkinson who inspired innumerable young scholars. I am thankful to Ron Blom, Rémy Crassard, Tara Steimer-Herbet, Catherine Heyne, Julien Charbonnier and Paul Zimmerman. The Republic of Yemen, General Organization of Antiquities and Museums (GOAM), Al-Mukulla Museum in Hadramawt Government and associates Ietha Al-Amary, Khalid Badhofary, Abdelbaset Noman, The American Institute of Yemeni Studies (AIYS) including former Resident Director Chris Edens, and Canadian Occidental Petroleum (later Nexen Inc.) were similarly critical in making fieldwork in Yemen possible. Funding contributions have included support from the Social Sciences and Humanities Research Council of Canada (SSHRC) and the U.S. National Science Foundation (NSF). The Ohio

State University, University of Michigan, University of Toronto, University of California – Los Angeles, and Johns Hopkins University also played a pivotal role in hosting me at various times over the past decade.

Following fieldwork, the foundational idea of comparing ancient Yemen and the American West in this book first germinated in 2006 after a lecture I gave at the University of Nevada, Las Vegas that prompted discussion of similarities between these very different histories. A number of invited lectures similarly provoked discussions that improved this book, including at UCLA, American Schools of Oriental Research, the Deutsches Archäologisches Institut (Berlin), International Water History Association Conference (Delft), and University of California, Berkeley. For an extremely wide range of encouragement and support over the years I have many people to thank, including Joy McCorriston and Clark Spencer Larsen at the Ohio State University; Catherine D'Andrea at Simon Fraser University; Norman Yoffee, Henry Wright, Joyce Marcus, and Kent Flannery at the University of Michigan; E.B. (Ted) Banning and Michael Chazan at the University of Toronto; Ian Kuijt at University of Notre Dame; Elizabeth Carter, Aaron Burke, Willeke Wendrich, John Papadopoulos, Sarah Morris, Monica Smith, Charles Stanish, and William Schniedewind at University of California, Los Angeles (UCLA); and Benjamin Porter and Lisa Maher at UC Berkeley. A number of people spent considerable time reading and commenting on parts or the entire book, including Joy McCorriston, Alan Shapiro, Marian Feldman, Peter Magee, Glenn Schwartz, and Vernon Scarborough.

I am very grateful to my colleagues in the Department of Near Eastern Studies at Johns Hopkins University for their professionalism and collegiality. Many of the colleagues and students who are involved with my current fieldwork in Oman and Ethiopia also deserve thanks for their hard work, support, and flexibility that made space for this book, including Cinzia Perlingieri, Katie O'Meara, Benjamin Zaitchik, Martha Anderson, Ioana Dumitru, Jacob Bongers, Smiti Nathan, Frances Wiig, Jennifer Swerida, Wolfgang Alders, Helina Woldekiros, Joseph Mazzariello, and Laurel Poolman.

Finally, my heartfelt thanks to my parents Mervin and Dorothy Harrower, my brother William Harrower, and my fiancée Nicole Feldhan – I truly could not have done it without you.

CHAPTER 1

# Introduction

Comparing water histories of America and Arabia

> *You visit the earth and water it, you greatly enrich it; the river of God is full of water; you provide their grain, for so you have prepared it.*
> (Bible – New Revised Standard Version Psalm 65:9)

> *There was for Saba' in their dwelling place a sign: two gardens one on the right and one on the left. They were told, eat from the provisions of your Lord and be grateful to him. A good land you have and a forgiving Lord. But they turned away refusing, so God sent upon them the flood of the dam, and replaced their two gardens with fields of bitter fruit, tamarisks, and sparse lote trees.*
> (Quran – Surah Saba 34:15–16)

For thousands of years in many different contexts worldwide, people have sought to control and have been subject to the unpredictabilities of water. While the contexts of water histories around the world widely differ, many of the key elements – climate, environment, culture, politics, religion – are arguably very similar, yet are interconnected and expressed in very different ways. Amidst the long mundane rhythm of everyday human struggles to capture and control water, great achievements and terrible catastrophes often demarcate histories. The year 2013 marked the 100-year anniversary of the Los Angeles-Owens Valley aqueduct that drained and largely desiccated a landscape to supply what would become one of the world's largest cities. In 1928, fifteen years after the creation of the aqueduct, the collapse of the St. Francis Dam just north of Los Angeles – one of the worst disasters in American history – sent a 200-ft wall of water rushing down Santa Clarita Valley that killed as many as 600 people. This terrible catastrophe, which followed on Manifest Destiny, rapid colonization, and watering of the American West, is not as different as it might seem from the calamity described above in the Holy Quran. The collapse and final abandonment

# Introduction

FIGURE 1.1. The Great Dam at Ma'rib. This massive waterwork was constructed and reconstructed over more than 1,300 years. It spanned more than 600 m between bedrock outcrops and stood approximately 19 m high. Rather than impounding water, the north sluice (shown left, as recently reconstructed by a German team) and south sluice (shown right) at the dam's extremities diverted water into an extensive series of primary, secondary, and tertiary canals that irrigated as much as 9,600 hectares (photos by the author).

of the Great Dam at Ma'rib in Yemen (Figure 1.1 and Plate I) ca. AD 575 after more than 1,300 years of construction and reconstruction was similarly a pivotal turning point in the history of Arabia linked to the rise of Islam. In both cases, these important junctures are interspersed throughout long histories of human toil and struggles to harness water, which illustrate some of the central commonalities and contrasts among human societies of past and present.

Water and its histories reveal deep similarities and pivotal differences among human societies that are critical to understanding the human past and our future. Environments are often defined by water availability and periodicity; water is a frequent theme of religious traditions and a common point of politics. Anthropology has long been marked by a dichotomous tension between interests in commonalities among human cultures on the one hand, alongside emphasis on human cultures as unique, contingent, and exceptional on the other. Concordantly, this book examines the role of water and irrigation in long-term ancient histories of Southwest Arabia (3500 BC–AD 600) contrastively juxtaposed against other unique contexts worldwide, most prominently the American West (2000 BC–AD 1950). These two cases are strikingly different culturally and historically

# Introduction

and span dramatically different time scales. Rather than building an analogy that aims solely to demonstrate likeness and similarity between two very different spans of history, the following chapters contrast and juxtapose these extremely different cases to illustrate how they are unique in similar ways, and reveal some of the essential characteristics of water histories. Arabs and Arabia have long served as a central anthropological archetype of nomadic and tribal societies, whereas American frontier settlers and the American West have similar longevity as a historical stereotype of the mythical West and Western civilization. The natural and political importance of water is of well-known, deeply embedded significance in the history of the American West both in ancient and more recent times. In contrast, the ancient history of Yemen, including the important role of water, is far less widely documented. While shaped by profound differences and contingencies, these cases are mutually informative in exhibiting environmental, cultural, political, and ideological factors that are expressed, weighted, and interconnected through space and time in different ways.

There are a number of key reasons the unconventional juxtaposition of America and Arabia in this book is not only warranted but is necessary and effective (also further explored in Chapter 2). Scholars have long sought to explain factors responsible for the rise and fall of civilizations; however, with a dramatically expanding wealth of data available for regions worldwide, global comparisons are challenging as they often overlook critical historical and cultural particularities and contingencies. Amidst a wide range of approaches, from particularistic to universally comparative, studies that contrast two or a few histories or cultures have proved to be highly revealing (e.g. Adams 1966; Earle 1997; Geertz 1972; Sahlins 2004), and, I argue, have a critically important and expansive scholarly future. Histories of the American West (including as related to water) are some of the best documented and most studied histories of the world; they are widely known (albeit often mischaracterized) via American popular culture, and offer a powerful lens through which to view the role of water in other contexts (e.g. Hundley 2001, 2009; Kahrl 1983; Reisner 1986; Worster 1979, 1985; White 1995). Since ancient Yemen (3500 BC–AD 600) and the American West (2000 BC–AD 1950) are two intervals almost as outwardly culturally and historically different as any cases one could select, commonalities between these histories are well suited to reveal deep underlying patterns characterizing other histories worldwide. Finally, and perhaps most importantly, in a contemporary era of profound turmoil and concern focused on the Middle East, we confront what many troublingly portray as a clash of Western (Occidental) and Eastern (Oriental) civilizations, and Americans' and Arabs' vast misunderstandings of each other's histories and cultures contribute to conflict worldwide (Barber 1995; Johnsen 2013; Morris 2010, 2014; Pagden 2009). We arguably have far more in common than we realize and overestimate differences that are in part the result of explanations of the past that divide the world into East–West factions contributing to conflicting visions of the present and the future. While widely differing, antithetical views of recent histories of the Middle East are difficult to overcome, the ancient past offers powerful means to build shared interests and understandings that resist and counteract East–West framing and serve as a powerful foundation for dialogue, diplomacy, and peacemaking (Luke and Kersel 2012).

This book's core arguments focus on spatial analysis, spatial theory, and spatial politics of water resources. Throughout the southwestern corner of the Arabian Peninsula – what is today the Republic of Yemen – water figured prominently in the lives of the earliest human migrants to the region and retained deep importance through the rise of pastoralism, agriculture, and ancient states (Plate II). As in the American West, water's significance in such an arid region is difficult to overlook, yet details of Yemen's water histories and their wide scholarly relevance are scantly appreciated beyond the comparatively few archaeologists with experience in the region. In addition to water's wide thematic importance in Near Eastern archaeology and, ancient physical and human geographies analyzed in this book are employed to convey deeper cross-cultural understanding of water histories and societal dynamics worldwide. In terms of the beginnings of agriculture, I critique origins and spread "frontier" conceptions and related primary/secondary designations that have dominated archaeology for more than fifty years (Sauer 1952; Vavilov 1951). I contend that greater attention to the spatial role of water is needed to better understand early agricultural societies, and that spatial heterogeneity of water resources alongside perceptions, anxieties, and politicized narratives of water scarcity are often central to the ways complex polities in arid regions rationalize, justify, and perpetuate their influence through water control and major waterworks.

A wealth of evidence and methods analyzed in this book helps illustrate ancient Yemen's water histories, and their relevance worldwide. Empirical spatial analysis, social theory, epigraphy, ethnography, historical narrative explanation, and multiscalar landscape history offer insights on the sociopolitical dynamics of water in Yemen. Paleoclimatology, hydrology, geomorphology, geospatial science, and perhaps most centrally archaeological survey and excavation illuminate the environmental contexts of water politics. Contrastive juxtaposition, that is, pairwise comparison of cases to reveal

# Introduction

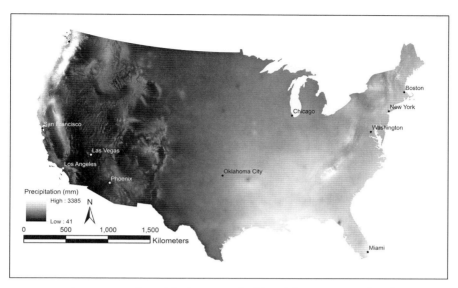

FIGURE 1.2. Average annual precipitation across the United States. Image is based on WorldClim data (Hijmans et al. 2005). The western half of the country receives far less precipitation, which makes rainfed agriculture precarious in many areas (image by the author).

similarities and differences, highlights how environmental and political dynamics of ancient Yemen and the American West, while outwardly very different, exhibit foundational commonalities. The physical geography of the eastern United States (Figure 1.2) is marked by considerable continuity in undulating topography and continental climates with hot, humid summers and cold winters, dense vegetation, and abundant rain and snowfall. Yet the same is not true of the western United States, which is far more arid, inhospitable and diverse with high mountain ranges, rugged topography, profound climatic differences, arid deserts, dense forests, and palimpsest of summer and winter timed precipitation. The American West is also home to great watercourses, such as the Columbia, Missouri, Rio Grande, and Colorado Rivers, as well as vast drylands, including the Mojave, Sonoran, Great Basin, and Chihuahua Deserts, which contributes to pronounced geographic diversity and spatial heterogeneity. Wide diversity and spatial heterogeneity is also true of Yemen (Figure 1.3), which is characterized by rugged terrain up to 3,652 meters that includes the highest rainfall areas of the Arabian Peninsula (which receive as much as 800 mm of annual precipitation) flanked by hyper-arid sandy deserts that are fed by massive flash floods from enormous highland watersheds. In light of these varied

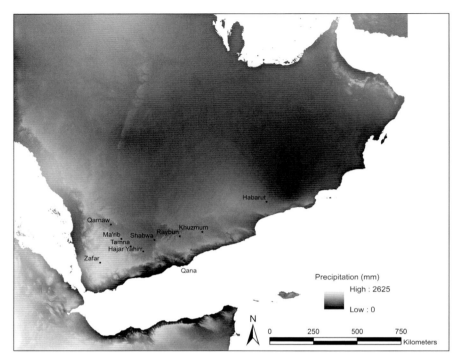

FIGURE 1.3. Average annual precipitation across southern Arabia. Image is based on WorldClim data (Hijmans et al. 2005). The highlands of Southwest Arabia in some places receive as much as 800 mm of precipitation per annum facilitating rainfed agriculture, yet lower elevation areas require supplementary water (image by the author).

American and Arabian topographies, Chapter 2 examines the past and future of comparative methods in anthropological archaeology. Attention and critique concentrates on traditional conceptions and explanations for the beginnings of agriculture and the emergence of the world's earliest states, with a particular focus on spatial patterning of water. Chapter 3 then goes on to juxtapose water histories of ancient Yemen and the American West set within a global comparative context of ancient hunting-gathering, pastoralism, crop cultivation, and small- and large-scale irrigation. In conjunction with acknowledgment of incalculable global diversity, characteristics shared among widely disparate cases are seen as particularly revealing.

When viewed through the lens of water histories, key transformations in Southwest Arabia including the beginnings of agriculture (Chapter 4) and the rise and decline of ancient states in Yemen (Chapter 5) are substantially clarified and unraveled. Domesticated animals appear as early as the sixth

# Introduction

millennium BC, followed by crops and irrigation by the mid-fourth millennium BC. Archaeologists have long framed the appearance of the earliest plant and animal rearing societies as the origins (invention) and spread (adoption) of rainfed farming, to which irrigation and pastoralism were later added. Recent investigations illustrate a far more complex picture in which crop cultivation and animal herding were closely tied to water-rich areas; and rather than simply receiving domesticates from elsewhere, new lifeways were reconfigured and reinvented to suit very different environmental and social contexts. As irrigation systems in Yemen developed through time over subsequent millennia, food production practices increased in scale and technological complexity and became increasingly interconnected socially, politically, and ideologically with natural water availabilities and conceptions of shortage and abundance. Near the end of the second millennium BC, roughly 2,000 years of experience with irrigation propelled the rise of five powerful kingdoms, Ma'in, Saba, Qatabān, Awsan, and Hadramawt, around the margins of Yemen's Ramlat as-Sab'atayn Desert interior – the lowest rainfall portion of the region. In a groundbreaking study published twenty-five years ago, Brunner and Haefner (1990) used German MOMS (Modular Optoelectronic Multispectral Scanner) satellite imagery to map 26,000 hectares of ancient irrigation and postulated a total of 44,500 hectares of once irrigated oases along Yemen's inland desert that would have supported roughly 200,000 people. These ancient kingdoms and their achievements in water control are impressive by any archaeological standard; however, their histories are scantly known beyond a relatively small cohort of archaeologists who specialize on the region, and the factors responsible for their rise and decline remain obscure and controversial. Beyond desert oases, smaller-scale terrace agriculture and runoff cultivation also sustained many people in highland areas as they do today, but the earliest, most powerful cities quite surprisingly emerged in Yemen's driest areas. Rather than states developing because of the unavoidable need for massive irrigation works, I argue it was not only the environmental obstacle of water scarcity per se but social construction of the perceived environmental necessity and its solution (large-scale water control) that promoted large, complex, self-perpetuating aggregations of people. It was not the need for centrally managed large-scale irrigation (which in neither the American West nor ancient Yemen was unavoidably necessary) that propelled the rise of complex polities, but rather the spatial heterogeneity of water (comparative abundance in some areas and comparative scarcity in others) that polities used to dominate agricultural production, guide the flow of commerce, and perpetuate their influence.

Agency is most seminally recognized in individuals (Giddens 1984) and more recently in objects (Feldman 2010), yet I argue polities also take on a proactive, self-perpetuating character as collections of environmental, economic, technological, political, and ideological rhetoric and logic. Water is just one of the variables often implicated in trajectories of history that enables and propagates differential power. In both the American West and ancient Yemen, agricultural production focused not in areas where rainfed agriculture was possible, but in hyper-arid areas where attention focused on geographies of water scarcity and the need to colonize water-scarce areas rationalized massive state-constructed irrigation schemes that helped generate state identities, religiosities, and sovereignties. Contrastive juxtaposition of these distinct histories helps illustrate the societal dynamics of water and how a combination of scientific and humanistic research techniques are best suited to generate deeper, nuanced understanding of histories that are superficially incomparable yet share foundational commonalities.

## Water histories and Orientalism

Portrayals of the Oriental East by scholars of the Occidental West have a long and contentious history; yet enduring critique of Western bias and prejudice has unintentionally come to reiterate a highly problematic, binary East–West dichotomy. An indisputable turning point in the study of the Middle East, Edward Said's (1978) *Orientalism* stridently challenged Western scholarship on the East and revealed wide ranging improprieties from pompous ethnocentrism to self-serving racism. Said's seminal commentary exposed deep subjectivities of research and literature that long served to bolster and sustain British, French, American, and other colonialist and neocolonialist designs for the Middle East. The transformative value of *Orientalism* and Said's subsequent work is undoubtedly extraordinary. Yet, as Daniel Varisco (2007: 291) remarked in his lengthy and judicious review of Said's famous book and its consequences, "*Orientalism* is frequently praised for exposing skeletons in the scholarly closet, but the book itself provides no blueprint for how to proceed." Said's analysis centers on critique rather than outlining means to more appropriately or affirmatively investigate histories of the region. His work and its scholarly descendants challenge a wide swath of scholarship and literature as unduly essentializing; as eloquently extended, for example, in Said's (1993) *Culture and Imperialism*. Yet in emphasizing the creation and reification of stereotypes of the East, Orientalism as denunciation overlooks similarly disparaging caricatures the Occidental West spewed against its own impoverished and unseemly populations within the West (Makdisi 2014); and Orientalism often neglects opportunities to explore what might be shared or amicable among seemingly antipodal East–West histories and cultures, which are depicted in perpetual conflict (Turner 1994). In essence, Orientalism's condemnation so thoroughly and so successfully eviscerates Western scholarship on the East that it incapacitates and renders inept any analysis that disavows the diametric power geographies of East and West, and the polemic established comes to reiterate and reproduce the very East–West dichotomy Said set out to expose as so deeply misguided and flawed (Varisco 2007: 290–305).

What is it to be Western? What are Western History, Western Civilization, the Western Hemisphere, and the American West? Are these cultures and histories truly categorically different than those deemed Oriental and Eastern? Is the essence of Western ultimately to be found exclusively in Greek and Roman classical civilizations and their descendants in Europe? Pop-culture images and Hollywood stereotypes of the American West more recently borrow and re-create ideals of heroic, triumphalist Western culture. Interestingly, arguments that seek to define a Western type perpetuate its antithesis – a category or type of non-Western perspective. The colonized and the colonizers become inescapably interlocked with views of one relying on views of the other. Continuing efforts to evade reifying archetypes of the East by pointing out bias of the West have come to rely on the notion that there must be some sort of non-Western perspective that departs from Western bias and thus falls victim to the same misconceptions that Said sought to undermine. As Stockhammer (2012) argued, Bhabha's (1994) postcolonial conceptualization of hybridity problematically implies that somewhere we can find cultures that are less hybrid, less adulterated, and more authentically or typically pure. It would seem that we know, or we think we know, what Western is and means so that analysis that eschews the opposition of East and West is seen as misinformed and misguided. Yet misrepresentations of Eastern Others accordingly rely on a vainglorious superficial foundation of archetypical Western histories that are so well rehearsed and choreographed that they obscure recognition of commonalities and differences. Even more problematically, Eastern and Western archetypes impair our ability to envision shared interests and futures that in light of current violence, turmoil, and concern focused on the Middle East are increasingly essential, including with respect to water (Moore 2011). If we aim to confront and avoid bias, then one important means to do so is by more thoroughly considering the similarities and differences between what are seemingly diametrically opposed Eastern and Western geographies.

One of the most influential early scholars in the study of water and ancient civilizations, Karl Wittfogel's writings on ancient waterworks exemplify the highly problematic distinction scholars often draw between Western and Eastern societies. Drawing on Marx's Asiatic mode of production, Wittfogel (1957) claimed that the organizational requirements of large-scale irrigation led to the world's earliest states and a form of governance he called Oriental Despotism. While many of his central assertions have been discredited on a variety of grounds, his work has dominated studies of ancient irrigation for more than half a century. Many (myself included) have still felt compelled to further repudiate Wittfogel's model (e.g. Adams 2006; Harrower 2009; Wilkinson and Rayne 2010) in part because it has yet to be replaced by a widely acknowledged alternative and therefore continues to play a major role in structuring scholars thinking about water and complex polities. Surprisingly, Wittfogel's theory has even been revived in attempts to explain water histories of the nineteenth- and early-twentieth-century American West (Worster 1985), in direct contradiction to his central premise about categorical differences between Western and Oriental societies. Nevertheless, Wittfogel (1957) and the preeminent anthropologist Julian Steward (1930, 1949) were instrumental in recognizing the importance of water control among early states. While Steward simply considered irrigation a potential cross-cultural parallel worthy of further investigation, Wittfogel forcefully proposed a deterministic explanation. Wittfogel eventually deemphasized the distinction between Western and Eastern types and began referring to "Hydraulic" rather than "Oriental" societies, but he retained the unicausal basics of his model – that the need for large-scale waterworks was the primary cause behind the rise of the world's earliest civilizations (Wittfogel 1972). One of his central assertions – that large-scale irrigation invariably *requires* centralized bureaucratic coordination – has been thoroughly invalidated (Mabry 2000), yet Wittfogel unfortunately remains a recurrent distraction in studies of irrigation as analysts continually feel obliged to renounce his explanation for the origins of civilizations (e.g. Adams 1981: 243–244, 2006; Butzer 1976, 1996; Hunt 2007: 105–128; Wilkinson and Rayne 2010). Ultimately, a more sophisticated, accurate, and nuanced theory of irrigation's role is required, but most studies have focused on particular historical cases, and those with a cross-cultural focus have yet to achieve widespread affirmation. Given the rapidly expanding and overwhelming wealth of information on water-use among ancient civilizations worldwide (e.g. Marcus and Stanish 2006; Mithen 2012; Scarborough 2003) and the importance of cultural particularities and historical contingencies (e.g. Kirch 1995; Lansing 2006), comparison of two or a few cases (rather than global synthesis) is arguably a highly revealing mode of analysis (e.g. Adams 1966; Wilkinson 2014). Using contrastive juxtaposition of ancient Yemen and the American West to illustrate its counterpoint to the hydraulic hypothesis, this book offers an alternative interpretation of water's influences among civilizations of arid regions. I argue that nascent complex societies exploited spatial heterogeneity of water and, through political rhetoric and social logic related to anxieties about scarcity, complex polities often came to rationalize state authority over highly concentrated agricultural production in ways that perpetuated state sovereignty.

## Water histories and the archetypes of America and Arabia

The role of water and irrigation in American and Arabian histories and cultures is marked by both wide differences and foundational commonalities; neither are they entirely different nor essentially the same. Both the prevailing assumption that outward differences make such histories wholly distinct and idiosyncratic, and conversely the notion they could be informatively assigned to, and explained as, discrete types of societies are both deeply flawed. Instead, effectively revealing similarities and differences of American and Arabian water histories requires deconstructing and defamiliarizing the generalizing portrayals and persistent archetypes that structure not only our understandings of those we view as others but just as importantly understandings of ourselves and our own diverse backgrounds. Societies when viewed as sustained by economic, technological, political, and ideological logic perpetuate themselves often without prescient leadership. Polities are not only structure and habitus to be replicated, but are comprised of constantly shifting canonical narratives that persuade people to understand themselves through interpretations of histories alongside anxieties about potential crises and opportunities of the future.

I am myself a product of Western histories albeit of the Canadian rather than the American West. My family arrived in Canada from England, Scotland and Poland during the nineteenth and early twentieth centuries and both my mother's and father's families moved west to Saskatchewan to homestead. On my mother's side my great grandfather Albert Hill was trained as a meat cutter in Devonshire, England and came in 1910 to join his two older brothers William and Richard on their homesteads near Imperial, Saskatchewan. With quarter section (160 acre) homesteads side-by-side the two brothers built one small shack straddling the property line to fulfill the requirement of living on, farming, and "proving up" their claims. Some of the most productive land that my family farmed, and still farms, lies on either side of Bulrush Lake – a shallow variably expanding and contracting body of water about 3 km long and 1 km wide flanked by marshes. As a boy I remember that some of the tallest wheat, standing nearly as high as I was, often grew along Bulrush Lake. My family, like farmers in the Middle East many thousands of years ago, recognized these seasonally inundated areas as highly fertile and productive. Histories of the Canadian West substantially differ of course from those of the American West. Yet being Canadian, I find, is a lot like having an older brother, one is often vividly witness to the differing views and identities of siblings.

The American frontier settler and Arabian camel-rearing nomad, whether cast as heroes or villains, persistently shape our understandings of histories and the contemporary world. These popular motifs are reiterated so often as to become nearly axiomatic representations that are deeply tied to and often illustrated through relations with water. The American Dream is a western dream; stereotypically noble, pioneering American settlers forging across the West in covered wagons as entrepreneurial yeoman homesteaders to populate a land supposedly devoid of civilization (Limerick 1987). Freedom, individuality, ingenuity, hard-work, piety with an adamant commitment to vigilante, frontier justice often demarcate the American West. The calls of government, railroads, profiteers, and newspapermen fueled the ambitions and migrations of prospective farmers playing on their hopes of owning a prosperous spread of land. In the throws and aftermath of the Civil War, of slavery, of the Indian Wars, American collective identity and sovereignty were built, in part, through the refrain of Manifest Destiny and aspirations to conquer the vast opportunities of the West. Correspondingly, the Arabian desert nomad is archetypally resourceful, self-reliant, honorable, pious, courageous, perfectly adapted and predisposed to hospitality across inhospitably harsh, desiccated terrain. Prayer, poetry, tribal and religious genealogies (Ho 2006), the long-term metastructural continuity of pilgrimage, gathering, sacrifice, and feasting bound together widely dispersed peoples of otherwise widely differing backgrounds (McCorriston 2011). In both America and Arabia, collective identities and societal rationale were generated through explanations of the past and rationalizations of the future; women, minorities, and slaves were frequently sidelined in narratives that centered on heroic male prototypes.

These archetypical histories, while they might superficially appear to be a product solely of media and popular culture, emanate from a multitude of sources including religious, scholarly, and commercial representations.

# Water histories and the archetypes of America and Arabia

As Richard White (1994) revealingly examined, two very contrasting figures of the 1890s – the distinguished historian Fredrick Jackson Turner and the famous showman "Buffalo Bill" Cody – both presented the western frontier as emblematic of American history. The former portrayed the West as an opening and closing window of opportunity to populate a purportedly empty land, while the latter reenacted adventure and violent conflict in a land that clearly was not empty. A wide range of late nineteenth century American literature simultaneously energized "boomers" the fortune seekers who fled eastern cities to claim homesteads in Oklahoma and across the West, as well as "sooners" the claim-jumpers who would often illicitly usurp law-abiding homesteaders' claims (Emmons 1971). Narratives advocating homesteading were frequently reinforced through a combination of religious and economic arguments, including supposed biblical dominion of man over nature, Manifest Destiny, the protestant work ethic, and the simple profit motive. While historians have more recently recognized Turner's frontier thesis as a substantially overwrought interpretation of western history (Limerick 1987), American heroes *are* almost invariably and quintessentially western frontier heroes; and even across the American East, George Washington and Andrew Jackson were known as pioneering frontiersmen, Meriwether Lewis and William Clark as renowned explorers, and Davy Crockett a legendary heroic woodsman.

American cinema similarly plays a major role in generating and aligning American identities with western frontier histories including in relation to water. An unmistakably influential genre, early Hollywood western movies frequently deal with water, including the anxieties associated with wealthy landholders monopolizing water across the arid West. The early western film *Riders of Destiny* (1933), starring John Wayne, tells the story of a wealthy landowner who illicitly controls the water supply and a covert government agent (Singin' Sandy Saunders) who arrives to save the day. In *King of the Pecos* (1936, the year the Hoover Dam was completed, Figure 1.4) a Texas cattle baron controls water vital to local ranchers and John Clayborn (John Wayne) arrives to break up the monopoly. Many others, including *Law of the Ranger* (1937), *Oklahoma Frontier* (1938), *Stampede* (1949), *Big Country* (1958) starring Gregory Peck, *El Dorado* (1966) starring John Wayne, *Once Upon a Time in the West* (1969) starring Claudia Cardinale and Henry Fonda, and *Chinatown* (1974) starring Jack Nicholson and Faye Dunaway similarly center around water and the anxieties of water shortages and monopolization of water. We need not glorify nor malign these movies and their more recent brethren to recognize that they reflect, mythologize, and continue to shape understandings of American history and culture.

FIGURE 1.4. The Hoover Dam named after U.S. President Herbert Hoover was completed in 1935 and was at the time one of the largest human-made structures in the world. Built along the Colorado River by six private companies under contract to the U.S. Bureau of Reclamation, the dam stands over 200 meters tall and created what is still the largest water reservoir in the United States. This massive construction was finished under budget and ahead of schedule and its success sparked a half-century fury of dam building across the American West (photo from U.S. Government National Archives).

Scholarly and popular literature on the American West similarly reiterates archetypes of a heroic Western frontier. More than 15,000 books of all sorts, for example, have been published about esteemed sixteenth President of The United States, Abraham Lincoln (Figure 1.5) who was an indisputably important figure in American history, including with respect to water, homesteading, and colonization of the West. Extensive scholarly tomes, with books in retort, innumerable biographies of Lincoln, biographies of Lincoln's friends, children's books, children's coloring books, and many others contribute to a monumentous literature about Lincoln; a 2010 book and associated movie even depict Lincoln as a vampire hunter. These books and films demonstrate the depth and breadth of research, scholarship, and wide pop-culture recognition of American history and are only a

# Water histories and the archetypes of America and Arabia 15

FIGURE 1.5. Monument of books written about President Abraham Lincoln. Located at the Ford Theatre Center in Washington, DC this massive tower is constructed from replicas of some of the 15,000 books written about esteemed President Abraham Lincoln (photo by the author).

tiny fraction of the wide repertoire of material on the American West. Far less literature describes ancient Arabia, including water histories of ancient Yemen. Yet, as examined in the following chapters, many of the environmental, economic, social, political, and religious themes and rhetoric found in depictions of Arabia strikingly parallel more well-known archetypes of the American West.

Archetypal portrayals of Arabia, Arab tribesmen, and nomads have also long proliferated through religious, scholarly, and other sources. Like the American West without cowboys, if it were deprived of tribal nomads the Arabian Peninsula would almost cease to qualify, in American and Arab imagination, as Arabia. Tribal affiliations, genealogies, and stereotypes have long played an important role in Yemeni history, culture, and politics (Dresch 1989; Dresch and Haykel 1995; Ho 2006). The Bible and the Quran both frequently describe the interactions of nomads and settled folk, variably depicting nomads as sometimes righteous and at other times as misguided heathens. The fourteenth century Arab historian Ibn Khaldūn, ancestrally from the Hadramawt region of Yemen, highlighted nomadism in describing the history of civilization as structured by the shifting fortunes of *badu* (nomads) and *hadar* (settled folk) as cycles of *asabiyyah* (group-feeling) carried successive groups of nomads to power (Dawood 1969).

Water plays an undeniably critical role across the Near East with customs, rightful access, and rituals often centering on water. Jewish *mikveh* traditions prescribe immersion in water prior to entering a temple as well as after sex, menstruation, childbirth, and other instances. Christian baptism facilitates salvation and declares belief in the death, burial, and resurrection of Jesus Christ. Islamic *wudu* ablution washing of the face, arms, head, and feet ensures purity necessary before prayer. The Arabic term *sharia* denotes Islamic law but literally can be taken to mean path to follow or path to watering place (Weiss 1998: 17). Islamic law ideally requires equitable, open access to water from natural sources so that access can only be restricted for water captured in wells, canals, or other waterworks (Naff 2009). Water (and to a certain extent food) must be freely provided to travelers and their animals, which contributes to rural bedouin populations' oft-reputation for hospitality. I have argued previously that these traditions extend deep into the past, perhaps to the earliest water management, since there would be little incentive to invest in waterworks without traditions that limit unfettered overuse (Harrower 2008a). Investments in water management, however, would be potentially dangerous without simultaneously maintaining some element of access for highly mobile or travelling populations. Such traditional regulatory guidelines are particularly important where essential resources, such as water in deserts, exhibit high spatial and temporal heterogeneity (that is, patchy relative abundance in some areas and near absence in others). Local traditions, nevertheless, often diverge from general principles and internationalized norms. The widely practiced *salat al-istisqa* (prayer for rain), a supplication that is part of the *hadith* (teachings and practices of the Prophet Mohammed), is often led by an Imam who appeals to God for rain (Abu-Zahra 1988; Başgöz 2007). In the village of Al-Jabin in western Yemen, Hehmeyer (2008) reports on the local use of sign magic and God's supreme name to call for rain to fill communal cisterns. In the Hadramawt, ritual visitations (*ziyarah*) to tombs of revered ancestors include the tomb of *Mawla Matar* (Patron of Rain, Figure 1.6) where pilgrims gather annually to sing, dance, recite poetry, and pray for

# Water histories and the archetypes of America and Arabia

FIGURE 1.6. The tomb and sanctuary of *Mawla Matar* (Patron of Rain) positioned within one of the few mountain passes along the coastal escarpment of Hadramawt where summer monsoonal fog and rains rise up from the Indian Ocean (photo by the author).

rain and prosperity (Rodionov 1997). These diverse traditions highlight the practical and religious importance of water and the widely varied range of beliefs and customs that have shaped and continue to shape water histories.

Interestingly, framing of the American West has also traditionally involved long-enduring narratives about the interactions of mobile and settled populations and their use of land and water. Just as Arab nomads are revered in some narratives and abhorred in others, Native Americans were variably depicted as vicious killers in some cases and brave and noble guardians of nature in others. In both regions throughout history, encroaching settled peoples had vested interests in portraying mobile populations as primitive, uncivilized, and not making proper use of lands that were often violently reappropriated. The storyline of the American West as a land either vacant or idle operated in tandem with the myth that settled European-style farming was invariably the most economical and therefore the only justifiable use for Western lands. As has been detailed by historians of the American West (further discussed in the following chapters) many areas are simply not well suited to agricultural practices devised for more temperate European climates. Small-scale agricultural traditions of Native Americans of Arizona, California, and elsewhere across the region prevailed for roughly four millennia prior to Europeans arrival. Yet native practices were not only discounted as primitive and inefficient; the very existence of Native American farming was often summarily dismissed, which served to justify reappropriation of lands for immigrant homesteaders and rationalized American sovereignty. Indeed, the stereotypical vision of equitable, entrepreneurial capitalism operating virtually independent of the government intervention across the West certainly does not accurately describe post-1850s western agriculture where politics and massive government irrigation subsidies have propelled otherwise unsustainable practices (Hundley 2001, 2009; Wahl 1989; Worster 1992).

Just as critique and deconstruction of past scholarly and popular representations of the American West have led scholars to revise their understandings and archaeological research across the United States (Dixon 2014), critical appraisal of representations of Arabia in literature and media are similarly indispensable in reformulating understandings of Yemen. A wide breadth of material produced by travelers and explorers attests to water-use during the medieval past of Yemen. The tenth century Yemeni scholar Al-Ḥasan Ibn Aḥmad Al-Hamdānī in his *Sifat Jaziirat al-Arab*, Geography of the Arabian Peninsula (Müller 1884) and ten volume treatise *Al-Iklil*, The Crown (Faris 1938) offers a variety of important commentary. The later work concentrates on the history and genealogies of the Kingdom of Himyar (ca. 100 BC to AD 520) and helpfully, for archaeologists, describes some of the castles, monuments, and irrigation works he considered most significant including the Great Dam at Ma'rib (Faris 1938: 34). The thirteenth century account of Ibn Al-Mujawir who travelled through Yemen on the Hajj (probably from Iran) similarly offers a range of geographic, economic, and cultural information including commentary on food and agriculture (Smith 2008: 12). The fourteenth century explorer Ibn Battuta who left North Africa on the Hajj and journeyed over vast swaths of the world during the succeeding thirty years also reports on his time in Yemen including in Ta'iz where he met Rasulid Sultan Al-Mujahid Nur Al-Din Ali (Mackintosh-Smith 2002: 86). All three of these observers, Al-Hamdānī (Müller 1884) and Ibn Al-Mujawir (Margariti 2007: 50–52) and Ibn Battuta (Mackintosh-Smith 2002: 87) comment on the famous Tawila water storage tanks (cisterns) near Aden, Yemen reflecting their significance to water control of the time. Its remains unclear when these tanks were first built, but a version of them may have been constructed as early as the first half of the first millennium AD (Margariti 2007: 50–52). Indeed, the first few centuries AD saw a great number of dams, barrages, and other waterworks constructed across highland Yemen (Charbonnier 2009, 2011; Charbonnier and Schiettecatte 2013). Specialists in Arab history and culture, most notably Daniel Varisco (1983, 1996, 1997, 2009), have also helpfully focused on ethnographic and medieval water-use, irrigation, and agriculture in Yemen. These and other historic accounts substantially inform the chapters that follow.

In addition to historic literature, more recent late nineteenth and early twentieth century reports of scholars and travelers in Yemen yield a range of helpful insights related to water. While a comprehensive review is beyond the scope of this book (see also Chapter 5) a number of materials are particularly noteworthy. In 1843 Joseph Arnaud visited Ma'rib and Sirwah and made an informative plan map of ancient Ma'rib's famous dam (Arnaud 1874). During explorations of Yemen from 1882 to 1894 Austrian orientalist Edward Glaser (1913) also visited the dam at Ma'rib and surveyed its northern and southern sluice gates expanding on Arnaud's early work. Such early reports thus frequently recognized the technical accomplishments of ancient irrigation, but the major hallmarks of ancient South Arabian civilization including writing were most commonly attributed to incursions of foreigners from elsewhere in the Near East. Conventionally racist late nineteenth and early twentieth century accounts often viewed the region's present Arab inhabitants as having ousted the region's earliest civilizations thereby disconnecting achievements of the past with the supposed barbarity and stagnation of the present (e.g., Dingelstedt 1916). Fortunately, such misguided representations focused on race eventually gave way to more informed archaeological research. Gertrude Caton-Thompson and Elinor Gardner (1939) conducted some important early work on irrigation over the winter of 1937–38 in eastern Yemen's Hadramawt region. They concentrated near the town of Hureidha in Wadi 'Amd where they examined alluvial silt sections, mapped an irrigated area spanning 7 sq. km and traced a canal feeding the area for approximately 16 km. In 1947 Egyptian archaeologist Ahmed Fakhry (1951) visited the region and reported on irrigation works of Ma'rib and Sirwah. An relatively innovative overview of irrigation works of the Kingdom of Qatabān in Wadi Bayhan was produced by Richard Bowen (1958) of the American Foundation for the Study of Man (AFSM) expedition to Yemen. Bowen's air-photo-assisted surveys documented vast floodwater irrigation systems including canals, sluice gates, and banked fields illustrating, as we know today, that the earliest civilizations of the region were supported by flash floodwater irrigation systems that captured highland runoff. Sir Edward Evans-Pritchard (1940, 1949) subsequently, and quite famously, drew heavily on African and Arab populations as exemplars of segmentary, tribal societies in which conflict aligned shifting, opportunistic collections of social groups against one another. While this "segmentary lineage system" model gained considerable traction for many decades, critical appraisals in Yemen and elsewhere have shown it to be a vastly oversimplified representation that overlooks the importance of situational contexts and individual agencies (Dresch 1986, 1988).

Beyond these early scholarly contributions, a range of twentieth century Western popular culture has also simultaneously contributed to archetypes of Arabia that echo colonialist histories, including views about conflicts over water. In a thought provoking book that analyzes the 1962 Hollywood film *Lawrence of Arabia* Steven Caton (1999), an anthropologist whose work has often concentrated on Yemen, shows how the film both reiterates, and to some extent defies, major precepts of colonialist discourse. Based on the adventurous exploits of T.E. Lawrence a British officer who built alliances and coordinated Arab attacks on Ottoman forces during the First World War, the epic movie won Academy Awards for Best Picture and Best Director. As Caton outlines, Arabs are portrayed in harmony with nature while Lawrence frequently seems to supersede the confines of his hostile surroundings. Although the film stars a British hero, he is revered for adopting Arab dress and understandings of the desert, and yet simultaneously reflects the romanticized, rugged self-reliance so common in Hollywood Western movies (Caton 1999: 189, 202). Imagery, action, and conflict revolving around water, or lack of water, are a center-point of the film. In one scene early in the movie, Lawrence's bedouin guide Tafas leads him across vast sandy and mountainous expanses of desert to a well. A violent confrontation ensues over tribal rights to use the well, recalling early Western movies' representations of a lawless, drought ridden American frontier (Caton 1999: 188–89). Caton, in one passage, focuses his analysis on this scene:

> *I have been arguing that the desert becomes a protagonist in this film, but the paradox is that the director is at the same time striving to exert a total, even obsessive, control over it ... We are looking up the dark walls of a deep, round and stony well shaft. At the center are a circle of blue light and two figures opposite each other. One is Tafas, holding onto a rope, at the end of which is attached a leather water bucket. The other is Lawrence, with his compass dangling from a strap around his neck, which we see for the first, but not the last, time as a symbol of his rationality, of his ability to orient himself in the desert. These characters are contrasted through parallel postures: the Arab relying on little more than his body, his unaided sight, and*

*his almost intuitive knowledge of the terrain (thus, like the noble savage, he is close to nature); whereas the European, whom we have seen to be physically helpless, nevertheless is powerful by virtue of mechanical instruments like his revolver, binoculars, and compass (which make him further removed from nature and thus civilized).* Caton 1999: 88

As the scene develops, Tafas draws water from the well, from which both Lawrence and he drink. Tafas explains to Lawrence this is the well of another tribe, the Harith. Then Tafas spots a figure far on the horizon riding a camel fast toward them and runs to retrieve his revolver from his saddle. Just as Tafas aims to fire, he is suddenly hit from afar with single shot, and falls, lying motionless – dead.

This scene and others in the movie involving water revealingly depict the film makers' preconceptions about hostilities and conflicts over water in Arabia. Interestingly, these depictions strikingly contradict the fundamental basics of tribal custom and Islamic law. As described earlier in this chapter, a deep legacy of tribal custom and Islamic law requires sharing access to water with people and their animals, particularly when travelers are passing through strange lands (Faruqui 2001; Naff 2009). Certainly customs can be broken and Islamic traditions do not allow travelers unlimited and unfettered use; but, the movie depicts monopolization of water as a customary, commonplace practice and perennial source of conflict when such exclusionary control of water is explicitly forbidden. In effect we see some of the same anxieties surrounding monopolization of water that are depicted in early Hollywood Western movies, yet in *Lawrence of Arabia*, amongst Arabs, such conflicts are portrayed as a perpetual and never resolved.

Colonial overtones, misunderstandings, and misrepresentations of water-use are similarly interconnected with archaeology and call for continued, cautious, and circumspect research in the region. Although the term "postcolonial" archaeology erroneously leaves the impression that the colonial era has entirely passed, the neocolonial underpinnings of Near Eastern archaeology remain significant in shaping understandings of ancient histories (Bernbeck 2012; Meskell 2002). Caton only briefly mentions Lawrence's connection to archaeology – at the dawn of the war Lawrence was a promising postgraduate archaeologist who had studied at Oxford and had considerable experience traveling and working in the Middle East (Wilson 1990). These experiences were what made Lawrence exceptionally valuable as a military and intelligence operative; his understanding of the region, its people, language, and its past were rare amongst the British. The audacious spirit of adventure is similarly reflected in Wendell Phillips's (1955) book *Qataban and Sheba: Exploring Ancient Kingdoms on the Biblical Spice Routes of Arabia*, which chronicles one of the most important early archaeological projects in Yemen. Phillips's entertaining account of the American Foundation for the Study of Man (AFSM) expedition from 1950 to 1952 portrays Yemen as unexplored frontier with Wendell Phillips (still only in his twenties) wearing the quintessentially Arab *keffiyeh* headscarf, cowboy boots, and a Colt 45 six-shooter at his side. Widely reported in *The New York Times*, the AFSM expedition spent only weeks in Wadi Bayhan excavating Tamna', capital of the Kingdom of Qatabān, before moving on to dig at the even more spectacular Awwam Temple at Ma'rib, purported home of the legendary Queen of Sheba. Phillips drew on the support of the British Protectorate of Aden to gain a foothold in the region and with copious private financial backing assembled an impressive team of leading experts in the ancient Near East including William F. Albright, Frank P. Albright, Albert Jamme, Gus Van Beek, and Richard Bowen. As briefly mentioned above, the latter scholar focused specifically on irrigation in Wadi Bayhan and completed an illuminating study based on only six weeks of fieldwork (Bowen 1958). Even during the early stages of archaeological research in the region, scholars recognized the technologically advanced nature of ancient irrigation systems and they frequently debated the respective impacts of irrigation and incense trade (Serjeant 1960); yet they were often still quick to attribute the impetus for irrigation to foreigners (e.g., Bowen 1958: 87). Today's archaeologists no longer collect treasure for Western museums nor do we serve as spies or petroleum prospectors, but we do still retrieve something even more valuable – knowledge of cultures and histories – which uniquely qualifies us to educate and assist in building mutual understandings that are cognizant of colonialist legacies and foundational to contemporary peacemaking and alliance building.

## Geopolitics of East and West: Commonalities and contemporary conflict

As introduced in the preceding pages, this book examines water histories of ancient Yemen intermittently juxtaposed aside the better-known water histories of the American West. To the extent that these two very different cases share underlying commonalities, they help reveal the essential characteristics of water histories worldwide and build critically needed common ground between understandings of America and Arabia in a time of profound global turmoil. There are of course enormous differences; for example, the history of the American West is one of incursive expansion while ancient states in Yemen are for the most part indigenous. It should be clear, therefore, that the purpose of efforts to contrast and juxtapose is not merely to highlight similarities, but, just as importantly, to identify and acknowledge wide differences. Societies are never completely in harmony nor entirely in conflict with nature, neither are they wholly exploitive and despotic (Wittfogel 1957) nor entirely collectively beneficial and consensually equitable (Lansing 1991, 2006). The past 200 years of American history illustrate comparatively short-duration, spatially wide (global) impacts on a great many peoples' lives. In comparison, the nearly 4,000 years of ancient Yemeni history that is the central focus of this book spans a much longer duration, smaller area, yet perhaps similar number of human lifetimes. Particularly when regarded as persistent collections of environmental, economic, social, political, and ideological rhetoric and logic, societies and polities offer a helpful lens through which to consider the diverse trajectories of humankind. In ancient Yemen and the American West, the formats of political discourse widely differed. Caton's (1990) work on contemporary poetry in Yemen highlights traditions that must have also had precursors in more ancient times. In comparison, print media, newspapers, and other literature played a major role in promoting the movements of pioneers and homesteaders across the American West (Witschi 2011). Contrastive juxtaposition of these distinct water histories is one means of reconfiguring and defamiliarizing perspectives to help us understand what differs and what is shared in the trajectories by which we arrive in the present.

Archaeologists over the past few decades have increasingly scrutinized the modern political involvements of archaeology, yet scholars have most often focused and warned of manipulations of the past when the positive importance of archaeology in international dialogue, diplomacy, and peacemaking, particularly in the Middle East, is far less often emphasized (Bernbeck 2012; Boytner et al. 2010; Luke and Kersel 2012; Meskell 1998, 2012). Cooperation is necessarily constructed on the foundations of mutual understandings of the past that provide essential starting points for communication and interactive dialogue. As Edmund Hull, the former U.S. Ambassador to Yemen from 2001 to 2004 (who happened to be in the

Pentagon during the attacks of September 11, 2001) commented on his time posted in Yemen ...

> In a sense, our greatest impediment was not the insecurity in which we worked or the paucity of resources, but rather the mutual suspicions that corroded the partnership we were attempting to build. (Hull 2011: xviii)

His commentary conveys the very real need to understand, in more than superficial ways, both American and Arabian histories and cultures so that similarities and differences inform our current and future relations. Yet even the provocative title of Hull's book *High-Value Target: Countering Al-Qaeda in Yemen* evokes understanding Yemen as an adversary rather than an ally. Nevertheless, his comments echo for me conversations during a brief meeting in 2005 with cultural attaché staff of his successor, Ambassador Thomas Krajeski. Embassy staff spoke enthusiastically about a program to translate and disseminate classic American literature in Arabic including, for example, the 1939 John Steinbeck novel *The Grapes of Wrath*, which chronicles the tribulations of the Joads – a family forced to flee Oklahoma for California because of drought and economic hardship during the Great Depression. This endeavor seemed to us like a great idea, but when we asked if there might be funds to translate acclaimed Arabic literature into English the room fell noticeably quiet. After a moment of hesitation, it was grudgingly acknowledged that unfortunately there were no immediate plans to translate Arabic literature. Embassy staff were keenly aware not only of the wide misunderstanding of the United States prevalent among Yemenis but also the similarly wide misapprehension of Yemen among Americans. Notwithstanding efforts such as those of the Bureau of Educational and Cultural Affairs, U.S. diplomatic efforts were (and still largely are) directed more at disseminating favorable portrayals of the United States than toward promoting reciprocal dialogue. While recent histories of the Middle East are understandably controversial, the deeper ancient past is less so and archaeology offers a critically important and powerful basis on which to build understanding and cooperation on the foundations of shared knowledge of histories. Beyond the U.S. Department of State, other branches of the U.S. Government do expend significant funds annually on international humanistic research and cultural heritage, including, for example, the National Endowment for the Humanities, and the National Science Foundation (Directorate of Social, Behavioral and Economic Sciences). These programs, however, are only a miniscule fragment of enormous annual expenditures on military and intelligence. While the long-term impacts of scholarly research including archaeology in the Middle East are difficult to quantify, this book (which includes research supported in part by the National Science Foundation and the Social Sciences and Humanities Research Council of Canada) argues that mutual understanding fostered by investments in humanistic research are indispensable in combating misrepresentations of histories that are a foundational and seemingly unending ideological fuel of extremism and violence.

In terms of water, a great breadth of recent material calls attention to drought and looming water crises worldwide (Barlow 2007, 2014; Barlow and Clarke 2005; Fishman 2012; Gleick 2014a; Pearce 2006; Shiva 2002), including in the United States (Glennon 2010; Reisner 1986), the Middle East (Allan 2001; Black et al. 2010; Gleick 1994; Kliot 1993; Murakami 1995) and specifically in Yemen (Caton 2013: 284–93; Moore 2011; Ward 2009). Predictions often include dire shortages and political turmoil, with increasing violent conflict often forewarned for the Middle East. Indeed, recent conflicts in Syria (Gleick 2014b) and Yemen (Moore 2011) are connected with, or at least contributed to, by water shortages. Water crises (and warnings of imminent shortage) undoubtedly warrant concerted action, particularly in emergency situations such as in Yemen today where millions of people lack adequate food, water, shelter, and basic medical care. Longer term solutions are just as vexing, and water histories of Yemen outlined in this book offer substantial caveats. While promoting water-use sustainability is certainly a worthy goal (Orlove and Caton 2010), long term solutions require a good deal of caution as policies and practices aimed to relieve shortfalls can lead to unanticipated consequences as societies adapt and come to depend on artificial availabilities. Even though they operated for more than a thousand years, irrigation systems of Yemen's ancient kingdoms induced massive sedimentary changes that contributed to their eventual abandonment and were/are extremely difficult (if not impossible) to redress. More recently, well-intentioned efforts to develop Yemen's agricultural productivity through introduction of diesel pump wells (beginning predominantly in the 1980s) propelled the neglect of terrace agriculture and began the rapid drawdown of aquifers with heavily subsidized diesel fuel that now significantly contributes to ongoing national conflict (Lichtenthäler 2003; Moore 2011). Knowledge of ancient irrigation is greatly valuable in understanding contemporary water issues in Yemen (e.g., Al-Hakimi and Pelat 2003); but unfortunately past technologies are not a quick-fix as they are invariably socio-politically situated within (now internationalized) water and food production economies as well as local environmental and cultural histories that cannot simply be unwound.

Geographies of water, and more recently oil, illustrate the spatial interconnections of resources, histories, and cultures as intertwined with local, national, and international geopolitics. Even the powerful government agencies that built thousands of dams across the American West mostly during the first seventy-five years of the twentieth century, namely the U.S. Bureau of Reclamation and the U.S. Army Corps of Engineers, eventually came to recognize that while some were greatly successful and contributed to the rise of the United States as a global superpower, many were misguided and were driven more by politics than by rational, balanced assessments of water needs (Reisner 1986; Rowley 2006; Worster 1985). Nevertheless, water across the West remains enormously and understandably controversial as many have come to rely on artificial availabilities (Hundley 2009). As William Kahrl, author of *Water and Power: The Conflict over Los Angeles' Water Supply in the Owen's Valley* (1983), put it …

> The Owen's Valley story has something for everyone. Who do you dislike? Big Government, rich people, media, environmentalists, people who don't like environmentalists? All of these are part of the story, and all of them are related to issues that are really fundamental to the way we organize ourselves as a society. William Kahrl quoted in Stringfellow. (2013: 51)

Across the Middle East, natural geographies and availabilities of water and oil are similarly central to geopolitics. In the Sultanate of Oman, for instance, changing practical and religious conceptions of water (Limbert 2001) and the discovery and production of oil (Limbert 2010) have had pivotal historical impacts.

Like oil and water, the historic dichotomy draw between Western Occidental and Eastern Oriental civilizations has often been portrayed as involving inevitable conflict even by scholarly (Barber 1995; Huntington 1996; Pagden 2009) not to mention more popular media sources. Is this dichotomous portrait of East and West really as immutable as many contend? Are deep misunderstandings and violent conflicts between the West and East (recently dominated by geographies of water and oil) simply inevitable?

This book's focus on juxtaposition of water histories leads to the wider conclusion that many of the world's present and future challenges are eternally vexing in the absence of some basic shared understandings of America and Arabia that disavow dichotomous views of East and West. As an archaeologist working in Yemen, vast misconceptions were vividly apparent. We spent long, arduous days living and exploring for months at a time from our remote desert tent camp in the rugged highlands of eastern Yemen. We learned a great deal from the local bedouin we hired as guides and workmen. They lived modestly across rocky unforgiving terrain, herding goats and camels – inexorably self-reliant and graciously hospitable. During lunch one day in 2004 we crouched, as usual, in the shade of a small rockshelter to rest, drink water, and munch tepid egg sandwiches supplied by a nearby (at that time Canadian-owned) oil camp. Our eclectic group of American graduate students, Yemeni colleagues, and local Yemeni bedouin pondered the wanderings of peoples thousands of years ago. Ancient foragers, hunters, and herders often chose the very same rockshelters to rest and repair arrows, leaving scatters of broken stone tools and pecked rockart images of animals on seemingly everlasting limestone rock walls. As the conversation turned to current events and America's role in the Middle East, I wondered what our local hosts, including our Yemeni bedouin workmen, might think of these issues. Some locals had worked with us for many long days over numerous years. One of our most enthusiastic hosts, a young man named Ahmed woke everyday hours before dawn and walked for miles by moonlight from his camp with wife and child to start work with us at dawn. We, as archaeologists, arrived with a wide assortment of expensive GPS equipment and laptop computers, and constructed an elaborate tent camp (with a generator for electricity) in the desert where we stayed in search of vestiges of the past. The disjunction between our backgrounds was vast, but we made deep friendships and gained an invaluable sense of our very different experiences of the world. After 9/11 and the recent U.S. invasion of Iraq I was very curious, albeit a little hesitant to ask, what Ahmed might think of these events.

"Do you know who George Bush is?" I asked.
"Yes", Ahmed quickly replied "He is the leader of the world."

I could hardly summon the response needed to correct him, and I wondered how he had arrived at that impression? Perhaps he was simply telling us what he thought we wanted to hear? I certainly cannot claim that such views are commonplace; but if that was truly Ahmed's view, once he had arrived at that impression it became relatively easy to unjustifiably credit the United States for many of the world's accomplishments or alternatively to blame us for innumerable shortcomings including enormous wealth in the face of enormous inequities. Many scholars similarly divide civilizations into Eastern and Western types that are seen as fundamentally divergent and perpetually in conflict. Stanford archaeologist Ian Morris, for example, in his recent book *War! What Is It Good For?* recounted the ancient past to argue that wars throughout history have counterintuitively served to reduce violence and the United States can and should act as an international "globocop" (Morris 2014). His arguments like many others before him are predicated on the long-standing assertion that categories East and West truly distinguish fundamentally different types of societies that perpetually battle for preeminence (Morris 2010). In light of Ahmed's comment, some (perhaps many) around the world may similarly view international geopolitics as Morris does as an East/West battle for supremacy. Unfortunately, such inflexibly dichotomous us/them views and inability to see commonalities are foundational to the rhetoric that underlies violent conflicts in Yemen and more widely throughout the Middle East. Even though many Arabs and many Americans are ill-equipped to recount anything but a superficial, stereotypical understanding of each other's histories, this East/West framing is viewed as so fundamental and taken-for-granted that it is seldom challenged. Rather than struggling to explain Ahmed's response or endeavoring to directly challenge Morris' account of world history, this book compares across the East/West divide and I hope in a small way can help remedy wide misunderstandings of Yemen to better convey underlying commonalities and differences to archaeologists and beyond.

CHAPTER 2

# Comparison and juxtaposition in archaeology

Water, agriculture, and state formation in space and time

> *Indeed, juxtaposition is perhaps a better term than comparison, for anthropology is far better at rendering situations comparable across place or time, thus forcing a change of perspective, than at actually comparing them.*
>
> (Pál 2013: 371)

Water's enduring importance is evident throughout histories of ancient hunter-gatherers, agriculturalists, states, and civilizations. With a rapidly burgeoning range of information available on water and ancient societies worldwide, the configuration and goals of comparative methods in archaeology require continual reappraisal. This chapter examines the forms and aims of cross-cultural comparisons of water-use in anthropological archaeology with specific attention to methodological developments in spatial analysis and spatial theory, and a thematic focus on early agriculture and state formation. Amidst wider consideration of these issues, I argue that rather than comparing societies only based on similarities, contrastive juxtaposition of societies that are extremely different is also highly informative. In transportation, defense, flood control, ritual symbolism, provisioning of animals, crop rearing, and household purposes, water figures prominently in a vast array of ancient contexts (Mithen 2012; Scarborough 2003; Solomon 2010). A considerable literature examines the role of water among indigenous and ancient societies, including water's impacts on the movements of hunter-gatherers (Kelly 1995), the settlement choices of agriculturists (Stone 1996) and the food producing economies of ancient states (Marcus and Stanish 2006). Comparisons of ancient and contemporary water management, with attention to physical and social landscapes, helps reveal similarities and differences among a wide diversity of histories (David and Thomas 2008; Mabry 1996; Mithen 2012). Since 1950 radiocarbon dating has revolutionized archaeologists' understandings of timelines and chronologies. Spatial technologies, including satellite imagery, Global Positioning System (GPS) receivers, and Geographic Information System (GIS) software, are now similarly revolutionizing archaeologists' understandings of spaces, places, and ancient geographies, including in relation to water. Questioning traditional origins/spread, primary/secondary, core/periphery dichotomies revitalizes views of ancient geographies that stagnate on conventional decades-old framing.

Faced with a necessarily fragmentary record of ancient material culture, archaeologists have perpetually struggled to compare and explain the long arc of human histories in different contexts worldwide. Since the dawn of anthropology as a discipline, the value of ethnography (studying contemporary peoples) to understand the ancient past was immediately recognized. The renowned anthropologist Julian Steward, who is well known as founder of cultural ecology and for his work with Native Americans of the western United States, was among those captivated less by evolutionary taxonomies of societies and more by the direct historical approach to archaeology that traces from ethnography of a region backward in time (Steward 1942). Steward also famously hypothesized, as part of his multilinear evolutionary theory of culture change, that societies inhabiting similar natural environments were likely to develop similar economic adaptations. He viewed subsistence adaptations, closely tailored to environments, as the essential "culture core" of a society (Steward 1955a). Since many of the world's earliest civilizations appeared alongside major rivers in otherwise arid regions, he considered irrigation a potential cross-cultural parallel worthy of investigation but he never arrived at a fully formulated explanation of why and how water proved so important (Steward 1930, 1949, 1955b, 1977). Efforts to understand similarities and differences among societies, inspired in part by Steward, led to the still hotly debated bands-tribes-chiefdoms-states evolutionary classification of sociopolitical organization (Service 1962). Despite efforts to disavow directionality, such classifications have been criticized for implying a ladder of progress (e.g., Yoffee 1993, 2005) and for contributing to rote labeling of societies in ways that ascribe sets of characteristics that arguably do little to contribute new understanding (Pauketat 2007). Nevertheless, studies focused on ancient tribes, chiefdoms, and states as societal types continue (e.g., Drennan and Peterson 2006; Marcus 2008; Parkinson 2002: Redmond and Spencer 2012) and particularly when viewed as descriptive, heuristic terms rather than as immutable, universal types of societies these categories do arguably retain considerable value (Feinman 2011: 22, 28). Related lines of comparative archaeology searched for regularities or laws of culture change (Binford 1962) and debated how best to employ ethnographic analogies to assist in understanding archaeological remains (Ascher 1961). Nearly from the outset, the search for laws of culture change was strongly criticized (Flannery 1973) and has led to few, if any, widely accepted cross-cultural generalizations (cf. Binford 2001). Similarly, the goal of devising methods to ensure analogies drawn between ethnographic and archaeological contexts are valid and reliable has long remained a topic of debate, including in the Near East (e.g., Verhoeven 2005; Wendrich and van der Kooij 2002). Binford (1968, 1972, 1985) famously argued that one should compare ethnographic and archaeological contexts through deduction and hypothesis testing without using analogies. However, as Alison Wylie (1982, 1985) emphasized, even though Binford and others disclaim use of analogies, archaeologists' arguments nevertheless frequently rely on analogical reasoning. Ann Stahl (1993) reminded archaeologists to pay careful attention to both the similarities *and differences* between source (ethnographic) and subject (archaeological) contexts. Yet after decades of debate there no clear and reliable means of ensuring the accuracy of ethnographic analogies has emerged. Ultimately, explanations of histories frequently rely on somewhat subjective evaluations of narrative emplotment and often depend, quite simply, on whether or not experts find the evidence marshaled compelling and arguments convincing. Lars Fogelin (2007) identified seven traits of effective explanations in archaeology, namely empirical breadth, generality, modesty, refutability, conservatism, simplicity, and multiplicity of foils; but here again ways to pursue explanations with these characteristics remain, unavoidably, somewhat subjective. In a more recent volume, *Comparative Archaeology of Complex Societies*, Smith and Peregrine (2011: 7–9) identify a range of comparative approaches along a continuum from systematic (many societies or cases examined according to few variables or themes) to intensive (few societies or cases examined according to many variables or themes). As further described in this chapter, the approach I adopt, which compares ancient Yemen and the American West, falls on the intensive end of this spectrum, yet includes comparisons with other contexts worldwide particularly as related to water in early agriculture and state formation.

In cultural anthropology, multi-sited ethnography and juxtaposition have (re)emerged over the past few decades as modes of comparative research (e.g., Coleman and von Hellermann 2011; Falzon 2009; Marcus 1995) and these approaches have substantial untapped potential in archaeology. As informed by these approaches, I argue that comparison of very different cases can be highly informative and one need not aim to show that two cases are the same or even closely similar to draw understanding from them. George Marcus (1995, 1999, 2009) has played a substantive role in the emergence of multi-sited ethnography in ways that eschew meta-narratives (grand overarching explanations) of either individual cultures or classifications of human societies as a whole. Related postcolonialist approaches have proven particularly attractive to historical archaeologists, for example, in helping to counter triumphalist colonial histories (Paynter 2000) and for considering archaeologies of sovereignty (Smith 2011). One of the most well-known early scholarly applications of juxtaposition as method comes from Margaret Mead's (1928) best-selling book *Coming of Age in Samoa* in which she draws on her ethnographic study of adolescence and sexuality in Samoa to reflect on similar life events in American culture. In their influential book, *Anthropology as Cultural Critique*, George Marcus and Michael Fischer (1986) similarly argue for juxtaposition and defamiliarization, yet criticize Mead's approach for her relatively cursory and belated integration of American culture. In essence Marcus and Fisher (1986) argue in favor of a half-and-half approach in which two cases are best balanced against one another ...

> The strength of ethnography and ethnographic criticism is their focus on detail, their enduring respect for context in the making of any generalization, and their full recognition of persistent ambiguity and multiple possibilities in any situation. These are precisely the characteristics put at risk in projects of criticism in which one or the other case is presented statically by its removal from the full cultural context in which it occurs and is recorded ethnographically. How, then, to achieve a kind of criticism by juxtaposition which makes telling points, but not at the cost of decontextualization and stereotyping either case represented? (Marcus and Fischer 1986: 159–160)

How can one ensure full recognition of the full cultural context in which neither case is stereotyped or decontextualized? The implication that one might distill the true essence of a history or a culture by conferring a significant or conventionally acceptable amount of time or text speaks against a central precept of anthropology that one cannot easily condense and extract a culture as a singularized entity. Marcus and Fisher (1986: 163) acknowledge that more than two cases are likely needed to better situate and triangulate a binary juxtaposition, but how could one sufficiently ensure *these* examples were appropriately set in context? Even where they still persist, contemporary hunting and gathering populations have been heavily impacted by interaction and contact with agriculturists and cannot be viewed as pristine, isolated vestiges of the past (Headland and Reid 1989).

The challenge of contextualizing and balancing one case against another is precisely the obstacle Marshall Sahlins encountered in his 2004 book *Apologies to Thucydides: Understanding History as Culture and Vice Versa*. Sahlins compares the Peloponnesian War (431–404 BC) with a Fijian Polynesian War (1843–1855) to reveal the commonalities of these two very different cases, and illustrate his argument that historians often pay too little attention to culture and anthropologists pay too little attention to history. However, as Sahlins (2004:2) reflexively notes, his book is far less detailed and simplified with regard to Ancient Greece than for the South Pacific (the region in which much of his field research has concentrated). Yet I would argue he need not apologize, as there is no compelling need for two cases to be balanced against one another with equal analytical time or text devoted to each. Indeed, George Marcus' (1995) more recent arguments promoting multi-sited ethnography allow far more comparative flexibility and abandon the need to aim for balance between two cases, thereby opening the door to a much wider repertoire of potential comparisons.

Just as multi-sited ethnography has moved beyond restrictive dualistic approaches in which only two ethnographies are compared (Coleman and von Hellermann 2011; Falzon 2009), to prove useful in archaeology multi-sited approaches and juxtaposition can and should involve far more than simply analyzing more than one archaeological site or region. Acknowledgment of historical contingencies and cultural particularities requires that categories of societies, if employed at all, are viewed as descriptive heuristic tools in which one cannot *a priori* assume that societies designated tribes or chiefdoms, for example, necessarily resemble one another with regard to any particular trait or practice. The important role of contexts, audiences, and analysts as interlocutors recommends a diversity of comparative frames beyond merely two contrasting supposedly analogous cases, or sets of cases purportedly representing a categorical type. In the present case, the American West is so vastly better-known and historically documented it would be remiss to aim for a balance with histories of ancient Yemen. Instead, defamiliarization of the American West via juxtaposition with ancient Yemen breaks some of the barriers between what are outwardly entirely different, incomparable histories. The approach of the following chapters thus reenvisions the interconnectivities of water in ancient Yemen amidst a spatially and temporally wide comparative frame.

## Spatial analysis and spatial theory in studies of water histories

Spatial technologies and spatial theory offer a powerful combination of tools and perspectives for considering geographic dimensions of water histories. In conjunction with temperature, water is the central variable that defines climates and vegetation cover. Particularly in arid regions, water exerts critical influences in cultural, ritual, and religious life. David Clarke's (1977) edited volume, *Spatial Archaeology*, long ago emphasized the importance of spatial perspective, formal models, and quantitative spatial analyses. More recently, archaeologists have drawn on social/spatial theory (e.g., Lefebvre 1974; Soja 1989) and various currents of landscape archaeology (David and Thomas 2008) to become more widely concerned with qualitative views of spaces, places, and spatiality (e.g., Blake 2004). Particularly given the fluid and heterogeneous nature of water, spatial perspectives offer a wealth of opportunities to examine interconnectivity and patterning of human activities and histories (e.g., Ertsen 2010). A wide range of geospatial data are now available on precipitation, groundwater, surface water, and even more recently spatial patterning of evapotranspiration. From a tear-drop, to monsoonal fog, to a deluge that floods an entire landscape, water exemplifies the importance of scalability and vantage point. The importance of scale in human geography (Moore 2008), recommends close attention to scale and the analytical impacts of borders, boundaries, and categories (Dungan et al. 2002). Acknowledging the malleability and the often boundless and seamless nature of interaction in the past as well as the present substantially enhances understandings of ancient geographies.

From archaeological survey and settlement patterns analysis to phenomenological landscape archaeology, differing conceptions of archaeological geographies, space, and spatiality have long contributed to widely differing research questions, methods, and results. While systematic archaeological surveys offer informative baseline data for analyzing the distribution of archaeological remains relative to water, opportunistic landscape archaeology conveys deep interpretive views of water across terrain. Field investigations often extrapolate from firsthand experience in relatively small areas to wide regional geographies. It was not until the 1960s that archaeologists began to recognize archaeological survey, for example, Robert McCormick Adams (1965) air-photo-assisted surveys of Iraq, as more than just a means to find sites to excavate. Drawing on developments in quantitative geography (Haggett 1966), advocates of settlement archaeology (Trigger 1968), spatial archaeology (Clarke 1977), and regional analysis (Johnson 1977) took up the challenging task of modeling and explaining site geographies. Water for household purposes and for agriculture was quickly recognized as an important variable (Trigger 1968). Analytical techniques included rank-size analysis of site sizes (Johnson 1980), nearest neighbor analysis of site clustering (Pinder et al. 1979), and Thiessen polygon analysis of site territories (Renfrew et al. 1974). One analytical approach, site catchment analysis, directly borrows on the geographical concept of a drainage basin or watershed. An archaeological site's catchment quite simply designates the area from which a site derives sustenance, most primarily water and food but also firewood, building materials and other resources or raw materials used on a regular basis (Roper 1979; Vita-Finzi and Higgs 1970).

Some remain skeptical of spatial analysis and may never be convinced (see Llobera 2012), yet technologies such as satellite imagery, GPS, and GIS offer a wide range of analytical opportunities that can powerfully inform, and be informed by, interpretive landscape archaeology and spatial theory. After receiving considerable attention in the 1970s, interest in settlement pattern and spatial analysis declined somewhat in the 1980s and early 1990s. This downturn can be attributed to both the time-consuming (pre-computer era) challenges of implementing quantitative spatial analyses, alongside the vigorous critique advocates of interpretive landscape archaeology (e.g. Tilley 1994) leveled against processual archaeology for purportedly overemphasizing subsistence and settlement in lieu of social, political, and ideological dynamics (see Flannery and Marcus 1996; Hodder 1986). However, we need not view archaeological remains merely as dots on maps within concentric catchment radii or mechanically defined Thiessen polygons. Archaeological geographies can be far more richly portrayed amidst complex topographies that structure water flow (Harrower 2010), terrain that shapes human movement (White and Surface-Evans 2012), and territories that delimit visibility of tombs (Bongers et al. 2012), encampments (Garcia 2013), and settlements (Jones 2006). Few archaeologists recognize that "blue-line" features on topographic maps used to designate stream channels and rivers are often very subjectively defined based on interpretation of air photos (Kvamme 2006: 7, 21). Measuring the distance from sites to stream or river networks is therefore a needlessly arbitrary exercise that can and should be replaced by more advanced GIS water flow modeling that better represents directions and accumulations of flow as a continuous raster layer of grid cells. Archaeological remains can then be quite easily compared in a far less capricious manner with the distribution of water across landscapes (Harrower 2010; Harrower et al. 2012). The utility of these spatial tools to consider water across landscapes lies not only in quantitative approaches but also in data management, visualization, and qualitative GIS (Cope and Elwood 2009).

Despite common-points of interest, attempts to reconcile and integrate views and practices of spatial analysis with those of interpretive landscape archaeology have proven challenging (Gillings 2012; Llobera 2012). Yet there remains far more middle ground and compatibility than often acknowledged. Reflexive skepticism that acknowledges the malleabilities of spatial analyses helpfully bridges divides between scientific and humanistic archaeologies. Views of earth from space, for example, have been vigorously critiqued using Haraway's (1991) concept of omnipotent "god-trick" for offering distanced and detached representations (Aitken and Kwan 2009). Yet the recent popularity of Google Earth in archaeology is in large part attributable to its wide accessibility, ease-of-use, and operationally seamless multiscalar flexibility (Ur 2006) suggesting these tools are far less inaccessible and opaque than some argue.

The various meanings and implications of the term satellite imagery "resolution" helpfully exemplify the malleability of spatial representations. The impact of pixel size on legibility of satellite imagery is familiar to anyone with even passing interest in spatial technologies. However, the important concepts of spatial, spectral, radiometric, and temporal resolution are far less widely understood but nevertheless important. Pixel size is directly related to the size of an entire satellite imagery scene. As spatial resolution increases (i.e., pixel size decreases with common values ranging from 250 m to 0.5 m) this almost invariably and necessarily comes at the cost of less expansive coverage of a region. In terms of spectra, most early satellite photographs taken on film were panchromatic (black and white), but since the 1970s multispectral images have captured light beyond the visible spectrum that helps distinguish different rocks, minerals, vegetation, and other human-made features. Early multispectral satellite images consisted of relatively few multispectral layers or bands (e.g., Landsat-1 launched in 1972 had only four bands) while more recent hyperspectral satellite sensors have far more bands (e.g., NASA's Hyperion sensor has 220 bands). This far greater number of bands results in far greater spectral resolution. Essentially, when the same range of the electromagnetic spectrum is divided into a greater number of narrow slices, it increases analysts' ability to distinguish between different materials not discernable to the naked eye. Radiometric resolution refers the range of values a pixel in each band or layer can take, for example, 0–255 in 8-bit imagery versus 0–65,536 in 16-bit imagery. A greater range of values confers a greater ability to differentiate objects on the ground, but leads to larger file sizes and often necessitates decreased spatial and/or spectral resolution. Finally, temporal resolution quite simply refers to the interval by which a satellite revisits or reimages an area (e.g., eighteen days for the original Landsat-1 imagery). Unlike most other analysts, archaeologists (other things being equal) most often prefer older imagery that records landscapes prior to recent damage and development.

Once these basic elements of satellite imagery are understood, one begins to recognize the various ways they shape conceptions of landscapes and the ancient past. With recently increasing spatial resolution imagery, archaeologists' attention has been drawn to smaller and smaller objects, for instance, circular tombs and other small-scale monuments across southern Arabia (Deadman 2012; Harrower et al. 2013). High spatial resolution imagery is helping archaeologists detect and map tombs over areas far larger than those that can be visited and mapped through traditional on-the-ground archaeological fieldwork (Schuetter et al. 2013). Just as the binocular vision of human eyes allows sight in three dimensions, overlapping stereo satellite images can be used to extract Digital Elevation Model (DEM) representations of terrain. These satellite imagery based representations of topography enable both quantitative evaluations and qualitative visualizations, for example, of tombs and other monuments inter-visibility and prominence as well as their associations with water (Harrower et al. 2014a). Archaeologists have also long used multispectral satellite imagery to classify landforms and landcover (e.g., Harrower et al. 2002). As geographer Paul Robbins (2001, 2003) has emphasized, these methods call attention to the subjectivities and politics involved in conceptualizing and defining types of landscapes, soils, vegetation, and changes over time. The number of categories or classes, the boundaries, borders, scales, and areas of interest all serve to define and alter analytical outcomes (Dungan et al. 2002; Wong 2009). While the concept of a watershed or catchment area superficially appears to be objectively definable, catchments can be delineated at almost any scale for the area above any given point(s) across a landscape. The broad malleability of watersheds thus recommends flow analyses that determine the direction and accumulation of water flow in ways that avoid arbitrary or discretionary choices about where and at what scale to define catchments. Particularly when informed by spatial theory on construction of places and spaces, spatial technologies therefore offer a wealth of opportunities to consider engineered hydraulic landscapes (Earle and Doyel 2008) including spatial heterogeneity of water and its role in facilitating reproduction of societies and polities.

## Water histories of ancient Yemen: comparison and juxtaposition in space and time

As representative and reflective of societal change, water histories are shaped by a wide range of interrelated dynamics – terrain, climates, environments, social, political, and religious variables – that change and oscillate through space and time. The remainder of this chapter introduces some of the main highlights of ancient Yemen's water histories set within context of current issues and debates in studies of ancient agricultural origins and state formation with a specific focus on comparison and the future role of landscape-scale spatial analysis and spatial theory.

Over the past several decades, paleoclimatology, geoarchaeology, and spatial technologies have shed considerable new light on water environments, and human adaptation to, and use of, water resources across the Near East and Arabia. A burgeoning range of ice core, sea core, speleothem, lacustrine, and other terrestrial records has dramatically enhanced understanding of past climates of the region (Bar-Matthews and Ayalon 2003; Bernhardt et al. 2012; Maher et al. 2011; Phillipps et al. 2012) including specifically in southern Arabia (Burns et al. 2003; Cremaschi and Negrino 2005; Fleitmann et al. 2003; Lézine et al. 2010; Parker et al. 2006). Geoarchaeological research including studies of water management, paleosols, and alluvial geomorphology have made similarly substantive contributions to understanding ancient Yemen (Berger et al. 2012; Brunner 1997a, 2008; Pietsch et al. 2010, 2012; Wilkinson 1999, 2006). These investigations have defined with increasing clarity an early Holocene pluvial period and a major shift to more arid conditions near 3500 BC with oscillating aridity thereafter. While air photos and topographic maps traditionally provided qualitative means of evaluating spatial patterning of archaeological remains relative to water, recent advances in satellite imagery and GIS technologies have allowed a far wider breadth of qualitative and quantitative spatial analysis (e.g., Berking et al. 2010; Bolton et al. 2006; Gillings 1995; Harrower 2010; Harrower et al. 2012; Hritz and Wilkinson 2006; Hritz 2010). In Yemen's Hadramawt region, these tools show physical landscape changes in patterns of deposition and erosion (Berger et al. 2012; Harrower et al. 2012) that occurred in concert with the emerging expertise of the region's earliest irrigators (Harrower 2008a, 2008b). Social and technological elaboration of irrigation over more than two subsequent millennia in the face of shifting hydrological and geomorphological conditions formed the agricultural foundations of Yemen's ancient desert kingdoms (Harrower 2009; Vogt et al. 2002; Wilkinson 2006, 2009).

# Water histories of ancient Yemen

In tandem with hydrology, social, political, and religious dimensions of water-use were also of critical importance across ancient Southwest Arabia. Water appears as a frequent political and ideological theme in pre-Islamic culture, a pattern echoed in many other arid contexts worldwide. Perspectives of spatial theory that consider space and place as venues for the production and enactment of politics and culture (Lefebvre 1974; Soja 1989; Tuan 1977) offer a deep window into ancient waterscapes and histories. For the American West, John Brinckerhoff (J. B.) Jackson in a series of books and essays including *The Necessity for Ruins* (1980) described the importance of landscape, memory, vernacular architecture, monuments, and ruins in shaping everyday experiences and generating American identities and culture. Houses, public buildings, and urban and rural layouts of streets and tracts of land, monuments to revered or representative historic figures, such as widely pervasive small-town statues of Civil War soldiers, explain the past while structuring understandings of the present and future. Although less immediately intelligible and legible to audiences of archaeologists thousands of years later, we can see comparable cultural landscape markers in Yemen's distant past. Some of the earliest surviving constructions in the region are dolmen monuments built as early as the middle fifth millennium BC along major wadis of eastern Yemen (McCorriston et al. 2011). These mysterious constructions were assembled of large stone slabs sometimes weighing as much as 200 kg that were frequently decorated with pecked geometric designs. More than a thousand years later during the mid-fourth millennium BC our earliest evidence of irrigation and crop agriculture appears in southern Arabia. Incipient irrigators probably first targeted springs and other water-rich areas where small-scale water control alleviated the challenges posed by the era's untimely shift toward aridity. In at least some parts of Yemen, early irrigators built small circular cairn tombs, similar to those found across the Arabian Peninsula, as early as 3200 BC (Figure 2.1). These tombs first appeared in southern Arabia at nearly the same time as irrigation and were built in topographically prominent locations that not only served as resting places for the dead, but additionally expressed memory of ancestors and pronounced claims to land and water (Harrower 2008a). J. B. Jackson who was also well known for his role in promoting the use of air photographs in viewing and understanding the American West undoubtedly would have approved of the use of satellite imagery to study such tombs. In his 1951 opening to journal *Landscape*, Jackson's inaugural essay *The Need of Being Versed in Country Things* argued not only that rural areas of the American West played a central role in defining American culture but also that views from the air and

FIGURE 2.1. Bronze Age Tower Tomb perched above Wadi Sana, Yemen. These tombs often overlook irrigable alluvial sediments where some of the region's earliest evidence of irrigation dates to the mid to late fourth millennium BC (photo by the author).

aerial photography uniquely reveal the historical interdigitation of nature and culture. Air photos and satellite imagery have similarly proven (and will undoubtedly continue to prove) important in understanding ancient Yemen, including for mapping ancient tombs and analyzing their spatial distribution in relation to water (Harrower et al. 2013, 2014)

After more than 2,000 years of irrigation in the highlands of both western and eastern Yemen, near the end of the second millennium BC large towns and eventually cities began to appear in lowland areas along the margins of Yemen's Ramlat as-Sab'atayn Desert interior. These large compact settlements with tall, multi-storied mud-brick buildings were flanked by smaller villages, tombs, ritual sanctuaries, fields, and irrigation systems generating an indelibly prominent cultural landscape (Breton 1999). By roughly 700 BC, powerful incense trading kingdoms produced a burgeoning range of inscriptions in Ancient South Arabia (ASA) script (MacDonald 2010; Stein 2013) including examples attesting to the deep importance of water and early leaders' role in managing and claiming credit for the bounties of irrigation (Harrower 2009; Stein 2010). Construction inscriptions describe the digging of wells and the building of canals, cisterns, and other irrigation works, and legal texts that define appropriate land uses frequently invoke gods as authorizing, protecting, or directly ordering particular actions (Avanzini 2004; Clark 1976; Pirenne 1971, 1977). These efforts by leaders to co-opt secular and cosmological recognition for control of water and the proceeds of irrigation show how substantially water shaped ancient politics. Even many hundreds of years after the fall of Yemen's pre-Islamic civilizations Al-Hamdānī recalled the many grand waterworks and other architectural achievements of bygone pre-Islamic kingdoms, including the famous dam at the Sabaean capital of Ma'rib (Faris 1938: 34).

Contemporary religious traditions, perceptions, and water-use across the Near East today similarly convey some of the patterning and legacies of water in the past. As de Châtel (2007) explored in her journey across North Africa and the eastern Mediterranean, water is inexorably interconnected with beliefs and social identities of Jews, Christians, and Muslims. Following on earlier polytheistic traditions, each of these religions impacted Yemen, including during a short interval of monotheism (Yule 2013a) prior to the dramatic rise of Islam. Indeed, the central role of water in Islam with its long enduring influences in the lives of local peoples and empires demonstrates the wide contextual significance of religion in water histories (Faruqui 2001; J. C. Wilkinson 1990). In Hadramawt region of eastern Yemen, ritual visitations to tombs of venerated ancestors include most famously Qabr Hud. This tomb and surrounding settlement dedicated to pre-Islamic prophet Hud (Ho 2006; Knysh 1997) is quite expectedly located in one of the region's most water-rich areas. Similarly, in Yemen's western highlands, the recent interface of new technologies, growing populations, tribal affiliations, and national politics have long structured patterns of water-use, perceptions of equity, and water allocation (Lichenthäler 2003; Varisco 1983).

## Water, space/time, and the beginnings of agriculture

Transitions to pastoralism and crop agriculture in ancient Yemen illustrate a multicausal historical pattern of dynamics that are highly informative in understanding agricultural origins worldwide. The region exhibits a specific local expression of factors that recur in transitions to agriculture globally, including climatic and environmental change, demography, economic risk, social relations, politics, and ideology. Unraveling the complex gesticulation of these disparate forces of change in different regions and historical contexts is central to long-running debates about the beginnings of agriculture. The deep insights southern Arabia, including Oman and the United Arab Emirates provide (e.g., Cleuziou 2007, 2009; Cleuziou and Tosi 2007; Potts 1990, 2012), remain underrecognized and vastly underexploited beyond the purview of regional specialists (Magee 2014). Due to contemporary geopolitical affiliations, including alignments of language and religion, Yemen is commonly grouped with the rest of the Middle East, Near East, or Southwest Asia and it is often presumed that agriculture must have spread or diffused into the region from the north. Surprisingly, it is farther from Jerusalem to the port city of Aden in southwest corner of Yemen (2,300 km) than it is from Jerusalem to Budapest (2,200 km). Few, if any, would argue that transitions to agriculture in Hungary could be explained in terms of histories of the Levant. However, it is often tacitly assumed that agriculture simply spread into southern Arabia or, alternatively, the region is simply overlooked (or ignored) in reviews of Near Eastern agricultural origins and thus falls into an archaeological interstice that is nowhere included in global overviews.

There are a wide range of reasons why less archaeologically known regions, including southern Arabia, are critically important for understanding agricultural origins. The long-standing depiction of agriculture as a discovery that originated and spread around the world from a handful of core areas (Bellwood 2004; Sauer 1952; Vavilov 1951) is an oversimplified portrayal that concentrates on plant and animal biology and domestication yet does far less to explain the complex historical dynamics that structured societal transitions to agriculture. Ongoing dialogue on the origins of agriculture in the leading journal *Current Anthropology* exemplifies some of the seemingly intractable differences among competing conceptions of agriculture's beginnings. A range of competing general explanations were highlighted in a 2009 issue from a symposium that initially centered on the impacts of population pressure (Cohen 2009) yet moved on to discussions of migration and diffusion (Bellwood 2009), climatic variability (Bettinger et al. 2009), human behavioral ecology and risk management (Gremillion 2009; Winterhalder and Kennett 2009), feasting (Hayden 2009), and local sociohistorical conditions within regions (Barton 2009; Bruno 2009; Iriarte 2009; Kuijt 2009; Zvelebil 2009). Each of these various explanatory perspectives have long-running and controversial histories, which signifies to many researchers that a multicausal combination of factors is likely at play (Barker 2006; Zeder and Smith 2009). Two years later another series of papers from a symposium of leading scholars was published in *Current Anthropology* with an introduction that noted the meeting brought together "a volatile mix scholars, from many times and places ... did not determine why agriculture originated ... and did not even agree on whether its causes were global or local" (Price and Bar-Yosef 2011: S169). At least ten different areas were identified as potential original centers of domestication and a great deal of emphasis was placed among the various papers on local conditions within regions. Indeed, in this same journal only a few years later vigorous continuing debate for long studied regions, namely the Near East (Asouti and Fuller 2013) and Europe (Robb 2013) led scholars to argue that in both of these regions local social and historical contingencies played the most important role. If so, our repertoire of case-study examples needs to expand beyond so-called core regions to include lesser-known geographies, such as southern Arabia, which followed atypical social and historical trajectories. Critical issues, including why peoples along the southern Red Sea eschewed agriculture for many thousands of years despite demonstrable interaction with agriculturists to the north, remain to be acknowledged beyond a relatively small cohort of researchers (Harrower et al. 2010). In the search to discover the world's earliest agriculture, regions to which agriculture is often *presumed* to have spread including most of Africa, Arabia, and Central Asia have languished in relative archaeological obscurity. Debate focused on domestication (e.g., Larson 2014) has often centered on biologically and genetically vexing issues of how to officially define a particular plant or animal as domesticated, and whether or not domestication happened rapidly within small core areas or more gradually over more diffuse geographies (Fuller et al. 2014). While these issues are of substantial importance, they depend not only on the idiosyncratic biology and genetics of particular plant and animal species but often also on the spatiotemporal vantage point and subjective perspective of analysts. What constitutes a "core" or "center" and what constitutes "rapid" or "protracted" is a matter of spatiotemporal point of view (Harlan 1971) that is shaped by subjective appraisals of what should be included or excluded in areas variably viewed as small or large (Bar-Yosef 2013: 50). Areas at the margins of traditional archaeological foci, including, for example, the island of Cyprus (Simmons 2007), greatly inform understanding of core regions precisely because they are often overlooked. Similarly, even the boundary between hunter-gatherers and agriculturists is far more of a blurry heuristic distinction than a clear, objectively definable categorical difference (Harris 1989; Smith 2001). Since evidence is often malleable enough to be molded to fit or contradict different general models, we are unlikely to ever achieve wide consensus regarding explanations of early agriculture in lieu of more detailed appraisals of evidence from lesser-known regions.

Gathering baseline evidence and building understanding of the many regions that are often considered peripheral is, I argue, just as likely to substantially enhance our ability to evaluate general models and produce widely accepted explanations as cyclical debates about regions that are vexing precisely because they are already well documented. For Yemen and Ethiopia, colleagues and I have argued that both multiregional influences and local historical contingencies played central roles amidst a palimpsest of climatic, environmental, demographic, economic, social, and ideological factors (Harrower et al. 2010). We also maintained that much of the conflict between different general models emanates from widely differing spatial and temporal scales of analytical vantage point rather than actual mutual exclusivity and incompatibility of different models. Some scholars are focused on the social interactions of individuals over seasons, years, and decades in villages, while others aim to explain climatic, environmental, or demographic ramifications over centuries and millennia spanning continents. Essentially, when we speak of the "origins and spread of agriculture" we are employing a particular "invention and diffusion" framing of the issue that is more than sixty years old (Sauer 1952; Vavilov 1951) and are often referring to and seeking to explain very spatiotemporally different phenomena with a long outdated conceptual framing.

Water is undoubtedly among the themes of wide, albeit underappreciated, importance in studies of early agriculture that is interjected in many of the aforementioned climatological, economic, demographic, social, and ideological issues. Three and a half decades ago Andrew Sherratt (1980) cogently reviewed the role of water in early cereal cultivation, yet one of his central arguments – that European rainfed farming is often considered a default agricultural norm when most early cultivation relied on ground and surface water – has yet to be widely acknowledged. Scholars working in the Levant have only recently begun to concentrate on Neolithic water-use and more broadly recognize the need for attention to small-scale water management, including agricultural terraces (Barker et al. 2008; Finlayson et al. 2011; Gebel and Fujii 2010; Kuijt et al. 2007; Mithen and Black 2011). Landscape perspectives that examine issues including the distribution of sites relative to water, and proactive management of water resources such as irrigation and terracing offer many revealing opportunities to clarify how and why hunter-gatherers came to intensify their use of particular plants and animals. Importantly, water-rich areas and small-scale irrigation were crucial to some of the earliest agriculture in both ancient Yemen (Harrower 2008a; 2008b) and the American West (Mabry 2002). In both cases what eventually became the most important domesticated crops originated elsewhere and took thousands years to spread a few thousand kilometers (Harrower et al. 2010; Merrill et al. 2009). As examined in the following chapters, the unique and historically contingent local patterns in these two regions are mutually informative; and particularly given the far greater breadth of research in the American Southwest, it can help enhance and propel investigations of Yemen and adjacent areas.

Irrigation in ancient Yemen may have been inspired by contemporary systems in adjacent regions, but technologies and social arrangements needed to be dramatically adjusted, even reinvented, to fit very different natural and political circumstances. Rather than being on the derivative receiving end of water management practices originating elsewhere, Southwest Arabia's unique histories interconnect the same constellation of factors, landscape, environment, technology, politics, religion, and culture, in very different formulations. They provide a distinct historical example and perspective that complements what is known about other times and places – including those seemingly as far-removed as the American West. A variety of ancient systems in adjacent regions, such as riverine irrigation in Egypt (Hassan 1997) and Mesopotamia (Adams 1981), runoff systems in Iran (Gillmore et al. 2009) and the Levant (Miller 1980), or more proximately the precursors of *aflaj* irrigation that supported the earliest agricultural settlements in Oman and the United Arab Emirates (Boucharlat 2003; Cleuziou 1996; Magee 2005) may have influenced the range of irrigation systems that emerged in Yemen. However, technologies in these neighboring regions are all very different in comparison with terrace agriculture, hillslope runoff, and flash floodwater technologies prevalent in Yemen, which are uniquely formulated to the region's arid tropical terrain, climate, and environments. Yemen notably lacks large perennially flowing rivers, that were a central focus of ancient Egyptian, Mesopotamian, and Indus irrigation, and ancient waterworks are therefore arguably less obscured (or at least obscured in different ways) by alluvial deposition. Rain falls predominantly in the summer, rather than in winter months as is the case in more northern areas such as the Levant and Iran. Very few underground infiltration galleries, known as qanats in Iran and as falaj in Oman and the Emirates, can be found in Yemen, and they contribute only a tiny fraction of Yemen's water supply. Regionally distinct social, political, and religious forces also played an enormous role. Just as politics and religion drove the move to claim land, control water, and homestead the American West, so too did a comparable, yet uniquely expressed range of political and ideological forces propel the transformation of land from hunting and gathering to pastoralism and crop rearing many thousands of years ago in Yemen.

Ultimately, given the wide and locally contingent diversity of transitions to agriculture, global theorizing about agricultural origins is best informed by local evidence from more than just a small number of so-called primary "core" regions. The rapidly burgeoning collection of documentation from around the world makes globally synthetic models prone to the perils of overlooking critical evidence and painting an oversimplified picture of migration and demographic expansion when the realities within regions are far more complex. If local historical contingencies and cultural particularities are really as important as many recent commentators argue, then neither analysis of individual regions nor globally synthetic reviews that deal in an abbreviated, cursory manner with a plethora of cases are appropriate. Instead, I argue, contrastive juxtaposition of two or three cases set within a wider context of global issues and debates is likely to prove, in the long-term, most revealing.

## Water, space/time, and the rise of complex polities

In contrast with explanations for agricultural origins, explanations proposed for the rise of the world's earliest states are almost always historically constructed and multicausal. Unwinding the interconnectivities of environments, demography, trade, warfare, politics, and the various similarities and differences among regions is undoubtedly a considerable challenge. Even in very early research scholars identified water and irrigation as one of the centrally important factors implicated in the genesis of ancient states (Steward 1949). A wide literature now grapples with the influences of irrigation among ancient states (e.g., Hunt et al. 2005; Lucero and Fash 2006; Mabry 1996; Marcus and Stanish 2006; Mithen 2012; Ortloff 2009; Scarborough 2003). Whether or not irrigation had significant economic and social ramifications among early states is no longer a matter of dispute. Rather, the nature, extent, and precise historical influences of irrigation among ancient complex societies and their trajectories are more predominately issues of controversy. Water and irrigation are clearly part of a complex repertoire of factors shaping ancient life. It is not whether water and irrigation were important but the specifics of how they contributed to make histories similar and different, how the pieces of the puzzle fit together, that has become central to understanding water's dynamics among ancient societies.

Much like investigations of ancient agriculture, archaeologists' studies of ancient state formation have traditionally focused on a small number of so-called primary cases that are long-thought to have spawned the rise of all subsequent, secondary states (Marcus 2008). This pattern of inquiry, while productive, has had significant ramifications for resultant understandings, including of irrigation. In the two earliest centers of ancient civilization, Egypt and Mesopotamia, irrigation often took place along major rivers that have buried many of the earliest farming systems under thick deposits of sediment. Although archaeologists have made considerable strides in mapping settlements and irrigation systems in both regions they encounter many challenges in retrieving a long-term sample that illustrates how irrigation originated and changed through time. As Huot pessimistically noted with reference to the Ubaid period immediately preceding the origins of states in his southern Mesopotamia study locale, "we must completely abandon all hope of mapping the irrigation network of these ancient times" (1989: 24). While the prospects of mapping southern Mesopotamian land and waterscapes are considerably less dire given the now wide availability of satellite imagery (Hritz 2010; Pournelle 2007), archaeologists concerned with the role of water in state formation still face significant challenges in unraveling long-term patterns of water-use (Rost and Hamdani 2011). Similarly, conceptually peeling back the many layers of alluvial sediment deposited over thousands of years along the Nile to identify early water-use presents comparably vexing difficulties (Butzer 1976; Hassan 1997; Wilson 2012). Other less archaeologically known regions, including but not limited to Yemen, exhibit very different histories alongside very different evidentiary opportunities and challenges that powerfully complement studies of so-called primary states.

Ancient Yemen (3200 BC – AD 600) and the American West (AD 1800–1950) are strikingly different culturally and historically, yet parallels and contrasts among water histories widely disparate in space and time illustrate how constellations of environmental, social, political, and religious factors combine to shape societies' interrelationships with water. Just as the histories of the American West are deeply intertwined with water, including ideologies of conquest and massive state-sponsored irrigation schemes (Worster 1992), so too are those of Yemen's ancient past in which conquering and watering the desert served as a centralizing political narrative for more than a thousand years (Darles et al. 2013; Nebes 2004). In counterpoint to the hydraulic hypothesis, the history of ancient Yemen (and the American West) show rather than political centralization developing because of the unavoidable need for massive irrigation systems, it was not water scarcity itself but ideologically reinforced reliance on costly waterworks as a solution to perceived water shortfalls that made water so important. Attention focused on geographies of water scarcity, specifically the need to settle, colonize, and control water-scarce areas, rationalized enormous irrigation works that in turn helped generate national identities and religiosities, and justified state sovereignties. Despite their profound differences, in both ancient Yemen and the American West agricultural production focused not in water-rich areas where rainfed agriculture was possible but in hyperarid areas where large state-constructed irrigation systems politically and ideologically propelled agricultural intensification. Massive irrigation schemes and associated identities facilitated state control and monopolization of water across the American West even though enormous federally funded dams and aqueducts belie the deep and comparatively underexploited rainfed agricultural potential of the American East (Worster 1985). Similarly, in ancient Yemen massive desert flash floodwater irrigation systems (along with frankincense trade and pilgrimage to state temples) drove the genesis of five great kingdoms (Ma'in, Qataban, Saba, 'Awsan, and Hadramawt) near the beginning of the first millennium BC. Immense irrigation systems, including the Great Dam at Ma'rib that stood for nearly 1,300 years, became a central part of religious and political rhetoric that eschewed the rainfed agricultural potential of highland Yemen where the vast majority (more than 75 percent) of locally produced food is grown today. In both cases it was not only water scarcity but the spatial distribution of water, geographies of scarcity, and centralizing rhetoric and social logic that justified massive irrigation systems, and promoted national identities, religiosities, colonization, and expansion.

There are, of course, not only similarities but also massive differences between ancient Yemen and the American West. In contrast with archaeologists' earlier arguments, most now agree Yemen's ancient civilization was largely autochthonous having devised its own writing system, unique political structure, and economic foundations. The American West was colonized by foreigners who violently displaced Native Americans and built on the enslavement of innumerable Africans. These colonial histories remind us of marginalized groups who are often overlooked in discussions of the ancient past. The voices of women, minorities, and everyday peoples are less accessible to archaeologists studying histories thousands of years ago, but nevertheless are just as important as elites in shaping histories. Moreover, the cultural, historical, and religious specifics of ancient Yemen and the American West are almost entirely different. Water has a propensity to become deeply intertwined in politics and ideology as illustrated in many cases around the ancient world (Oestigaard 2011), for instance, in water rituals of ancient Egypt (Amenta et al. 2005), among the ancient Maya (Lucero 2006), and ancient Khmer of Cambodia (Fletcher et al. 2008). The deep economic, social, and religious role of water is similarly exhibited in ancient Yemen in distinctive ways that eventually contribute to Islamic traditions and water laws. These, of course, cannot be richly explained through the American West, but the American West does help exemplify how and why environments, politics, and religion become interconnected with water in unique, historically and culturally contingent ways.

## The future of comparison, juxtaposition, and spatial archaeology

This chapter (and this book) argues for a distinct approach to comparison in archaeology that draws a balance between the advantages of analyzing individual histories versus widely synthetic global overviews. It combines and aims to help reconcile the seemingly incompatible methods of quantitative spatial analysis and qualitative spatial theory particularly as they pertain to studies of water histories. I question and challenge the time-honored primary/secondary, origins/spread categorizations that have long framed studies of early agriculture and state formation and recommend a geographically wider range of foci than the earliest and most monumental histories toward which archaeologists' attention most often gravitates. Contrastive pair-wise juxtaposition of cases that are outwardly very different offers new perspectives and avoids the troublesome problem of aiming to prove that cases are the same or closely similar when all histories and cultures are to some extent unique. While there are a vast array of comparative approaches capable of contributing new understanding of ancient societies (Smith 2011), the past success of pair-wise comparisons including Adams' (1966) comparison of the earliest urban societies in Mesoamerican and Mesopotamia, Sahlins' (2004) comparison of ancient Greece and historic Fiji, and Geertz's (1968, 1972) comparisons of Indonesia and Morocco, suggest a promising future. As archaeological evidence accumulates, broad global overviews become less achievable and less likely to offer compelling explanations to scholars with deep expertise in evidence from particular regions. The approaches adopted for impressive recent masterworks by prominent figures in archaeology, including Bruce Trigger's (2003) *Understanding Early Civilizations: A Comparative Study*, which analyzed seven different civilizations, or Kent Flannery and Joyce Marcus's (2012), *The Creation of Inequality: How Our Prehistoric Ancestors Set the Stage for Monarchy, Slavery and Empire*, which reviewed a very wide range of cases to make arguments applicable worldwide, become less and less feasible for younger generations of scholars faced with a deluge of important new literature almost daily. As Robert McCormick Adams (2004) described in his review of Trigger's aforementioned book, so much time and energy was expended examining the validity of comparing the seven different societies selected that it ultimately detracted from the overall effort to provide a collective synthetic analysis. There will always remain some level of healthy tension between generalizing nomothetic and specifying idiographic approaches to archaeological research. Yet in an increasingly troublesome contemporary world wrought by xenophobia and violent conflict, better comparative understanding of similarities and differences through which we draw distinctions between ourselves and others is crucial to effectively confront challenges of the future.

In conjunction with contrastive juxtaposition, spatial analysis and spatial theory offer a range of powerful tools and perspectives to consider the ancient past. Acknowledging the wide middle ground between quantitative spatial analysis and qualitative spatial theory both strengthens and diversifies archaeological research. Water is one of the world's most indispensable resources. Its spatial plasticity make it perpetually manageable and malleable, its variability and periodicity defines climates and environments, and water often plays a crucial role in culture, ritual, and religion. Scalability, borders, boundaries, and categories are of central importance to considerations of places, spaces, and landscapes and even quantitative spatial analyses encounter substantial subjectivities related to scale and data classification. Perspective and vantage point are similarly central to spatial theory. Modern and historical geopolitics have long structured archaeologists' research and they continue to shape disciplinary alignments, interests, and funding support for archaeology. As a professor of mine once remarked, the apparent spatial distribution of archaeological sites often has as much to do with the distribution of archaeologists as it does with people of the ancient past. This observation recommends that we expand our explorations to areas that may lack the earliest and the most fantastic discoveries, to gain wider appreciation of underexplored contexts and global perspective.

CHAPTER 3

# Water histories of ancient Yemen in global comparative perspective

> *Suppose now that a new army of frontier farmers – as many as could occupy another belt of 50 miles, in width, from Manitoba to Texas, could, acting in concert, turn over the prairie sod, and after deep plowing and receiving the rain and moisture, present a new surface of green, growing crops instead of dry, hard baked earth covered with sparse buffalo grass. No one can question or doubt the inevitable effect of this cool condensing surface upon the moisture in the atmosphere as it moves over by the Western winds. A reduction of temperature must at once occur, accompanied by the usual phenomena of showers. The chief agency in this transformation is agriculture. To be more concise.* Rain follows the plow.
>
> (Wilber 1881: 68)

Water interconnects a wide range of environmental, historical, political, and cultural dimensions of social life. The drive to apprehend nature expressed in different ways in different times and places is in some ways unique to particular historical cases, yet does exhibit significant commonalities across contexts. Understandings of water environments, for instance, are invariably shaped by political ideals. The climatological theory of the late 1800s "rain follows the plow" – that cultivation of the American West would release soil moisture and permanently increase precipitation – exemplifies linkages among political rhetoric, social logic, and water. Among this concept's proponents were noted scientists, writers, and publishers, including Professors Cyrus Thomas (Southern Illinois University), Samuel Aughey Jr. (University of Nebraska), and Frank H. Snow (University of Kansas), whose support lent credibility to media that vigorously promoted railroads, homesteading, and settlement of western drylands (Emmons 1971). This convenient yet misguided theory was also taken up at nearly the same time to promote settlement of Australia's desert interior (Ferrill 1980).

Not only do some of the same adaptive challenges recur in arid regions, but politicized conceptions of environments are frequently interjected in both modern and ancient times to shape food production economies.

Water histories of ancient Yemen are atypical, yet informative, in illustrating global patterns including interconnectivities of water, culture, and politics. Arabs and Arabia have quite notoriously served as a central archetype of tribal societies (Dingelstedt 1916; Evans-Pritchard 1949) from which scholars have drawn often misguided views of nomads and pastoralists. Similarly, early American settlers and American West long served as a continuing stereotype of farmers as pressing forward a mythical frontier separating savagery from civilization (Limerick 1987). In both instances the representational repercussions in shaping understandings of societies and water are considerable. Setting juxtaposition of America and Arabia in a wider historical frame helps reveal the role of water among hunter-gatherers, pastoralists, agriculturists, and ancient states worldwide.

Many of the categorical constructions of archaeology that have long structured our investigations of the ancient past are overdue for reappraisal, including Wittfogelian views on societies' interrelationships with water. Archaeologists have traditionally concentrated their energies in areas of the world with the earliest most striking finds, and since agriculture and complex societies appear comparatively later in southern Arabia in comparison with the eastern Mediterranean it is often erroneously presumed that the region must have been a secondary recipient rather than an originator of agriculture and political complexity (Harrower et al. 2010; McCorriston 2013). Conventional distinctions between core/periphery and primary/secondary regions in transitions to agriculture and origins of states have come to obscure the contingencies and complexities of local cultural and historical change. Archaeologists' efforts have long been predicated on V. G. Childe's (1952) early conceptualization of Neolithic and Urban Revolutions, yet precisely what such transformations entail in any particular region is a matter of wide variability. Arguments that we need to better recognize pastoral nomadic states that are not founded upon cities (Frachetti 2012; Honeychurch 2014), suggest that the origins of urbanism may need to be further decoupled from models for the beginnings of civilization (Cowgill 2004; Smith 2009). Similarly, the categories wild versus domesticated plants and animals long used to define the Neolithic Revolution are useful as descriptive tools yet nature does not produce conveniently discrete, mutually exclusive types (Harris 1989; Rindos 1984). Biological, ecological, and cladistic concepts used to define species often blur on closer inspection. Similarly, scrutiny of categorical distinctions between foragers, pastoralists, and agriculturists reveals far more mixing and pliability than commonly assumed (Smith 2001). As historian of the American West Richard White (1995) argued in his book, *The Organic Machine: The Remaking of the Columbia River*, nature only exists as it is understood in relation to culture; people work and experience their surroundings in interaction with things understood as natural or wild. For ancient Yemen, designation as secondary recipient of agriculture and civilization overlooks the unique local script (Ancient South Arabian), architectural, artistic, and religious traditions, sociopolitical organization and the region's distinct irrigation technologies. However, it would be similarly remiss to contend that histories of Yemen were *entirely* autochthonous as the region was impacted by a complex combination of local and multiregional (global) influences. Irrigation agriculture in Yemen was inspired to some degree by practices in adjacent regions. At least some of the domesticated plants and animals upon which early societies came to rely were introduced from elsewhere (including sheep and sorghum) and by the time irrigation appeared in Yemen during the fourth millennium BC substantial scale irrigation was well underway in the Levant (Braemer et al. 2009), Egypt (Mays 2010), Mesopotamia (Tamburrino 2010), and Iran (Wilkinson et al. 2012). However, Southwest Arabian terrain, environments, and social contexts posed unique challenges, and the region followed atypical trajectories through foraging, pastoralism, crop agriculture, and civilization throughout which water availability and water management were crucial. Southwest Arabia, therefore, can not only assist in revealing the local and interregional connections during an era of ancient globalization, but additionally helps reveal parallels among water and agricultural histories worldwide.

Water is an illuminating theme through which to examine histories of ancient societies as water intervenes in a wide variety of environmental, economic, demographic, social, and political dimensions of peoples' lives. Technically speaking, water manipulation technologies can be viewed as falling along a continuum of water management intensity. In Southwest Arabia a wide range of techniques and technologies were used, included digging wells and cisterns, exploiting hill-slope runoff or flood-recession waters, to flash floodwater or spate irrigation, terraces, dams, canals, and underground infiltration galleries (Varisco 1996). In any particular circumstance, technologies vary in a complex manner according to terrain, climate, environment, social, cultural, and political factors; yet despite wide diversity there are broad cross-cultural parallels, such as tendency toward centralized management as scale increases (Mabry 2000). In counterpoint to Wittfogel's hydraulic hypothesis, it was not, I argue, an unavoidable need for centrally managed large-scale irrigation that contributed to the rise of complex societies in arid regions, but rather spatial heterogeneity of water that polities exploited to rationalize highly concentrated agricultural production in ways that perpetuated state sovereignty.

## Irrigation, hunting, and gathering

> Elementary forms of supplementary watering may be almost as old as consciously conducted, archaeologically recognizable agriculture itself.
> *(Robert McCormick Adams 2006: 17)*

Even from the earliest peopling of the world many tens of thousands of years ago, water was a significant factor in shaping human movement, foraging, and residential mobility. While evidence of water management in contexts without agriculture is rare, it is certainly not absent. Thus we might even extend Adams's observation and argue that water control for drinking and other household purposes as well as to promote growth of natural vegetation is not only as old as, but even earlier than, agriculture. For populations in arid regions water availability is crucial not only for human consumption but additionally because it fosters vegetation and tends to attract game. Ethnographic research among Australian and African foragers has demonstrated, for example, the importance of proximity to water in influencing residential mobility (Kelly 1995: 126–27); and archaeological predictive models for ancient North American foraging populations frequently identify proximity to water as a primary determinant of settlement locations (Kvamme 1985). Since these associations demonstrate that water was an important matter of concern, it is not unexpected that some foraging populations took steps beyond passive reliance on water availability and devised water diversion techniques to ensure the success of desirable plants and animals.

Moving far back in time to consider the world's earliest hunters and gatherers, Yemen has recently become a center-point of interest and debate as proponents of the Southern Dispersal Hypothesis have argued the southern Red Sea (rather than exclusively the Sinai Peninsula) was an important gateway of early human migration out of Africa (e.g., Boivin et al. 2013; Derricourt 2005; Field et al. 2007; Petraglia 2003). While climatic and sea level changes have long played an important role in studies of the timing and geography of early human migrations, the spatial availability of water has more recently been recognized as a specifically important part of ancient climates and environments. Finlayson's (2013) Water Optimization Hypothesis draws on spatial analysis of 357 sites occupied between 200,000 and 10,000 years ago to propose that early humans favored intermediate semiarid environments that were neither rain forests nor arid deserts. While this hypothesis undoubtedly deserves thorough consideration that is not possible here (including evaluations of many preservation, site discovery, and paleoenvironmental issues) it does further point to the foundational importance of freshwater availability. In Arabia, Middle Paleolithic sites discovered in piedmont foothills of the Tihama along Yemen's Red Sea coast (Delagnes et al. 2013) and from the margins of Mundafan Paleolake of the interior of Saudi Arabia (Crassard et al. 2013a) reinforce the importance of water among early populations. Very ancient experiences adapting to water resources contributed over time to careful scheduling of activities in accordance to water, and perhaps enhancement of natural pools to encourage water retention, but such low impact activities are very unlikely to be archaeologically identifiable for such ancient times.

Beyond reliance on natural water availabilities, ancient Yemen and the prehistoric American West are two of the primary instances (along with Australia) of irrigation among populations at the cusp of agriculture. The Owen's Valley of eastern California – a region that was famously drained of much of its water to supply the city of Los Angeles – was originally home to Paiute ("Water" Ute) Indians who diverted water into small channels from local creeks and rivers. Julian Steward who studied the Owens Valley Paiute (Steward 1933, 1938) considered them a nonagricultural population. He maintained in his provocatively titled paper *Irrigation without Agriculture* that the Paiute used small ditches and earthen channels to divert water toward plots of seeds and tubers, but "They did not till the soil, plant or cultivate. They merely intensified by irrigation what nature had already provided" (Steward 1930: 150). Steward took an interest in the topic because it pertained to the contention that irrigation was involved in the world's earliest cultivation and domestication of plants and subsequent civilization (Steward 1930: 149; 1949). He considered number of possible explanations for the presence of irrigation among the Paiute including an independent origin or diffusion from Native Americans elsewhere in the Southwest (Steward 1930: 154–56, 1933: 248–49).

Was irrigation practiced among Native American populations without agriculture? More recent appraisals of historic accounts have shown that the Paiute in some areas did plant crops such as maize, beans, and squash, and diverted water to promote the growth of a variety of local wild plants (Lawton et al. 1976; Stoffle and Zedeño 2001). An even wider range of ethnohistoric evidence recounts "semi- or quasi-agricultural" (Bean and Lawton 1993) practices including intentional burning to induce vegetation succession, irrigation, and planting of foods including grasses among

Native Californians (Blackburn and Anderson 1993). In a range of contexts the tilling, irrigating, sowing, and harvesting practices that typically qualify as agriculture were present without plants typically designated domesticates (Anderson 1993). Interestingly, the starchy carbohydrate-rich tubers of purple nut-grass (*Cyperus rotundus*) and yellow nut-grass (*Cyperus esculentus*) that were irrigated by some Paiute populations were also favored foods of some Aboriginal Australian groups and are thought to have been a staple for the late Pleistocene residents of Wadi Kubbaniya in Egypt (Wendorf et al. 1989; Wetterstrom 1993: 175–76). These marshy adapted sedges can be vegetatively propagated by simply cutting and replanting uneaten tubers and are known under the right conditions to produce enormous yields of 3.3 kg/m$^2$ that meet (or even surpass) yields of modern cultivated cereals (Wetterstrom 1993: 175). Based on early fourth millennium BC finds, Zohary and Hopf (2000: 198) argue this plant is among the earliest cultivars in Egypt. Yellow nut-grass is historically known to have been eaten in Arabia and may have been important in ancient times. Although now considered a weed in many countries, yellow nut-grass is still grown in some places including in Valencia region of Spain where it is mixed with water and sugar to make the famous iced drink *Horchata de Chufa*, which quite possibly may be attributable in part to contacts with Arabia.

In stark contrast with traditional views that conceptualize agriculture as a discovery or invention, close scrutiny of indigenous plant use (including horticulture and irrigation of wild plants) makes clear that the distinction between hunter-gatherer and agricultural societies is far less a definitive categorical boundary and far more a blurry heuristic boundary. Indeed, a range of scholars have marshaled strong evidence against the notion that a clear, mutually exclusive categorical distinction can be made between foragers and farmers. Headland and Reid (1989) challenged the view that recent, late Holocene foragers ever existed independent of partial reliance on food production or trade with food producers. David Rindos (1984) and David Harris (1989) both forcefully argued that the wide diversity of plant exploitation strategies used by ancient foragers and farmers are best viewed as a continuum or plant–people interaction and domestication. Smith (2001) coined the term "low-level food producers" to refer to groups with a range of food acquisition strategies along this continuum; and a recent reappraisal of ethnographic data by Bulbeck (2013) shows quite heavy reliance on wild foods among incipient farmers.

The traditional view that agriculture was invented and appeared abruptly in small core areas is highly questionable upon closer scrutiny, including for the Near East (Zeder 2011). Using recent botanical and genetic evidence,

# Irrigation, hunting, and gathering

Dorian Fuller and colleagues (2010, 2011, 2012) have argued that agriculture appeared around the world in diffuse, protracted patterns. Despite the difficulties and uncertainties of designating plant remains as officially domesticated, some have argued in rebuttal that Near Eastern agriculture did appear in a more traditional sudden, core-area pattern (Abbo et al. 2010, 2012). Yet, the simple fact that after fifty years of analysis there remains such vigorous debate itself indicates that the subjectivities of differing spatiotemporal perspectives play an important role. Complex, debatable, fuzzy boundaries between wild and domesticated plants, and by extension between foragers and farmers, indicate that rather than searching for mutually exclusive categories, acknowledging the ambiguities and particularities of context is important. At the local scale of village life, in seasons, years, or even decades, shifts toward reliance on domesticated plants and animals can appear gradual and spatially diffuse. Yet from the perspective of regions or continents over centuries and millennium the shift from foraging to farming sometimes can appear to be concentrated in relatively small areas where changes seem comparatively abrupt (Harrower et al. 2010).

In light of the malleable, fuzzy, scale-dependent boundaries between categories of hunter-gatherer and farmer, vantage point and historical contingency of so-called secondary cases become as important as those deemed primary. In the case of the Paiute, there was a clear political dimension – if Native American populations were not farmers, or were erroneously depicted as having learned farming from Europeans (see Stoffle and Zedeño 2001), then this contributed to the justification for forcibly displacing them. Similarly, as Sherratt (1980) observed, ancient agriculture has often been judged according to how closely it approximates traditional European rainfed-style farming, which is often viewed by default as the agriculture's most primordial form. However, in the Near East site locations suggest early cultivation was often practiced near springs, alluvial fans or other water-rich areas very unlike temperate-zone European practices.

The complexity of distinctions between foragers and farmers similarly arises in studies of ancient Yemen. Irrigation structures and terrace walls offer some of the earliest evidence of moves toward agriculture during the mid-fourth millennium BC (see also Chapter 4). Should these early irrigation structures be considered definitive evidence of farming? Or might these structures have been used to water wild plants? Whether or not they qualify as farming, such constructions represent practices on the cusp of plant food production and are therefore of substantial importance. Particularly since we lack associated archaeobotanical remains, it is difficult to determine what exactly was irrigated, but circumstantial evidence from the region along with the rarity of irrigation among foraging populations globally suggests domesticates may have been involved. Throughout the Near East, foragers were displaced by pastoralists many thousands of years ago and therefore are missing from the ethnographic record. Since documented cases of irrigation without cultivation are globally/cross-culturally limited, it seems unlikely that ancient Southwest Arabian groups first irrigated naturally occurring plants. Indeed, one would expect that given the labor necessary to irrigate a plot of land, other methods of promoting plant success, such as tilling or reserving seed for sowing would be worthwhile. By the time of our earliest dates for irrigation in Southwest Arabia (during the fourth millennium BC) domesticated wheat and barley were present in the region (Ekstrom and Edens 2003), and it therefore seems a relatively minor advancement from irrigation to actively planting and harvesting.

Beyond North America, the only other well-documented examples of irrigation among foragers come from hunter-gatherer populations of Australia who employed comparable small-scale water management strategies. Campbell (1965) reports that populations along the Roper River would divert water moving into and out of lagoons with temporary dams made of logs, sticks, wooden stakes, and bark, which attracted birds and fostered valuable food plants. Tindale (1977: 345, 347) similarly reports that two Northern Territory groups, the Iliaura (Alyawara) and the Wanja, traditionally blocked runoff channels leading from periodically flooded areas to encourage water retention and promote the success of edible plants. The Alyawara and other Australian aboriginal groups also intentionally set fires to induce vegetation succession and enhance the abundance of certain plant foods (Latz 2004; O'Connell et al. 1983). Why did the Alyawara not turn to more actively planting and tending (i.e., cultivating) plants? According to O'Connell the risks of doing so were greater than the potential rewards ...

> Given this [use of fire to assist wild plants], we might well ask why the Alyawara lacked domesticated crops, or more specifically, why they evidently made no attempt to improve the productivity of native plants through selective propagation. The question is especially interesting in light of the apparent importance of seeds in the traditional diet (Tindale, 1977), some of which, notably the millets (Panicum spp.), are morphologically and taxonomically similar to those domesticated elsewhere (Allen, 1974). The best answer may be that there was little advantage to be gained from the attempt. The productivity of plants throughout central Australia is closely tied to local rainfall, as are the movements of hunter-gatherers. Since rainfall is unpredictable both spatially and seasonally, hunters cannot be certain that any patch they improve by selective reseeding or

> intensive cultivation will receive enough precipitation to stimulate plant growth, or that it will be accessible from a water source large enough to support a camp for the time required to harvest and consume the crop. Under these circumstances, hunters probably did better in cost-benefit terms by maintaining their mobility. (O'Connell et al. 1983: 99)

Through emphasis on availability, mobility, scheduling, and risk management, these observations, grounded in Human Behavioral Ecology (Kennett and Winterhalder 2006), substantially inform understanding of incipient agricultural strategies in other arid regions, including ancient Arabia. Hackenberg (1962) offers a comparable explanation for partial reliance on irrigation agriculture among O'odham Indians of Arizona and concludes uncertainty and periodic drought inhibited greater reliance on cultivars. Even earlier, Kroeber (1935: 48–60) similarly marshaled environmental arguments for partial reliance on agriculture among the Hualapai of northwestern Arizona. Other Native American populations widely considered hunter-gatherers, such as the Apache, sometimes partially relied on irrigation agriculture including maize cultivation. Some Chiricahua Apache believed maize was recently introduced from Mexico (Opler and Kraut 1996: 373–75) while other Western Apache maintained maize was of much deeper antiquity in the area (Buskirk and Opler 1986: 56). Bean and Lawton (1993) argue it was neither harsh environmental conditions nor lack of awareness that inhibited agriculture among Native Californians but the sufficiency of food relative to population and cultural–historical factors that resulted in practices not commonly deemed agriculture.

In sum, water intervenes in an extremely wide range of plant exploitation strategies that fall along fuzzy boundaries between traditional categories of forager and farmer; and understanding of ancient Yemen significantly enhances understanding of other ancient contexts worldwide. The earliest evidence of irrigation in Yemen appears in conjunction with high residential mobility that left relatively ephemeral encampments and irrigation structures, yet as discussed in Chapter 4 it was increased aridity, variability, and uncertainty that contributed to the beginnings of irrigation rather than prevented it. Since the earliest documented irrigation appeared roughly two millennia after cattle and caprine pastoralism were established in the area, analysis of pastoral patterns of water exploitation are similarly important. Collectively, patterns of water-use in regions as distinct as Australia, North America, and Yemen highlight how environmental and historical contingency and the spatially, culturally, and politically imbued perspectives with which we view and define agriculture play substantive roles in our understandings of water histories.

## Water, irrigation, and pastoralism

> A long time ago there was a poor boy who tried to obtain secret power so that he might be able to get some of the things he wanted but did not have. He went out from his camp and slept alone on the mountains, near great rocks, beside rivers. He wandered until he came to a large lake northeast of the Sweetgrass Hills. By the side of the lake he broke down and cried. The powerful water spirit – an old man – who lived in that lake heard him and told his son to go to the boy and find out why he was crying. The son went to the sorrowing boy and told him that his father wished to see him ... "My father will offer you your choice of animals in this lake. Be sure to choose the old mallard and its little ones." ... The boy did as he was told. At the edge of the lake the water spirit's son collected some marsh grass and braided it into a rope. With the rope he caught the old mallard and led it ashore. He placed the rope in the boy's hand and told him to walk on, but not to look back until daybreak ... At daybreak he turned back and saw a strange animal at the end of the line – a horse.
> *Blackfoot story explaining the origins of horses* (Ewers 1955: 294–95)

The horse in Native American and the camel in Arabian culture typify colloquial views of bygone eras. The rapid seventeenth- and eighteenth-century adoption of horses across the American West – a subject of research nearly since the dawn of anthropology (Wissler 1914) – exemplifies the speedy, down-the-line spread of a domestic animal often lacking direct contact with Europeans who originally introduced them (Haines 1938a, 1938b). Plains Indians' rapid and dramatic adoption of horses, including the Blackfoot, illustrates how substantially animal husbandry can alter not only economic adaptations but the essential cultural dynamics of societies. One is prompted to consider the very different, yet similarly impactful pattern in which domesticated camels revolutionized travel, trade, warfare and water-use across the Arabian Peninsula during the late second millennium BC. The large-scale movement of frankincense from its peculiar highland habitats to markets throughout the eastern Mediterranean greatly enriched Southwest Arabian kingdoms, but it would have been nearly impossible without camels. Much earlier, near 6000 BC, the adoption of cattle, sheep, and goats across southern Arabia, which was accompanied by only scant indications of long-distance human migration, similarly transformed cultures and patterns of water-use. In eastern Yemen cattle-cult rituals marked by large gatherings for cattle sacrifice, ritual, and feasting depict dramatic ideological changes that came to revolve around these important herded animals (McCorriston et al. 2012).

# Water, irrigation, and pastoralism

In comparison with hunting and gathering, water is of heightened significance for pastoralists who must ensure an adequate supply of drinking water and forage for their animals. As the first groups shifted from wild to herded sources of food, the need to provision animals necessitated changes in patterns of mobility and territoriality. Incipient pastoralists moved from adaptation to persistent and recurrent patterning in the availability of wild game, to scheduling their lives around patterning of the water and forage resources their animals needed to survive. Historic and ethnographic evidence from the Near East depicts nomadic pastoralists accustomed to trade with neighboring settled farming populations. Trade with settled agriculturists facilitated heavy reliance on animals and afforded access to luxury goods produced in towns and cities. Considerations of this strategy, often deemed *specialized* pastoralism, and its development have generated a substantial literature (e.g., Bar-Yosef and Khazanov 1992; Gilbert 1983; Levy 1983; Linseele 2010). Lees and Bates (1974), for example, hypothesized that specialized pastoralism developed in tandem with irrigation agriculture as two divergent, symbiotic pathways of intensification derived from earlier mixed farming economies. However, more recent archaeological research across the southern Levant has shown that the long-term dynamics of interactions between nomads and settled farmers are complex, historically contingent with neither a directional pattern of progressive intensification/specialization nor adherence to simple economic rules (e.g., Barker 2012; Rosen 2011). Cheryl Makarewicz (2013) goes further to argue that medieval, ethnographic, and travelogue literature have perpetuated stereotypes of nomads and settled-folk that have structured archaeologists' views and studies of pastoralism from the Neolithic onward. From Ibn Khaldūn to Gertrude Bell (1907) recurrent images of noble Bedouin herders enduring along the harsh desert margins of civilization implicitly persist in ecological models that concentrate on pastoralism as survival and subsistence (Makarewicz 2013: 167–68). Indeed, these long persistent heroic tropes overlook a vast range of ancient social diversity, including among populations across southern Arabia.

In Yemen the earliest evidence for domesticated animals appears during the early sixth millennium BC (Martin et al. 2009; see also Uerpmann et al. 2013) roughly two thousand years before evidence of domesticated crops (Ekstrom and Edens 2003). As in Africa, a substantial interval of forager-pastoralism (that is, following the appearance of domesticated animals but prior to appearance of domesticated plants) is therefore of particular significance (Marshall and Hildebrand 2002). In Arabia's often hyperarid environments, foraging and hunting frequently concentrated in water-rich areas, and a crucial interval of social change must have occurred as the first hunting and gathering populations (or pastoralist immigrants) began herding animals and sought water to sustain them (McCorriston and Martin 2009). Herded animals would have interrupted wild animals' use of precious water sources and grazing areas, and herd competition would have contributed to potential conflicts requiring new understandings of water rights and territories. Drawing on nineteenth- and early-twentieth-century documents, Betts (1989) recounts the lifeways of Solubba populations of Arabia who only occasionally herded sheep, goats, camels, or more commonly asses, but survived predominantly through hunting gazelle, ibex, ostrich, and oryx. The Solubba were particularly renowned for their knowledge of remote desert areas and water sources. The sometimes friendly, sometimes adversarial character of their interactions with Bedouin neighbors evokes encounters the earliest pastoralists must have had with preexisting hunter-gatherers. Archaeological sites such as Umm Dabaghiyah in Iraq (sixth millennium BC, Kirkbride 1974) and Ash-Shumah on the Tihama coast of Yemen (seventh millennium BC, Cattani and Bökönyi 2002), where 69 percent and 92 percent of faunal remains were onager and ass respectively, point to a time when equid exploitation was more widely prevalent.

Cattle, the most water-demanding domesticated animal of the Near East, along with sheep and goat, were the earliest domesticates in Southwest Arabia (Fedele 2013; Martin et al. 2009; McCorriston and Martin 2009). While details of archaeological finds in the region are further discussed in Chapter 4, the basic physiological needs of cattle call attention to the adaptive strategies required to provision domestic animals. Early agronomic and development studies often depicted indigenous cattle pastoralists' practices as inefficient, yet subsequent reappraisals have revealed the effectiveness and resilience of large-herd, high-mobility, milk-over-meat tactics particularly in drought conditions (Breman and De Wit 1983; Western and Finch 1986). In arid regions without lakes or rivers, herds are often watered at springs, ponds, or other areas of natural water accumulation; pits or wells are also sometimes dug to access groundwater, or cisterns can be constructed to contain periodic flow (e.g., Dahl and Megersa 1990; Evans-Pritchard 1940: 57–59). Wendorf and colleagues argued that some form of water provisioning must have existed in Egypt since the seventh millennium BC, because without human assistance survival of cattle in the Western Desert would have been highly unlikely (Close and Wendorf 1992; Wendorf and Schild 1994, 1998). Some dispute this assertion as it presumes environmental conditions at the time were too arid to sustain wild cattle (Brass 2013). Cattle typically thrive when watered daily, but can metabolically adjust and maintain weight with less frequent watering. Some Maasi herders regularly walk cattle 16 km or more daily, or water them every second or even every third day, and cattle can maintain weight under such practices unless subject to food shortage (Western and Finch 1986). Forage is therefore of utmost concern. In a very approximate sense cattle husbandry requires about 400 mm of precipitation per annum, sheep and goats 200 mm, while camels can be sustained with as little as 100 mm (*cf.* Zarins 1992). However, studies of rangeland ecology offer more detailed information that links forage availability to precipitation (mean and standard deviation), insolation, topography (including runoff/run-on areas), landcover, vegetation dynamics, and rangeland history (Le Houérou et al. 1988). As estimated by Le Houérou et al. (1980) for the African Sahel, one mature zebu weighing roughly 250 kg requires approximately 10–12 hectares of rangeland in the Saharo Sahelian zone (100–200 m rainfall), 5 hectares in the Sahelian zone (200–400 mm), and 3.5 hectares in the Sudano-Sahelian zone (400–600 mm). Rainfall variability in the arid tropics has a well-documented tendency to increase as mean precipitation declines (Dewar and Wallis 1999). Since rangeland productivity is highly correlated with precipitation, and productivity responds dramatically to changes in rainfall, half the annual rain, for example, can lead to one quarter the available forage (Le Houérou and Hoste 1977). These characteristics combine to make heavy reliance on cattle an energetically efficient yet somewhat risky strategy that offers high returns in good years (Russell 1988), but requires considerable adaptive flexibility accounting for high transhumant mobility, tandem exploitation of small stock, and traditions that emphasize sharing, social connectivity, and alliance building. Indeed, recent studies of ancient African pastoralism have increasingly highlighted the importance of social and ideological dynamics, including cattle rituals, in the domestication and early husbandry of cattle in Africa (e.g., Brass 2013; di Lernia et al. 2013; Wengrow 2001). Wengrow and colleagues (2014) have even recently argued the origins of ancient Egyptian civilization ultimately lies in "primary pastoral communities" of northeastern Africa with roots as early as the fifth millennium BC. In Chapter 5 we return to such deep-time views of civilizations, including McCorriston's (2011, 2013) metastructural approach, which helpfully clarifies the long-term genesis of Southwest Arabian civilizations.

In conjunction with animal husbandry, groups often referred to as agro-pastoralists cultivate crops in ways that sometimes involve water management and irrigation. Particularly in arid regions, transhumance to ensure water and animal graze often necessitates patterns of mobility that make heavy reliance on rainfed cultivation and sedentary settlement impractical. Itinerant techniques such as flood-recession (décrue) cultivation are relatively common among African pastoralists. Turkana pastoralists who inhabit an area of northern Kenya with roughly 200 mm of annual precipitation traditionally grow sorghum along river floodplains, intermittent streams, and seasonally inundated lake shores (Adams and Anderson 1988; Morgan 1974). The Nuer of southern Sudan similarly rely on cattle and sorghum grown in seasonally flooded areas (Evans-Pritchard 1940). Other northeast African pastoralists practice spate irrigation where water is captured from hillsides and upland stream (wadi) networks. Bisharien (Beja) camel pastoralists of the Red Sea Hills (Sudan) cultivate sorghum using spate systems (Egemi 2000) as do agro-pastoralists of the Sheeb region, Eritrea who use tree branches and boulders to build small barrages and water diversion structures (Tesfai and de Graaff 2000; Tesfai and Stroosnijder 2001).

Irrigation among pastoralists invariably involves human consumption of irrigated foods rather than irrigation solely for animals. This issue is of particular importance in considering ancient Yemen, as pastoralism and irrigation appear together in contexts where we lack precise evidence of what was irrigated. In modern economies a great deal of food is grown exclusively for animals, but it is difficult to identify any traditional or indigenous circumstance in which crops or wild plants were irrigated for animals while humans exclusively consumed gathered, nonirrigated foods. Indeed, pastoralists sometimes irrigate but generally consume primary products (such as grain) themselves and supply the by-products (such as hay or straw) to animals. Given the trophic energy losses involved in irrigating plants for fodder and then consuming resultant meat, milk, or blood (rather than crops themselves), it is not surprising that irrigated plants are generally only used for fodder after they have provided humans with food. One might expect that mixed cultivation-herding strategies would hold increased importance when reliable trade for plant foods was not an option, or when foraged human plant food availability was declining or unreliable because of overexploitation or aridity.

## Water, irrigation, and incipient farming

It may appear paradoxical to affirm that it is in arid districts, where agriculture is most arduous, that agriculture began; yet the affirmation is not gainsaid but rather supported by history, and is established beyond reasonable doubt by the evidence of the desert organisms and organizations. So, whatever its last estate, in its beginning agriculture is the art of the desert. W. J. McGee (1895: 375)

For more than 100 years, archaeological and ethnohistoric evidence of indigenous irrigation across the American West has significantly informed understanding of agricultural origins. Early scholars such as W. J. McGee, the first president of the American Anthropological Association, noted the significance of the American Southwest for understanding the beginnings of agriculture worldwide. Although his assertion that agriculture began in deserts was a premature simplification, it does still hold an element of accuracy in some contexts, including the Near East. Almost seventy-five years later, Flannery (1969) argued that cultivation began in marginal (more arid) locales when groups pushed out of optimal areas attempted to artificially replicate the dense wild stands of cereals found in their more ideal homelands. While Flannery referred to the earliest cultivation as dry-farming he importantly noted that the earliest villages in the Near East, Central Asia, and Mesoamerica frequently appeared to be concentrated where early farmers could cultivate in high water-table or other water-rich areas (Flannery 1969: 81). After another forty years, archaeologists are still vigorously debating not only how and why, but also precisely where and when agriculture originated. For the Near East some adhere to the more traditional view that domestication of crops and agriculture appeared relatively suddenly in a core area (Abbo et al. 2010, 2012) while others argue a more diffuse and protracted pattern is evident (Fuller et al. 2011, 2012). In some respects what qualifies as sudden and what constitutes a core is a matter of perspective. Even a number of villages or communities interacting over thousands of square kilometers might from some vantage points be considered a core (Bar-Yosef 2013: 50). We do know that environmental conditions, aridity, and water availability undeniably played a role; yet even those who argue strongly in favor of climate as an instigator of the world's earliest agriculture concede that social factors and historical contingency were most central in structuring the subsequent post-Pleistocene spread of agriculture (Bettinger et al. 2009).

So, *did* agriculture in the Near East first arise in the desert? Or more precisely, what was the role of water in the first appearance and subsequent expression of agriculture? The study of ancient agriculture has long been structured by the assumption that irrigation agriculture descended from preexisting forms of rainfed cultivation. Indeed, this was one of the central suppositions of early research on agriculture in the Near East; since irrigation was presumably more work, it must have come later as an addition to dry-farming (Flannery 1969; Helbaek 1960). However, the view that dry-farming (or in other words rainfed) techniques are a primordial agricultural norm runs counter to Flannery's (1969: 81) own insightful observations about early cultivation most commonly occurring in areas with abundant ground and/or surface water. Indeed, close proximity to water is a nearly ubiquitous characteristic of early agricultural villages of the Near East (Byrd 2005; Finlayson et al. 2011; Mithen 2012; Willcox 2005). Early farming sites of the Pre-Pottery Neolithic A (PPNA) period of the Levant (9700 to 8700 BC) were often located in naturally water-rich areas including near springs such as Jericho (Bar-Yosef 1986), Netiv Hagdud (Por 2004), along Wadi Faynan (Barker et al. 2007; Mithen and Black 2011), or near annually flooding perennial rivers such as Abu Hureyra and Mureybet (Moore et al. 2000). Archaeologists traditionally often cite the 200 or 300 mm annual rainfall isohyets as the limit of Near Eastern rainfed farming (Bagg 2012). While most acknowledge that this boundary is not immutably fixed and varies over time, natural water availability depends on a far wider complexity of factors, including precipitation, isolation, landcover, runoff/run-on, and water-table characteristics that vary at seasonal, annual, decadal, centennial, and millennial scales. Early farmers were undoubtedly aware of the conditions under which wild cereals thrived and therefore most probably would not have initially relied solely on rainfall when other means, such as targeted cultivation in water-rich areas, were available to ensure water availability and high productivity. For example, periodically inundated alluvial fans, wadi beds, or riverbanks not only allow targeting of soil moisture, but are also more productive because of the nutrients carried by waterborne sediments. Inundation can wipe out existing plants and weeds providing a fresh and fertile seedbed for planting that (perhaps inadvertently) helps genetically isolate domesticates. While such strategies are not generally considered irrigation it is also inaccurate to refer to them as rainfed cultivation as they are more aptly described as floodwater, water-table, or runoff farming. Technically, the term dry-farming specifically designates cultivation in semiarid areas that relies on moisture retained in soil, as opposed to rainfed farming which refers to cultivation in areas with appropriately timed rainfall (Mabry and Doolittle 2008: 58; Widtsoe 1911), but few adhere to this subtle and somewhat counterintuitive distinction.

From reliance on wild stands of cereals and planting crops in naturally water-rich areas, evidence of water management, namely wells and cisterns for capturing water, and barrages to retain water on areas for cultivation appears more widely during the Pre-Pottery Neolithic B (PPNB, ca.

# Water, irrigation, and incipient farming

8700–7000 BC). Some have used the memorable phrase "domestication of water" to refer to developments that began during this interval (Garfinkel et al. 2006; Gebel and Fujii 2010). Steven Mithen (2010: 5270) provocatively asserts, "Ultimately, it was the domestication of water that allowed civilization to emerge." Examples of Pre-Pottery Neolithic water management, albeit sometimes controversial, include the ditch and walls at Jericho (Bar-Yosef 1986), barrages near Wadi Abu Tulayha in southern Jordan (Fujii 2007), wells on Cyprus (Peltenberg et al. 2000) and somewhat later during the PPNC submerged wells at Atlit-Yam off the coast of Israel (Galili and Nir 1993). Given the relatively modest nature of early constructions, water management may have also taken place at many other early settlements only to be destroyed by later water flows leaving no discernable remains. For example, at PPNB sites like Beidha, which is located near a spring in an area where local topography constricts runoff (Rambeau et al. 2011), it seems likely early settlers experimented with water control but no proof of such practices is thus-far evident. Ancient vestiges of water management have only recently captured the heightened attention of archaeologists due in part to the increasing prevalence of landscape methods (Wilkinson 2003a). While continued searching will undoubtedly reveal more remnant structures most were likely modest constructions made of rock and brush that rarely survive thousands of years.

By the Pottery Neolithic (ca. 7000 BC) more definitive evidence of irrigation (i.e., diversion of water onto areas for cultivation) is evident alongside the aforementioned water management practices. A more than 4 m deep, stone-lined well at the large 20 hectare settlement of Sha'ar Hagolan in Israel (Garfinkel et al. 2006) and terrace walls at Dhra in Jordan (Kuijt et al. 2007) attest to increasing investments in water control. Across the Near East, much of the evidence of irrigation during the Pottery Neolithic is rather indirect, including a plethora of settlements in areas of southern Mesopotamia that would have required irrigation (Wilkinson and Rayne 2010: 118). Some of the best direct evidence of irrigation has long come from small canals at Choga Mami, Iraq (Oates and Oates 1976) as well as hill-slope runoff irrigation along the Rud-I-Gushk drainage of Iran that probably dates to the Chalcolithic (Prickett 1985). These finds have recently been bolstered by evidence of irrigation from the site of Tepe Pardis (Iran) that may date as early as the sixth millennium BC (Gillmore et al. 2009).

In addition to physical evidence of ancient water management structures, analysis of archaeobotanical remains, including weed assemblages, phytoliths and stable isotopes are also of considerable utility in revealing the role of water in early cultivation. Analysis of complete archaeobotanical assemblages, including the weeds rather than solely the crops, has been pursued as a means to reconstruct crop husbandry practices and environmental circumstances. Although complex combinations of growing conditions govern weed floras, experimental results indicate a potential ability to distinguish different watering regimes (Charles et al. 2003; Jones et al. 2005, 2010). Cereal phytoliths have also garnered attention as potential indicators of water availability and irrigation. Experimental results have shown significant size and structure differences in phytoliths under irrigation (Madella et al. 2009; Mithen et al. 2008; Rosen and Weiner 1994). Carbon isotopes can similarly be used to evaluate water conditions experienced by crops (Araus et al. 1999; Ferrio et al. 2005; Flohr et al. 2011; Wallace et al. 2013). During photosynthesis plants often discriminate against heavier $^{13}C$ isotopes in comparison with lighter $^{12}C$. When in water-stress, closed plant stomata help conserve water and reduce discrimination against $^{13}C$ leading to higher $\Delta^{13}C$ values. Conversely, open stomata when water is abundantly available increases discrimination against $^{13}C$ and leads to lower $\Delta^{13}C$ values (Wallace et al. 2013). Irrigation might therefore be inferred when crops isotopically indicate wetter conditions than expected based on other proxies such as isotope values for nearby wild plants (Flohr et al. 2011: 125). While such techniques have yet to be utilized in studies of ancient Yemen, they do hold great potential for clarifying ancient irrigation practices and climate change.

In conjunction with aforementioned evidence from archaeologically better-known parts of the ancient Near East, Yemen and the American West also provide rich archaeological and ethnographic evidence of small-scale water management and irrigation that offers many comparative insights. Western Yemen is renowned for its steep terraced mountainsides and wide range of traditional irrigation systems, including spring flow (ᶜayn and ghayl,), surface runoff (mudarrajāt and shrūj), wells and cisterns (bi'r, birkah, ma'jil, sināwa), flash floodwater (sayl), and underground infiltration galleries (qanāts and aflaj). While roughly 80 percent of modern cultivated land is rainfed (ᶜaqar) rather than irrigated (Taha 1988: 14; Varisco 1996: 239; 2009: 389) water management is crucial in intensifying production, growing fruit and vegetable crops, and mitigating the effects of periodic water shortfalls. Interestingly, comparable strategies can also be found in other arid regions including the American West where many of the small-scale water management and irrigation techniques including check dams and terrace agriculture bear a striking resemblance to those in Yemen (Doolittle 2000). Mabry and Doolittle (2008) examine ancient floodwater, water-table, and runoff farming practices of the U.S.–Mexico

# Water, irrigation, and incipient farming

borderlands and emphasize that these techniques were far more common than rainfed farming, which was rare and restricted to high elevation areas. Indeed, planting crops in naturally water-rich areas such as springs, alluvial fans, or periodically inundated locations, sometimes in conjunction with small-scale water management, is one of the most effective forms of cultivation in arid regions. Spring-fed irrigation from small (ᶜ*ayn*) or larger (*ghayl*) flows is common in Yemen and spring water is often diverted into banked fields or cisterns for agricultural uses and human consumption (Varisco 1983). Numerous ancient and historic groups across the American Southwest also traditionally grew crops near springs, arroyos, and alluvial fans using a wide range of water management strategies. Floodwater farming among the O'odham (Papago) Indians (Nabhan 1979, 1986a) is particularly informative in understanding ancient Yemen. Nabhan (1986b), for instance, reexamined what the indigenous term '*ak-ciñ* arroyo mouth farming refers to in a geomorphological sense and observed that irrigators paid careful attention to stream gradients and targeted areas where gradients flatten resulting and areal dispersion of water and nutrient bearing sediments. As outlined in Chapter 4, ancient irrigators along the Wadi Sana drainage of eastern Yemen (Figure 3.1) similarly targeted gradient-change locations as early as the fourth millennium BC (Harrower et al. 2012). Terrace agriculture appeared in western Yemen at nearly the same time (Wilkinson 1999, 2005, 2006) suggesting experimentation with a variety of different techniques in different contexts. Agricultural terraces, a relatively common means of conserving soil and retaining water worldwide, are similarly known along the U.S.–Mexico borderlands where they have often been referred to as *trincheras* (a Spanish term meaning trenches, see below).

Issues and debates surrounding water management and the beginnings of agriculture across the American Southwest mirror those that dominate studies of ancient Yemen. The distinct nature of evidence and history of investigations in the two instances makes them mutually informative and complementary. In both cases the crops that eventually come to dominate (maize in the Americas and sorghum in Yemen) are introduced from elsewhere, but in both regions there remains wide disagreement about whether the arrival of cultivars was the result of human migration or diffusion. While generalized global models often favor origin and spread patterns of population expansion (Bellwood 2004, 2013; Diamond 1997) detailed analysis of local evidence from the American Southwest and Southern Arabia does not support globalizing arguments for immigration of farming populations (e.g., Harrower et al. 2010; Merrill et al. 2009). Importantly, we know

FIGURE 3.1. Middle Wadi Sana showing the main wadi channel flanked by alluvial silts and upland bedrock slopes and plateaus. These alluvial silts and the hillslopes and small tributaries watering them were invaluable for ancient grazing and eventually for irrigation (photo by the author).

considerably more about the arrival of cultivars in the American Southwest than we do about the first appearance of crops in Yemen. The earliest archaeobotanical evidence of plant domesticates in Yemen hinges on a single site, Jubabat al-Juruf, that places wheat, barley, lentils, and possibly millet during the fourth millennium BC (Ekstrom and Edens 2003), which is bolstered by comparably dated evidence of small-scale water management (Harrower 2008a, 2008b; Wilkinson 1999). Recent pollen evidence more firmly establishes the arrival of maize at Chaco Canyon, New Mexico by the mid-third millennium BC (Hall 2010) where researchers interests have similarly focused on water availability and agricultural potential (Benson et al. 2009; Dorshow 2012; Wills and Dorshow 2012). Conversely, Yemen offers rich ethnographic record of terraces and small-scale irrigation systems, many of which remain widely in use today (Al-Ghulaibi 2008; Pietsch and Mabit 2012; Varisco 1991; Vogel 1987). Information on indigenous terracing across the American West is far less readily available as such practices were often disregarded and rapidly displaced by European colonization (Doolittle 2000: 264–75).

For the U.S.–Mexico borderland area, a long running debate centers on why ancient terraces were constructed, particularly those of ancient *cerros de trincheras* (entrenched hilltop) sites of the Trincheras Culture (Fish et al. 2007). Some have argued for a defensive function (Hard and Roney 2007), others are inclined toward agricultural uses (Doolittle 2000), while still others have emphasized symbolic purposes (O'Donovan 2002; Zavala 2012). With more than a hundred sites known with archaeological terraces (Doolittle 2000: 281–288), it seems unlikely all could be explained by a singular, mutually exclusive purpose. However, arguments that agricultural terraces are simply too much work for too little reward fail to consider the wide prevalence of agricultural terracing in other arid regions. Hard and colleagues (Hard et al. 1999, 2008), for instance, argue that terraces at the site of Cerro Juanaqueña were not used for cultivation as they would have required about thirty person years of labor to provide only 3.6 hectares of cultivable land, which would only produce enough maize to sustain about six people for a year (Hard et al. 2008: 321). However, terraces need not involve laborious manual in-filing of sediment behind terrace walls, which would dramatically reduce estimated construction costs, nor do terraces need to provide the entirety of a community's food supply. When maize was first introduced, it may have made a relatively minor dietary contribution (Smith 2001) and could have initially served as a valuable luxury food (Hayden 2003; Logan et al. 2012). Moreover, terraces that are indisputably built for farming are widely prevalent in many arid and semiarid regions, including across the western highlands of Yemen, probably the most extensively terraced arid region in the world (Varisco 1991). The wide prevalence of agricultural terraces in Yemen clearly demonstrates they offered benefits, such as retaining water and limiting soil erosion, which more than outweighed the costs of construction. It is therefore difficult to dismiss an agricultural purpose for at least some, if not many, of the terraces found across the U.S.–Mexico borderlands on the basis they were supposedly too burdensome and too costly to be agriculturally worthwhile.

In summary, comparing ancient Yemen with contexts across the Near East and the American West significantly informs understandings of early agriculture and irrigation. Most fundamentally, the conventional assumption that irrigation was derived from earlier forms of rainfed farming is at the very least highly problematic. As Flannery (1969: 80–81) long ago argued, agriculture in the Near East probably did not first originate in the most naturally verdant areas (where gathering experiments have demonstrated ancient foragers could have collected massive quantities of wild wheat in very little time), but rather, crop agriculture was more likely born in more arid, marginal areas where early cultivators targeted comparatively water-rich locales. In water-rich parts of otherwise arid zones – such as near springs, seasonally inundated riverbanks, or areas of concentrated run-off, or high water-table – early cultivators endeavored to replicate (or even surpass) yields of high productivity wild grasslands. Early cultivators had thus moved from adaptation to persistent or recurrent patterning of wild cereals to tailor their activities around the conditions those cereals needed to survive and thrive just beyond their optimal homelands. Since the dawn of radiocarbon dating, archaeologists have long concentrated on temporal variability including oscillations of climates and environments that impacted food resources such as wild grasses. With a transformative new generation of spatial technologies now available, we are poised to far better address spatial variability, including spatial heterogeneity of key resources like water that shaped human histories. Even though scholars interested in the beginnings of agriculture in the Near East have long examined climatic and environmental change (e.g., Bar-Yosef 2011) and more recently concentrated on the role of water management (e.g., Finlayson et al. 2011), powerful spatial technologies now available call for multiscalar (local and regional) analysis of spatial patterning, including potentially deliberate ancient targeting of water-rich areas in otherwise arid zones. Indeed, studies of the American Southwest (Mabry and Doolittle 2008) and spatial analysis of early cultivation in ancient Yemen (Harrower 2008a; Harrower et al. 2012) suggest targeting of water was critically important and widespread. Most fundamentally, when viewed as an invention agriculture can be framed as a discovery that originated and spread, but wider recognition of local historical contingencies, including spatial heterogeneity of water, necessitates rethinking and overhaul of traditional core/periphery, origins/spread conceptions of ancient agriculture.

## Irrigation among chiefdoms, kingdoms, and states

> A scholar's contributions to science should be judged more by the stimulus he gives to research – by the nature of the problems he raises and the interests he creates – than by the enduring qualities of his provisional hypotheses … it is safe to say then even Wittfogel's most vigorous critics have advanced our understanding of the role of irrigation precisely because their interest had been directed to the subject and they had a theory which could be tested. (Steward 1977: 87–88)

# Irrigation among chiefdoms, kingdoms, and states

The hydraulic hypothesis – that centralized coordination needed to build large-scale irrigation systems spawned the world's earliest civilizations – has shown considerable longevity. It has long survived and continually structured archaeologists' thinking and studies of irrigation, some would say deleteriously, for more than half a century (for discussion see Earle and Doyel 2008). Most closely associated with the work of its most forceful proponent, Karl Wittfogel (1935, 1938, 1955, 1957, 1972), irrigation was also advocated by Julian Steward (1949, 1955b, 1977) as a factor that could link the widely disparate histories of early civilizations. Of the conditions crops require to thrive – arable soil, sunlight, suitable temperatures, and moisture – water, as Wittfogel (1957: 131–135) recognized, is the most malleable and is a (if not the) primary preindustrial means of boosting agricultural production. While scholars now more broadly recognize the inadequacy of unicausal, deterministic explanations and the many deficiencies of Wittfogel's formulation, including the highly problematic distinction he drew between Western and Oriental societies, most still broadly acknowledge significant long-term connections between irrigation and the development of early civilizations. Over time interest has gradually shifted away from proving or disproving the hydraulic hypothesis toward case studies of water and irrigations' role(s) in particular historical contexts; yet the hydraulic hypothesis has proven so foundational that it often still, almost inescapably, constrains studies of water and civilization (Adams 2006; Harrower 2009; Kirch 1994; Lucero 2006; Silverstein et al. 2009; Stanish 1994; Wilkinson and Rayne 2010). As esteemed geographer Karl Butzer (1996: 200) put it,

> The Wittfogel model, like Elvis, refuses to die. And like the impersonators of Elvis Presley who earn their keep by rocking around the clock, Karl Wittfogel's "hydraulic hypothesis"…continues to be repackaged in a variety of guises that assign a unique causal role to irrigation in the development of socio-political complexity.

Nearly twenty years after Butzer's urging that we finally lay Wittfogel (with flowers) to rest, there still remains a need for dramatically new theorizing, new case studies, and new cross-cultural comparisons and propositions not only to help evaluate what has been learned over nearly eight decades, but more importantly to definitively move research in substantially new directions. In addition to studies of individual cases and global overviews, contrastive juxtaposition of two or three cases (including *very different* histories such as the Ancient Yemen and the American West) have a far more important future role, I argue, than commonly recognized. In an era of advanced spatial technologies and spatial theory, the spatial distribution of water, including spatial heterogeneity across landscapes, and how polities exploit such patterns, are important and expansive topics of future research. It was not, I argue, the unavoidable need for centrally managed large-scale irrigation that propelled political complexity in arid regions, but rather the spatial heterogeneity of water, which polities exploited to justify large waterworks (or other forms of highly concentrated agricultural production) that perpetuated state influence.

In ancient Yemen irrigation played an important long-term role among complex polities, and the region offers unique insights that can inform (and be informed by) historical trajectories of other contexts, including the American West. Water histories of ancient and modern complex polities of the western United States are comparatively far more widely known and better documented. The ancient Hohokam, for example, centered around present-day Phoenix, Arizona, constructed at least 600 km of mainline canals, extending up to 30 km, which irrigated as much as 20,000 to 40,000 hectares (Fish and Fish 2012: 571). While Hohokam is not generally considered to qualify as a "state" level society (Mithen 2012: 200–222) these irrigation works are impressive by any standard and surpass by many measures the scale of systems built by some of ancient Yemen's desert kingdoms. Far more recent European irrigation systems across the American West vividly illustrate the cultural, political, and religious connectivities of large-scale water control that became, and still remain, hallmarks of contemporary American culture, identity, and sovereignty. On the Colorado River alone, fifteen dams have been built on the river's main channel, including most famously Hoover Dam (1936) and Glen Canyon Dam (1966), which created Lake Mead and Lake Powell, the two largest reservoirs in the United States. These massive structures, built by the U.S. Bureau of Reclamation, symbolized and rationalized federal government power and sovereignty over the West and fueled not only construction of hundreds of smaller dams on tributaries of the Colorado, but also thousands more dams on other western rivers (Rowley 2006). John Wesley Powell, one of the most recognized early commentators on geographies of water across the United States, explicitly warned against such massive artificial transfers of water between watersheds. Powell who was founding Director of the Smithsonian Bureau of Ethnology (1879) and Director of the U.S. Geological Survey (1881–1894) believed that catchment-centered management, including state boundaries based on watersheds, would more equitably and reliably apportion water across what few realized at the time was an exceptionally arid region. Particularly when considered in contrast to Yemen, the American West thus helps reveal the complex intersecting dynamics of water geographies and water politics that are highly germane and important worldwide.

One of the seminal contributors to understanding irrigation among ancient civilizations, Robert McCormick Adams' surveys of Mesopotamia (Adams 1965, 1981; Adams and Nissen 1972) have played a pivotal role in clarifying irrigation's influences among ancient states. Beginning in 1956, Adams and colleagues covered vast swaths of Iraq, mapping settlements, natural and artificial waterways and interpreting their significance in long-term histories. In direct contrast to Wittfogel, Adams (1960, 1966, 1981, 2006, 2012) has steadfastly maintained that irrigation at the cusp of state formation did not require centralized coordination, and that large-scale irrigation was a consequence rather than a cause of civilization. He once concluded,

> All in all, the irrigation system and the major institutions of the urban society seem to have coexisted with little to suggest their close interaction or interdependence. Rather than the state using its necessary control over irrigation as a source of wider political leverage, the evidence (admittedly limited and not conclusive) could be better interpreted as indicating that involvement in irrigation was one of the means by which the state sometimes sought to extend its control over the countryside. (Adams 1981: 246)

Adams' research and a sizable wealth of subsequent studies have shown how irrigation was deeply implicated in Mesopotamian histories as changing environments, water control techniques, and irrigation management shaped trajectories of polities' rise and decline over millennia (e.g., Bagg 2012; Postgate and Powell 1988, 1990; Rost 2010; Wilkinson and Rayne 2010). But Adams and his scholarly descendants have long avoided portraying irrigation and civilization as linked in any causal way. In a scientific sense, to verify the hydraulic hypothesis the appearance of large-scale centrally coordinated irrigation systems would need to be accompanied nearly simultaneously by a substantial increase in political complexity. Evaluations of this potential pattern critically depend on how one defines large-scale centralization, and what qualifies as a state or a civilization. Indeed, issues of spatial and political scale are central to debates about the role of water and irrigation in the long-term trajectories of ancient societies.

A substantial breadth of research has focused on Witffogel's (1957) assertion that large-scale hydraulic systems require centralized coordination (Downing and Gibson 1974; Earle 1980; Fernea 1970; Hunt 1988; Hunt and Hunt 1976; Kelly 1983; Lees 1994; Mabry 1996, 2000; Millon 1962; Mitchell 1973, 1976; Price 1994; Scarborough 1991). Perhaps most significantly defining and measuring what is meant by "large-scale" and "centralization" has proven a significant challenge (Hunt 1988). Scale is dependent on perspective and can be defined as the size of area controlled by an irrigating society, the size of area actually irrigated, the number of people served by the irrigation system, or the number or irrigators involved (Hunt 2007: 105–28). These, of course, can be difficult to measure archaeologically, but even with such definitional complexities set aside, there is nevertheless substantial reason to question the supposed need for bureaucratic management in many, if not most, contexts. Collectively, the wide array of aforementioned studies demonstrates, while there is a tendency toward centralization as scale increases, no simple deterministic association holds between large-scale irrigation and politically centralized management (Mabry 2000; see also Chapter 5). The Hohokam, for instance, constructed extensive networks of canals that irrigated thousands of hectares for more than a millennium without any apparent need for centralized bureaucratic oversight (Hunt et al. 2005). Similarly, studies of ancient Polynesian agriculture have illustrated the deep importance of agricultural strategies, including both irrigation and dryland cultivation, yet have demonstrated little need for centralized management (Earle 1980; Kirch 1994). Water was critically important to agriculture across ancient Mesoamerica but reviews of water-use in the region also do not support Wittfogel's vision of totalitarian, bureaucratic control of large-scale irrigation (Scarborough 1998; Scarborough and Isaac 1993). Instead, Lisa Lucero's (1999, 2003, 2006) work on the ancient Maya, for example, illustrates the interconnected role of water and ritual that helped rationalize and solidify elite power. In summary, evidence from numerous contexts worldwide contradicts the central postulate of the hydraulic hypothesis that the need for centralized despotic management of large-scale irrigation prompted the emergence of the world's earliest civilizations.

If Wittfogel's hypothesis has been thoroughly discredited, how then do we now go on to explain irrigation's role in the birth of civilizations? In a recent paper, Tony Wilkinson and Louise Rayne (2010) avoid the origins issue and continue along a similar line of reasoning as Adams in examining how later complex societies enabled the spread of large-scale irrigation systems ...

> ... the Wittfogel model that posits that hydraulic management led to the development of the early state and civilizations is regarded as overly simplistic. Here, rather than attempting to tackle this long-debated question, this article examines the evidence for the chronological spread of hydraulic systems from the dry lands of Mesopotamia and SW Iran to

more verdant areas where the manipulation of water via canals appears to provide a supplement to rainfall ... In contrast to Wittfogel's model which saw water management as playing a pivotal role in the development of early states, there is gathering evidence to suggest that the later empires enabled and indeed encouraged the spread of water systems throughout the old world, in part, by the exertion of political power over vast areas. Therefore, this article explores the evidence for the converse of Wittfogel's model, namely how the development of large territorial empires in the first millennium BC and AD enabled major systems of water supply to develop and spread. (Wilkinson and Rayne 2010: 116–17)

Many have similarly concluded large-scale irrigation systems in Mesopotamia followed rather than appeared in conjunction with the birth of the earliest states (e.g., Adams 2006; Bagg 2012; Pournelle 2007; Wilkinson 2013). In addition to a considerable body of evidence showing that early systems would not have required state coordination, this conclusion emanates in part, I argue, from justifiable reluctance to see irrigation as a deterministic impetus. The hydraulic hypothesis focuses on the unavoidable necessity of the state and removes any vestige of human agency. Ancient polities were supposedly compelled to organize centrally managed large-scale irrigation systems to boost food production. There are no alternate pathways, the process is not optional, and is entirely deterministic. But even though the hydraulic hypothesis is misguided, should water and irrigation be excluded as significant contributors to state formation? Even though the hydraulic hypothesis has been repeatedly refuted, no clearly articulated alternative explanation of water's influence has appeared to replace it. The hydraulic hypothesis thus continually and unhelpfully reappears in scholarly dialogue contributing perpetual attention to whether centralized control of irrigation was *required* or not when this issue merely distracts from reappraisal of water's role in the genesis of civilizations.

It was not, I contend, the need for centrally managed large-scale irrigation that propelled the birth of civilization but rather the spatial heterogeneity of water, which polities often employed to concentrate and dominate agricultural production, guide the flow of commerce, and perpetuate their influence. Water control was one among numerous avenues to power and political complexity and its particular influence was manifest through physical and ideological manipulation of spatial scarcity and surplus. We know, for instance, in northern Mesopotamia where complex polities developed arguably as early as in the south (Ur 2010; Ur et al. 2007) that irrigation was largely optional and that large-scale waterworks in the north for the most part appeared later with imperialist expansion (Wilkinson and Rayne 2010).

Yet it would nevertheless be remiss to conclude that crop production in the north took place haphazardly with respect to water, as cultivation in at least some northern Mesopotamia locales exploits low-lying, water-rich areas where moisture accumulates in soil profiles (Yukich 2013). Water quite clearly played a less important role in the north than in the south, yet was still an important factor contributing to political complexity. Based on a detailed long-term study of northern Mesopotamia settlement data, Wilkinson and colleagues (2014) argue that large urban settlements neither preferentially grew in the wettest or driest areas, nor during intervals of drought or wetness. They instead highlight the importance of agricultural risk and a broad "zone of uncertainty" where rainfall between 200 and 300 mm per annum meant rainfed farming could be practiced but was vulnerable to water shortfalls. In southern Mesopotamia, marshland environments, turtlebacks, and river levees enabled floodwater cultivation for the most part without large canals moving water long distances (Pournelle 2003, 2007). When and where irrigation systems were constructed in southern Mesopotamia, head-gates, canals, regulators, distributors, and outlets to banked fields could have readily been constructed on a cooperative community basis (Fernea 1970; Rost and Hamdani 2011). However, neither the possibility that cooperating local farmers could have constructed large-scale irrigation systems nor the equivocal nature of early textual evidence for coordination and oversight of irrigation necessarily mean the state was not closely involved in irrigation through, for example, land ownership, taxation, or other means of controlling agricultural production (Rost 2010). It was not actually managerial oversight of irrigation, but rather rhetoric of supremacy and sovereignty that claimed credit for the bounties of irrigation (Richardson 2012). Natural and artificial waterways not only boosted food production but also funneled transport of crop products and other trade goods via corridors that could be controlled (Algaze 2008). Studies of Hohokam ceramics, enabled by far greater long-term research accessibility than many parts of the Near East, have shown clear evidence that trade and social affiliations are (in part) linearly framed by canal networks (Abbott 2009; Abbott et al. 2006). Water networks of late fourth and third millennia southern Mesopotamia were of comparable scale and arguably would have similarly contributed to water-patterned social interaction. As Wilkinson (2013) argued, south Mesopotamian polities were as much a function of hydraulic landscapes, including flood control, transport, and water for domestic purposes and manufacturing, as they were a function of irrigation. Taking this a step further, I argue, it was not irrigation per se but spatial heterogeneity of water and its interconnections with political rhetoric and social logic that contributed to state formation. For instance, in ancient Yemen irrigation *was not a requirement of crop agriculture* in the region, yet it was an important rationale of state sovereignty and statecraft that exploited spatial patterns of scarcity and surplus of water across landscapes. Nowhere is this pattern of irrigation-linked social change and spatial history more clearly apparent and well-illustrated as the late nineteenth and early twentieth century American West, a pattern that in turn sheds new perspective on, and helps explain, ancient contexts.

Water histories of the American West vividly illustrate the importance of large state-sponsored irrigation schemes, bureaucracies, national identities, and sovereignty in arid region statecraft. As historians of the American West have eloquently chronicled, attention focused on water scarcity and water crises often overcame economics to perpetuate the political and ideological logic that propelled colonization and control of the West (Arax and Wartzman 2005; Hundley 2001; Reisner 1986; Worster 1985). The 1850s and 1860s were pivotal, having admitted California as a state in 1850 and established its southern border with Mexico in 1853, American sovereignty across the West remained tenuous. The Civil War intensified the need to unite a war-torn and bitterly divided populace; hope and aspiration were fueled by discovery, opportunity, land, and water. Many of the factors archaeologists often identify as critical – culture, politics, religion, economics, environment, technology – similarly define water histories of the West. With Lincoln's Homestead Act of 1862 land that was divided into sections (a mile by a mile) was given away 160 acres (a quarter section) at a time, summarily discounting millennia of Native American ownership. In theory, homestead applicants had to live on the land for five years and show evidence of having made improvements before they were granted title; yet in practice rules were often ignored, and wealthy landholders amassed thousands of acres of land that were eventually irrigated by federally funded water projects. The American Dream, was and is a Western dream, the aspirations of Yeoman farmers to own a spread of land was largely impossible in Europe at the time where most land was controlled by wealthy aristocrats. Horace Greeley's famous 1865 prompt "go west young man go west" was the call of government, railroads, profiteers, and newspapermen (Emmons 1971). In the aftermath of the Civil War, of slavery, of Indian Wars, U.S. collective identity would be built through aspirations to settle the West and conquer the desert. The rhetoric of protestant work ethic and entrepreneurial ambition of frontier settlers was mobilized to expand the reach of civilization and bring the message of God, even if violently, to the heathen.

A premier example of megaproject water politics, the 233-mile-long Los Angeles-Owens Valley Aqueduct first built between 1908 and 1913 and it nourished and enabled a burgeoning city (Hundley 2001: 141–71; Kahrl 1983; Libecap 2007). Design and construction of this colossal undertaking was overseen by a self-taught engineer, William Mulholland, who began as a humble laborer maintaining ditches in Los Angeles and eventually rose to become Superintendent of the LA Department of Water and Power. While the city had previously relied on the Los Angeles River, explosive population growth saw the city rise from roughly 1,600 people in 1850 to more than 100,000 residents in 1900. More than 25 million dollars, raised from city bonds issued to fund the aqueduct, was justified by what many argue was a largely spurious, supposed water crisis. Although the city had already grown more than hundred-fold in just over fifty years, most conceded the proposed aqueduct's water was needed not so much for current residents but to sustain continued growth. Proponents of the aqueduct estimated that the city could only sustain 300,000 people with local supplies of water, yet the city in fact reached 500,000 before the aqueduct was completed without encountering any major shortage (Hundley 2001: 153–54). The aqueduct was bracketed by questionable land deals (most notably those of Los Angeles Mayor Fred Eaton and associates) that secured both headwaters and the soon-to-be agricultural lands that would be irrigated with water supposedly needed for residential purposes. Through what some call visionary strength of purpose, and others deceit and subterfuge, the City of Los Angeles acquired water rights to 300,000 acres that flow (or used to flow) into eastern California's Owens Lake. Although the initial justification was to provide water to the people of Los Angeles much of the water was used to irrigate the nearby San Fernando Valley where the city's confidants had purchased land that, with water, skyrocketed in value. Reappropriation of land and water previously owned by Owens Valley farmers at the head of the aqueduct, and the enormous windfalls accorded to San Fernando Valley land dealers near the end of the aqueduct, spawned accusations of conspiracy and in 1924 angry farmers seized and dynamited part of the aqueduct (Walton 1992). Was all that water really needed in Los Angeles? There remains heated and vigorous debate about whether Owens Valley water was stolen by clandestine land dealers, or fairly negotiated and rightfully purchased (Libecap 2007). Yet when Mulholland was asked during the campaign for the aqueduct what would happen if it wasn't built, in a moment of surprising candor he tellingly replied, "If Los Angeles does not secure the Owens Valley water supply, she will never need it" (C. Mulholland 2002: 128).

# Irrigation among chiefdoms, kingdoms, and states

Surely water histories of Los Angeles and the American West are contextually unique, what can they tell us about ancient civilizations? As further recounted in the chapters that follow, water histories of the American West richly illustrate contextual dependence of water needs, national identities, sovereignty and the malleability and spatiality of water scarcity. Just as in ancient Yemen, the seeming imperative need for water is often subjectivity and politically constituted and Mulholland's comment, for example, illustrates the deeply malleable nature of purported shortage and crisis in water politics. Yet we need to avoid the tendency to see water control dichotomously either as manipulative conspiracies of elites to exploit uninformed proletariats, or as the self-organizing, harmonious collective action of equitable social consensus. The American West copiously exemplifies a multitude of disparate and seemingly contradictory water histories, including exploitation of water for enormous personal gain (Arax and Wartzman 2005), colonialism and violent conflict over water (Walton 1992), machinations of powerful state and federal bureaucracies vying for control of water (Hundley 2009), alongside benevolent public servants concerned with conservation of water resources as a public good (Worster 2001). Unfettered capitalism and environmentalism often clash across the American West in a tempestuous interplay as water resources all-the-while contribute to nearly untold civilizational prosperity (Miller 2009). These diverse, often conflicting views and vantage points offer helpful insights with regards to studies of the ancient past. Underrepresented peoples, women, Native Americans, enslaved Africans, Eric Wolf's (1964) "people without history," even impoverished settlers themselves, remind us of marginalized peoples of the ancient past who are frequently overlooked. Historians of the American West have cogently documented how state bureaucracies and the personalities within them gain such power and inertia that irrigation schemes that are sometimes economically inadvisable, even irrational, for societies as a whole are often propelled by politics and the influence of relatively small, vocal groups that inordinately benefit. Similar dynamics are apparent in the ancient past; we cannot assume merely because irrigation systems were built or operated for sustained periods of many hundreds of years that they were necessarily sustainable nor economically advisable and equitable. Given the enormous quantities of labor and resources invested in construction and reconstruction of the Ma'rib Dam, for example, it seems highly unlikely these returns were repaid and justifiable solely in terms of food production. The remarkably engineered waterscape of Ma'rib by its last few centuries (~AD 300–575) was not agriculturally necessary (Harrower 2009). It would have contributed only a tiny fraction of the region's food supply

(Darles et al. 2013) and was more important in its visual and symbolic presence that bolstered not only individual leaders' authority but also overall sovereignty and state control of the region. As further emphasized in the following summary section, contrastive juxtaposition of these histories better animates environmental and political dynamics of water in the archaeological past, including, but not limited to, water histories of ancient Yemen.

## Long-term water histories of ancient Yemen in comparative perspective

In juxtaposition alongside the American West, long-term water histories of ancient Yemen offer a range of insights deeply pertinent to understanding water's role among ancient societies worldwide. Water is not only crucially important as an economic resource variably available in changing environments, but is also situated within a complex web of social, political, and ideological interconnections. The historic adage "rain follows the plow" exemplifies how colloquial understandings of environments, political rhetoric, and social logic can quickly come to influence, even dominate, human action. From the very earliest Paleolithic appearance of humans in Arabia, water played an important role in shaping human mobility. Categorizations of human societies are invariably prone to oversimplify wide diversity, but when viewed as descriptive, heuristic guides they helpfully facilitate baseline comparisons. While water management among hunting and gathering populations is rare, the American West, Yemen, and Australia are three of the primary instances with evidence of irrigation among groups without domesticated crops and therefore exemplify the fuzzy, imperfect boundaries between the traditional categories foragers and agriculturalists. Societal relationships with water shift dramatically among animal herding populations as humans come to rely on drinking and grazing conditions their animals need to survive. The dramatic transformation instigated by adoption of horses among Native Americans of the Great Plains vividly illustrates the wide impacts of domesticated animals. As further examined in Chapters 4 and 5, comparably dramatic upheavals characterized the early sixth millennium appearance of domestic cattle and caprines as well as the late second millennium BC domestication of camels in Arabia. These animals prompted major societal reconfigurations, including with respect to mobility, trade, and rights to water. Archaeologists have long considered sedentary village life and rainfed farming hallmarks of the world's earliest agriculture. This supposition, however, is not necessarily warranted as considerable evidence suggests that early cultivators often favored water-rich areas such as high water-table bottomlands, periodically flooded alluvium, or river and lake shores. Ultimately, quantitative spatial analysis is required to more fully evaluate potential associations among ancient cultivation, settlement, and water resources and is poised to help resolve long-standing speculations about water's role in ancient human geographies. In eastern Yemen, the earliest irrigating populations were neither sedentary nor reliant solely on local rainfall and understandings of the region necessitate rethinking of traditional conceptualizations of agriculture's beginnings.

Understandings of water among ancient complex polities have long been dominated by Wittfogel and associated efforts to evaluate whether or not centralized coordination of irrigation was a major cause of ancient state formation. Almost all now agree centralized management was not necessarily a requirement of large-scale irrigation; aggregations of independent farmers collectively created large, locally managed systems that produced enormous quantities of food in numerous contexts worldwide (Butzer 1996; Mabry 2000; Scarborough 2003; see also Chapter 5). Moving beyond the hydraulic hypothesis requires new, more compelling cross-cultural propositions on interconnections between water and civilization. Approaches that combine the rapidly expanding range of spatial technologies alongside spatial theory and contrastive juxtaposition are arguably well-suited to move research in significantly new directions that more accurately explicate the long-term natural and political spatial dynamics of water. The following chapters concordantly argue that spatial patterns of water scarcity and abundance (spatial heterogeneity) in ancient Yemen, and the rhetorical ways complex polities exploited such spatial patterns, helpfully illustrate and explain the role of water in political complexity.

CHAPTER 4

# Water and the beginnings of pastoralism and agriculture in Southwest Arabia

> *American social development has been continually beginning over again on the frontier. This perennial rebirth, this fluidity of American life, this expansion westward with its new opportunities, its continuous touch with the simplicity of primitive society, furnish the forces dominating American character. The true point of view in the history of this nation is not the Atlantic coast, it is the Great West.*
>
> Fredrick Jackson Turner (1894: 200)

The storied American frontier – fur traders, miners, cattlemen, and farmers forcing westward to pioneer arid lands – has long framed understandings of American history and culture, including as long-ago portrayed in Turner's seminal 1893 lecture. On April 22, 1889 roughly 50,000 people stormed into six Oklahoma counties to claim homesteads. Famously known as the Oklahoma Land Rush, this race to own land quite literally created cities – Oklahoma City and Guthrie – in a single day. These lands were of course appropriated from Native Americans many of whom had been killed, driven-off, or forcibly relocated. Over the next several decades homesteading in Oklahoma failed to yield the windfall many had hoped. Erratic crop and cattle prices, harsh winters, and drought took their toll. During the infamous droughts of the 1930s many were forced to abandon their land as extreme dust storms choked cattle to death; in 1934 a massive dust storm even spread inches of dust many hundreds of kilometers away on Chicago, New York, and Washington D.C. (Worster 1979: 13). These vignettes, merely small parts of chapters in the vast history of the West, exemplify a broad arc of colonial expansion that has spawned impassioned views both greatly positive and negative.

America is colloquially the land of the pioneering frontier settler, and Arabia correspondingly the archetypal land of the noble camel-riding nomad – scrutiny and defamiliarization of these generalizing depictions reveals how they have shaped and defined explanations of the past including water histories. Disparaging portrayals of Oriental "Others" have, quite rightfully, been vigorously challenged (Said 1978; Varisco 2007) and they in many ways hinge on reciprocally favorable triumphalist views of industrious western pioneers (White 1991). Particularly over the last several decades historians and archaeologists have shifted their studies of the American West to challenge glamorized depictions and better include underrepresented groups such as African and Native Americans (Dixon 2014). While conceptions of western frontier settlers have had broad influences on American culture, romantic essentialism of Arab nomadism comparatively extends even deeper into the past. As Zwettler (2000) examines, at least as early as the fourth century AD the term *Ma'add* referred to a particular pattern of saddled camel-riding and bow-wielding nomadism and warfare. Nearly a thousand years later Ibn Khaldūn emphasized histories as turning on relations between nomadic and settled populations and his work has recently been revived to help explain the origins of Southwest Arabian civilizations (McCorriston 2013). The antiquity of the term "Arab" itself has been subject to a great deal of interest and debate (Hoyland 2001). Known as far back as Neo-Assyrian texts of the early first millennium BC, various uses of the term Arab refer to an ethnicity, nomadism, pastoralism, camel-rearing, or a geographic area, showing what it meant to be Arab shifted considerably through time (Retsö 2003). In both America and Arabia research involving these imagined paradigmatic characters has also often turned on understandings of frontiers, mobility, and migration.

Just as the American West has been viewed as frontier window of opportunity (Grossman 1994; Limerick 1987; Murdoch 2001), the prehistoric spread of agriculture from the Near East to Europe has comparably been modeled as wave-of-advance frontier (Ammerman and Cavalli-Sforza 1971) sparking decades of research and debate about movement and population expansion (Bellwood 2013; Rowley-Conwy 2011). For ancient Yemen, there similarly remains long running uncertainty about the spread of agriculture from supposed core areas of the Near East to what are often viewed as "peripheral" lands of southern Arabia (Crassard and Drechsler 2013). We know that nomadic hunting-and-gathering populations occupied Yemen a hundred thousand years ago or more before being displaced, assimilated, or transformed through contact with animal herding and crop-rearing populations. Is this process best envisioned as migration, diffusion, colonization, or globalization? Far more research has concentrated on the movement of domesticates to the north and west of the Fertile Crescent into Europe than has focused to the south, and a great many new insights undoubtedly lay ahead in Arabia.

Investigations over the past several decades have begun to reveal an image of early pastoralism and agriculture in Southwest Arabia that is marked by substantial changes in human relationships with land and water. The nature of the frontier, or interface, between foraging and agriculture remains nebulous and challenging to define, yet is nevertheless of great significance as a lesser-known example of transitions to agriculture. The earliest documented appearance of domesticates in Yemen, that is, cattle, sheep, and goats as early as the sixth millennium BC (Fedele 2013; Martin et al. 2009), is closely tied to water via climate and grazing territoriality. The earliest evidence of domesticated plants in the region falls roughly 2,500 years later near the end of the fourth millennium BC (Ekstrom and Edens 2003) with evidence of irrigation and terrace agriculture recognizable at nearly the same time (Harrower 2008b; Wilkinson 1999). How did these animals and then plants first come under human husbandry in southern Arabia? Did immigrants from the north arrive in a sparsely populated land? Or were domesticates adopted by local forging populations? Thus far the evidence weighs toward a culturally autochthonous emergence of pastoralism and then agriculture, albeit involving adoption of at least some foreign domesticates.

## The beginnings of Southwest Arabian pastoralism

The origins of animal herding in ancient Yemen bears significant resemblance and substantially informs understanding of comparable trajectories across the Near East and Africa where animals come to play a central role not only economically but socially, ritually, and ideologically (di Lernia et al. 2013; Hodder 2011; Wengrow et al. 2014). Interestingly, these parallel patterns of animal husbandry seem to develop along their own unique social trajectories largely independently.

My experience in Arabia began with The Roots of Agriculture in Southern Arabia (RASA) Project which explored the highlands of Hadramawt Governate from 1998 to 2008. Our investigations over many long days of fieldwork and subsequent laboratory analysis help document one of the regional landscapes in which pastoralism and agropastoralism originated. The RASA project, led by Joy McCorriston, initially centered on the search for early agriculture, yet we came to discover and record a much wider variety of ancient human activity from the Paleolithic through the Iron Age. This evidence depicts human relationships with water over a

# The beginnings of Southwest Arabian pastoralism

long interval that is particularly helpful in clarifying transitions from hunting and gathering to animal and eventually plant husbandry.

Paleolithic scatters of lithics often found atop limestone plateaus along wadis are the earliest evidence of human occupation in eastern Yemen. Paleolithic debitage exhibiting the famous Levallois technique was first reported in Hadramawt by Gertrude Caton-Thompson in the 1930s (Caton-Thompson 1953; Caton-Thompson and Gardner 1939). More recent and immeasurably more detailed analysis of stone tool assemblages recovered by both RASA and the French Archaeological Mission to Jawf-Hadramawt (HDOR) studied by Rémy Crassard (e.g., 2009a, 2009b) have dramatically clarified the character and diversity of lithic technologies. Crassard's work has defined a range of regionally distinct Levallois modalities; and even though the more than two dozen Paleolithic sites he has analyzed in the area are surface sites, which are difficult to date, his detailed comparisons with finds from Africa and the Levant place many materials 100,000 or more years ago (e.g., Crassard and Thiébaut 2011). Crassard and colleagues have more recently documented comparable middle Paleolithic sites along the margins of Paleolake Mundafan in Saudi Arabia that illustrate early human adaptation to water and changing Pleistocene climates (Crassard et al. 2013a). The ancient shorelines of Paleolake Mundafan are most famous to archaeologists for Neolithic projectile points, foliates, scrappers, and other tools first reported during the 1970s (McClure 1976, 1988). Now that considerably more is known about the Neolithic of Arabia, these finds are better recognizable as part of Rub al-Khali (Empty Quarter) Neolithic types dated to the first few millennia of the Holocene (Crassard et al. 2013b; Inizan et al. 1997), which includes materials excavated by RASA at Khuzmum Rockshelters in Wadi Sana (McCorriston et al. 2002).

Early Holocene lithics are indeed a center-point of vigorous debate about frontiers and interaction across the Arabian Peninsula (Crassard and Drechsler 2013). Early investigations led to speculation that projectile points included within assemblages designated Qatar-B (Inizan 1980, 1988; Kapel 1967) and a type of south Arabian projectile point referred to as Fasad (Figure 4.1) may have been derived from the Pre-Pottery Neolithic B (PPNB) of the Levant. Such connections, if they could be confirmed or refuted, would hold deep significance in better explaining the long-debated origins of the Neolithic in southern Arabia (e.g., Drechsler 2009; Zarins 1998) and could, in theory, demonstrate an impressive magnitude of PPNB influences across Arabia. However, based on the very distinct nature of the reduction sequences involved, some have strongly questioned purported

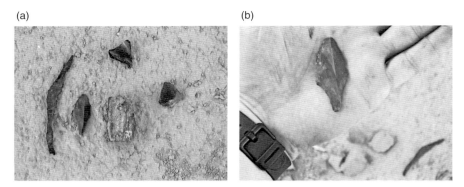

FIGURE 4.1. Fasad projectile point discovered along Wadi Sana. A corroded D-cell battery, bottle glass, and fragments of a tire were found nearby. Such are the challenges of archaeological survey in which very recent materials can often be found on the same ground surface as very ancient archaeological remains (photos by the author).

Levantine connections (Chapentier and Crassard 2013; Crassard 2009a). Others stand by their assertions that Fasad points, which are now referred to as Faya points at the site of Jebel Faya (UAE), do bear resemblance and ultimately a connection to Levantine types (Uerpmann et al. 2009, 2013). Even if similarities between lithics from southern Arabia and those of the Levant are superficial and are the result of entirely different reduction sequences, it seems too coincidental that such similar final products dated to approximately the same period (the likes of which are found nowhere else worldwide) could have originated entirely independently. There seems good reason to suspect, if the reduction sequences are different, that some flint-knappers purposefully chose a different strategy to arrive at a similar final product, or that one group was emulating another and used different methods to produce a very similar looking projectile point. Regardless, connections across the Arabian Peninsula, including those of peoples producing Fasad and Faya points (the latter now dated to the ninth millennium BC, Uerpmann et al. 2013) warrant further investigation and are not only important to scholars working in south but also across northern Arabia. Perhaps the most conclusive recent results come for Crassard and colleagues' (2013b) investigations in Saudi Arabia where they identified el-Khiam and Helwan points that are indisputably derived from the Pre-Pottery Neolithic (PPN). These finds for the first time firmly establish Levantine influences deep in the heart of Arabia. Were these some of the first pastoralists or pioneering farmers to move south? How did they interact with preexisting hunting-and-gathering populations? Did they come into conflict over use of precious water resources?

In 2000 the RASA team set up a tent camp in Wadi Sana and completed an intensive systematic survey of a few square kilometers surrounding a prominent inselberg (what might be called a mesa or a butte in the American West) located at the confluence of two wadis – Wadi Sana and its smaller tributary Wadi Shumlya. This limestone butte, known to local Yemeni Bedouin as Khuzma-as-Shumlya, was formed many millions of years ago as part of a deeply incised dendritic drainage network carved from the Paleocene Umm er-Radhuma formation creating in some places three limestone stair-step plateaus. The Khuzmum, as it is often called, remained a prominent landmark and camping spot for perhaps 100,000 years based, for example, on the 14 hectare scatter of Paleolithic tools, including copious Levallois material, found nearby. If Finlayson's (2013) Water Optimization Hypothesis is accurate and Paleolithic hunter-foragers favored semiarid areas with water that would help explain why the Khuzmum area was so attractive. The Khuzmum intersection was, and is, immediately recognizable to anyone travelling through this complex and confusing network of drainages and offers one of the locally most expansive areas of comparatively water-rich bottomlands. We cannot, of course, assume that occupation of the area was continuous as our earliest evidence is so difficult to firmly situate in time, but use of the area appears to have become somewhat less sporadic during the comparably more stable climatic conditions of the Holocene (Dansgaard et al. 1993). The relatively narrow channels of Wadi Sana and Shumlya widen near the Khuzmum as they converge, and drainage gradients flatten so that water flows (when they occur) momentarily slow, distributing sediments suspended in the water over a wide area. These alluvial sediments were brought and seasonally watered by runoff that collided and slowed at the confluence and began to deposit at first gravels and then finer sands and silts at least as early as the pluvial conditions of the terminal Pleistocene and early Holocene. Moist sediments fostered grasses and sometimes marshlands that attracted game. In addition to Paleolithic materials, early Holocene rockshelter encampments, Neolithic structures, cattle bone, small irrigation systems, Bronze Age tombs, Iron Age trilith monuments, and graffiti attest to a long series of occupations and uses. Our surveys discovered Fasad projectile points lying loose on the surface of alluvium in numerous locations, but lacking discoveries in stratified contexts we remain unable to offer a detailed account of their users' lives and livelihoods.

Were these Fasad peoples in contact with, or descended from, people of the Levant? While we can imagine and even devise computer simulations of cattle and caprine herders expanding outward from the Levant (Dreschler 2007), such conceptualizations are built on a much more recent Arabian archetype and as-of-yet we have no evidence that Fasad peoples were herders. Even if they were herders, they would have lacked trading partners who were farmers and would have needed to collect rather than trade for plant food, requiring a distinct herder-forager orientation that is lacking in ethnographic and most Near Eastern archaeological records. For eastern Yemen, somewhat more definitive, stratified evidence comes from RASA excavations of Khuzmum rockshelters radiocarbon dated to the middle seventh millennium BC (McCorriston et al. 2002). Although no Fasad points were found in these rockshelters, based on the abundance of broken proximal ends of Rub al-Khali projectile points, hunters must have returned to these small encampments many times over many years to camp and refit tips to their arrows. Although we have no direct evidence of their prey, the area must have made an attractive hunting ground perhaps for gazelle or ibex that would have grazed on nearby seasonal grasses.

In 2004 and 2005 RASA returned to our Wadi Sana tent camp to continue test excavations and complete a program of stratified random sampling up and down Wadi Sana. We were eager to know if the Khuzmum area was unique or if there were other ancient places of comparable importance nearby. Our sampling involved surveying twelve randomly positioned 100m wide strips across Wadi Sana and three more in the Ghayl bin Yumain basin that drains into it. Surveyors lined up 10 m apart and walked from the limestone plateau above one side of Wadi Sana down into the main channel and up to the plateau on the other side recording all archaeological remains, including most commonly lithic scatters and tombs. To retain consistency with our survey of the Khuzmum area, we retained the same spacing and system of dividing the landscape into seven landform types (Table 4.1; Harrower et al. 2002). Our results turned out to be unexpected and surprising. Notwithstanding its cultural significance as a landmark and way-station, statistically the Khuzmum area was not demonstrably unique. In particular, the density of major types of archaeological remains, including circular stone-slab structures, was not statistically different in comparison with other areas along Wadi Sana (McCorriston et al. 2005). Our findings demonstrated the utility of systematic survey and statistical analysis to clarifying spatial distributions that are often viewed very differently if judged solely by surveyors' impressions (McCorriston et al. 2005). However our results also simultaneously illustrated the inability of

TABLE 4.1. *Wadi Sana watershed landform class definitions using for GIS modeling*

| Class name | Definition |
| --- | --- |
| Bedrock Slope | Greater than 15° slope or cliff (sometimes covered in talus and/or scree) that separates upland plateaus from all other classes. |
| Scree Slope | Angular clasts often of a low (< 20°) gradient between bedrock slopes, terraces, and wadi sediments. |
| Plateau | Upland bedrock surfaces above bedrock slopes and cliffs, covered in primarily angular carbonate small cobble size clasts. |
| Gravel Terrace | Subrounded to rounded clasts often capping wadi silts and adjacent to wadi channels. |
| Bedrock Terrace | The youngest low angle (< 5°) or horizontal bedrock surface adjacent to wadi sediments and/or scree slopes, covered in primarily small cobble size carbonate clasts. |
| Wadi Silt | Pinkish tan colored areas of very fine sand and silt above wadi channels that often contain isolated lenses and scattered cover of gravel and/or scree. |
| Playa/Sabkha | Alluvial plain with gypsum and marl deposits found in the eastern Ghayl bin Yumain basin. |
| Wadi Channel | The lowest and most fluvially active area often demarcated by whitish gray rounded cobbles, boulders, and more prevalent vegetation. |

statistics to capture the important qualitative understandings of places that had long enduring significance in the ancient past.

One of our randomly selected transects located in a deep canyon with towering walls that forms the headwaters of Wadi Sana yielded particularly startling results. This transect was expected to be unproductive, as we initially presumed everything ancient would have been scoured away by powerful floods that periodically raced down the canyon. Instead, we discovered the site of Manayzah, at which excavations later yielded some of the earliest (early sixth millennium BC) evidence for domesticated animals (cattle and caprines) in Southwest Arabia (Martin et al. 2009; McCorriston and Martin 2009). Manayzah is moreover significant because of its assemblage of early Holocene lithics, which rather than illustrating connections with the Levant depict a uniquely Southwest Arabian range of technologies including fluted points (Crassard et al. 2006).

Near the Khuzmum we were similarly excited to discover more than forty cattle skulls placed in a ring during the mid-fifth millennium BC (McCorriston et al. 2012). These skulls found at the site of Shi'b Kheshiya were carefully positioned nose-down, teeth facing outward, with the largest skull centered in the middle. They attest not only to the economic importance of cattle but their associated ideological role in early pastoralist lifeways. While small in comparison with cattle in surrounding regions, these cattle – *Bos taurus* based on metric analyses conducted by Louise Martin of University College London – were prime adult animals selected for their size and status as victims of sacrifice rather than their expendability. The skulls are exceptionally well preserved and were probably pushed into soft mud over a very short period of days before delicate elements such as nasal bones were damaged or lost. Given that we lack evidence for drying, smoking, or salting, the meat was probably consumed immediately. The sacrifice would have commemorated a massive feast generating one day worth of calories (1990 kcal) for up to 5,000 people. Perhaps more likely, this feast may have served a somewhat smaller group of 1,000 people an enormous surfeit of 10,000 calories each.

Interestingly, ancient cattle sacrifice and rituals are also well known across the Near East and Africa. Most famously, rituals and daily practice at Çatalhöyük (Turkey) illustrate an exceptionally rich repertoire of imagery and action involving cattle (Hodder 2007, 2011). Somewhat closer to southern Arabia, feasting at the PPNB site of Kfar HaHoresh, Israel left a pit containing postcranial remains of wild cattle that could have fed up to 2,500 people (Goring-Morris and Horwitz 2007). In Africa, cattle were similarly a center-point of ancient life and by the late sixth and fifth millennia BC cattle became increasingly deeply interconnected with economic and ritual lives of northeast Africans (di Lernia et al. 2013; Wengrow 2001; Wengrow et al. 2014). It seems unlikely that practices thousands of years earlier and thousands of kilometers away could be direct progenitors of traditions in southern Arabia. More likely, the prevalence of cattle rituals and feasting indicates ritual often independently emerged as an ideological priority linked to economic dependence on cattle.

In ancient Yemen, cattle herders who gathered for ritual sacrifice and feasting at Kheshiya moved frequently and unlike Neolithic peoples of the Levant never lived in villages or occupied houses year-round. Instead, they built widely spaced and distributed small circular, slab-lined structures in vegetation-rich, wadi bottoms where their cattle could graze, and these structures became an important part of their rituals. Gathering, sacrifice, and feasting strengthened group identity, affirmed alliances and territories, setting the stage for the later development of irrigation-based agropastoralism and complex polities (McCorriston 2011).

Studies of African cattle pastoralism provide informative baseline data that helps illuminate the community dynamics of cattle ritual at Kheshiya. African cattle pastoralist families of roughly five to eight (including children) commonly own up to fifty or more cattle (e.g., Andom and Omer 2003: 548–49). Due to inevitable losses, they constantly need to acquire new animals not only through birth but also via trade, gifts, and marriage and other means to maintain their herds (De Vries et al. 2006). Offtake beyond 8 percent per year rapidly becomes unsustainable so in general relatively few animals are slaughtered and consumption of dairy products, or less commonly blood, is favored. Given these basic parameters we can estimate that a total herd of at least 500 cattle would be required to allow an annual 8 percent sacrifice of 40 animals represented at Kheshiya (McCorriston et al. 2012).

## Spatial dimensions of water flow and cattle grazing territories along Wadi Sana

Of the many challenges early herders faced in Southwest Arabia, ensuring adequate water and grazing lands was undoubtedly among the most pressing concerns, and geospatial analysis offers means to greatly clarify ancient environments, adaptations, and social relations. Herders in ancient Hadramawt would have relied on moist bottomlands along wadis to sustain their animals particularly cattle, which required copious grassy forage. Through archaeological survey, examination of natural sedimentary sections carved by erosion, and strategic radiocarbon dating, RASA generated a detailed record of Holocene environments. This record depicts an early Holocene pluvial interval followed by a pronounced shift toward aridity near 3200 BC. However, the specific ramifications of these changes for environmental and social landscapes are complex. Given the prevalence of ancient cattle bone we discovered eroding from alluvial sediments, we immediately knew conditions must have changed dramatically, as the area today offers almost nothing cattle can eat. How many cattle could Wadi Sana have sustained in the ancient past? And where did the animals and herds-people come from for the Kheshiya feast?

In addition to GIS, isotope analysis of cattle tooth enamel is one of the central ways the RASA team has examined water resources, grazing territories, and social relations of those who congregated for the Kheshiya cattle sacrifice (Henton et al. 2014). Even as we began excavating and making careful preparations to preserve the cattle skulls, we recognized the opportunity they offered for stable isotope analysis that could help reveal the animals' (and less directly the humans') life histories. After our team's many days of arduous work picking the hardened limestone-derived dirt around the skulls with dental picks, we eventually revealed the maxillary (upper jaw) teeth of each skull. Before carefully wrapping the skulls in plaster casting for transport, analysis, and storage in the Mukulla Museum we removed the third (last) maxillary molar from each skull. These samples were exported to the University College London where Elizabeth Henton conducted analyses that proved highly informative in clarifying their dietary profiles. The enriched pattern of stable carbon isotopes, consistent across all twenty-eight sample animals, showed the cattle consumed predominantly $C_4$ plants, most probably tropical grasses (Ziegler et al. 1981), rather than $C_3$ plants such as domesticated wheat or barley that had yet to appear in the region (Henton et al. 2014: figure 11). Additionally, the oscillating pattern of oxygen isotopes demonstrated the cattle were exposed to isotopically distinct water sources during their lifetimes as their enamel was laid down over time, perhaps due to transhumance or variable environments, and were reared in as few as 2 to as many as 4 different herds (Henton et al. 2014: figure 9).

Where did these herds come from? Where did they find forage? We know from cattle remains at Manayzah that the people of Kheshiya were not a frontier population that had recently colonized the region. They had been in the area, perhaps sporadically, for more than a thousand years. We thus turned to GIS to analyze grazing land availability and further explore the distribution of early herding populations in ancient Hadramawt. As outlined in Chapter 3, rangeland productivity depends on a complexity of factors, including precipitation, insolation, topography, landcover, vegetation dynamics, and rangeland history (Le Houérou et al. 1988). For the ancient past, some of these variables are more easily approximated than others, yet in conjunction with precipitation two of the most critical variables, landcover and topography-based runoff, are readily analyzed via satellite imagery in GIS.

The highlands of Hadramawt Governate today receive approximately 73 mm of precipitation per annum mostly in summer months (Bruggeman 1997: I.42), which is far less than needed to sustain cattle. Particularly given relatively high tropical temperatures (33°C average high in July and 21°C average high in January at Seiyun, Hadramawt), the area would require roughly a ten-fold increase in precipitation to comfortably support cattle without substantial seasonal migration and/or irrigated fodder. However, a tripling of annual precipitation to 220 mm/year would reach values comparable to those of modern Dhofar in western Oman and could be tolerable for cattle under certain circumstances. Cloud forest environments in which summer monsoonal fog supports a lush repertoire of vegetation presently extends over Dhofar's coastal escarpment above the city of Salalah (Hildebrandt et al. 2007). These environments, the historical homeland of Jebali cattle herding agropastoralists (Janzen 1986, 2000), undoubtedly spanned a substantially larger area during the early Holocene when the Intertropical Convergence Zone (ITCZ) extended further north across the Arabian Peninsula. Ancient cattle herders could have used a comparable transhumant strategy to prevent overgrazing and concentrated in autumn months along wadis where summer rains supported grasses. In dire circumstances they could have even fed dried sardines to cattle as Jebali did. However, unlike historic Jebali cattle herders, they would not have had farmers to trade with and would have needed to obtain all of their own plant food and forage.

Basic spatial understanding of grass availability can be generated using studies of African rangeland productivity and satellite imagery mapping in GIS. As discussed in Chapter 3, Le Houérou et al. (1980) estimate for comparable latitudes in Africa one mature zebu cow weighing roughly 250 kg requires approximately 10–12 hectares of rangeland in Saharo-Sahelian environments with 100–200 mm of annual rainfall. This means that a herd of 500 cattle would have required roughly 5,000 hectares of rangeland. Importantly, this is only an approximate guide and factors such as the grazing history that delimit patterns of vegetation and erosion would have also been critically important.

In the arid highlands of Hadramawt grass essentially requires two things, sufficient water and adequate soil. Since rainfall is relatively minimal, water availability is predominantly a function of runoff and soils only exist along drainages where water flow has deposited fine grained alluvium. To map runoff a Digital Elevation Model (DEM) that depicts terrain as a series of square grid cells can relatively easily be used to create maps of surface water flow using the eight-direction pour model (Figure 4.2; Harrower 2010; Maidment 2002). Quite simply, from each grid cell water can either pool in what is referred to as a "sink" or can flow in one of eight cardinal directions (N, NE, E, SE, S, SW, W, NW). Through accumulative summation of flow across a landscape one can quickly reconstruct water flow based on topography. In the present case, I used a DEM produced by NASA's Shuttle Radar Topography Mission (SRTM) that consists of 90 × 90 m grid cells to produce flow direction and flow accumulation maps.

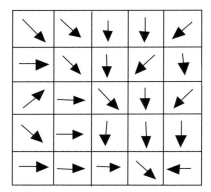 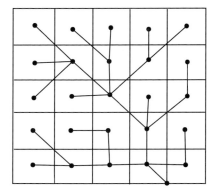

FIGURE 4.2. Water flow direction and flow accumulation modeling in GIS. In the eight-direction pour model, water flows in one of eight cardinal directions (N, NE, E, SE, S, SW, W, NW). Flow accumulation (right) is then defined by the cumulative summation of cells that aggregate across a landscape according to topography (figure by Clara Hickman based on Maidment 2002).

One then needs to determine how many 90 × 90 grid cells would need to accumulate to form a stream. While there are a variety of more complex ways of doing so (Heine et al. 2004) 5,000 accumulated cells is often used as an approximate rule-of-thumb (Maidment 2002) and was therefore used as a first measure for Wadi Sana. The resultant stream network was then buffered according to Strahler Stream Order to acknowledge that higher order streams would water and periodically flood a far wider area of sediments. The buffer distances for streams of different orders (1st =50 m, 2nd = 125 m, 3rd = 200 m, 4th = 275 m) were determined through visual inspection of satellite imagery. The 11,144 hectare area of wadi-bottom land within these buffers approximately maps locations with sufficient water to periodically sustain grass. To incorporate landform characteristics, the multispectral layers of NASA's ASTER (Advanced Spaceborne Thermal Emission and Reflection Radiometer) satellite imagery were used to generate a 15 m resolution digital landform map of the Wadi Sana watershed (Harrower 2006; Harrower et al. 2002). While some grass might have occasionally been available in other locations, Wadi Silts and Gravel Terraces would have been the two landform classes most capable of sustaining grasses (Plate III and Figure 3.1). To evaluate the combined impacts of water and landforms, I then calculated the overlap area of water-rich, wadi-bottoms with these two landforms, which gives a total of 2,130 hectares of relatively high productivity rangeland. Interestingly this amounts to less than half (43 percent) of the 5,000 hectares that would have been needed indicating that cattle and herders who participated in the Kheshiya sacrifice would have had to come from a substantially larger area than the Wadi Sana watershed.

Ultimately the beginnings of pastoralism in Southwest Arabia followed a unique pattern in which water played an important role through both grazing and the need for cattle to drink at least every few days. We will never know the precise geographic boundaries of grazing territories, which undoubtedly shifted through time in concert with environmental and social changes. However, geospatial analysis does provide some guiding insights that illustrate the wide-area social connectivity that must have been established and sustained by sacrificial feasting. In lieu of a regional political authority, such relationships would have been crucial in building and maintaining alliances that allowed mobility, clarified rights to territories, and promoted sharing and collective sustenance in times of hardship. A long interval of forager-pastoralism also set the stage for crop cultivation. This transition is again very different from that evident in other areas of the Near East and was similarly closely shaped by water availability and social arrangements of land and water rights and territories.

## The beginnings of Southwest Arabian irrigation

Following the establishment of pastoralism during the sixth millennium, our best records presently indicate a more than 2,000 year interval prior to the emergence of irrigation and crop-rearing in ancient Yemen. This transition is demonstrably shaped by a range of forces frequently invoked in explaining the emergence of agriculture including climate change, demography, subsistence economics, social dynamics, and ideological factors. Even though the earliest plant domesticates appear to have been introduced to the region, the specific societal expression of agriculture cannot simply be viewed as having been diffused through contact with or brought by immigrant foreigners (Harrower et al. 2010). Similarly, for U.S.-Mexico Borderlands, specialists working in the region have strongly challenged globalizing language-agriculture models that envision an expanding frontier pattern in which Uto-Aztecan speakers from Mesoamerica spread northward bringing agriculture (Bellwood 2013: 230–34) as such highly theorized models posit an association between language and subsistence that does not necessarily follow from linguistic, archaeological, and genetic evidence (Kemp et al. 2010; Mabry et al. 2008; Merrill et al. 2009, 2010). Correspondingly, for Yemen, even though some domesticates were introduced, this does not necessarily demonstrate migration nor does it explain the distinctive transition to pastoralism and then crop agriculture, given that no material links have been established with well-known PPNA and PPNB cultures of the Levant or other northern farming societies (Crassard and Dreschler 2013: Edens and Wilkinson 1998). Instead of agriculture arriving in so-called secondary, peripheral areas with colonists that displaced local peoples, far more complex, historically contingent and unique patterns of local and interregional interaction characterized transitions to agriculture in Southwest Arabia and the American Southwest. As examined in this chapter, atypical histories of early crop-rearing in ancient Southwest Arabia are marked by mobile agropastoralism that involved locally devised irrigation technologies tailored to local environmental and social contexts.

After arriving in Yemen in 2000 with the steadfast RASA project goal of discovering the beginnings of agriculture in Southwest Arabia, we made numerous important discoveries, yet were forced to dramatically revise our views of what agriculture in the region and across the Near East looked like and how agriculture was expressed archaeologically. Indeed, the material remains of agriculture across the region, including our area of research focus in eastern Yemen, are dramatically different than the more familiar, well-documented Levantine pattern of Pre-Pottery Neolithic villages. As we completed our aforementioned systematic survey of a few square kilometers around the Khuzmum and wider sampling of the surrounding area (Harrower et al. 2002; McCorriston et al. 2002, 2005), we began to recognize that the pattern of village and household life we expected was not to be found. Without clusters of houses forming settlements, it was not clear where we should be searching for the remains of the earliest crops and domesticated animals. The small subcircular stone structures we discovered were very widely spaced and appeared to have been only intermittently occupied. In western Yemen the pattern documented by Italian and American teams again appeared to be quite different. Early pastoralist sites, including Wadi al-Tayyilah 3, showed clusters of elliptical stone structures with remains of cattle dated as early as the sixth millennium BC (Fedele 2008, 2013). As in Wadi Sana, these structures are widely scattered, and the Neolithic village pattern found across the Levant is lacking (De Maigret 1990: 121; Fedele 2013: 48). Crops, including wheat, barley, lentils, chickpeas, peas, and possibly broomcorn millet, are first evident in Yemen at the sites of Hayt al-Suad and Jubabat al-Juruf during the late fourth and early third millennium BC (Ekstrom and Edens 2003). However, cultivation in western Yemen involved water management strategies, including terrace agriculture dated to the fourth millennium (Wilkinson 1999), that are quite different than those of eastern Yemen where terraces are not suited to the steep denuded, rocky terrain. In Wadi Sana, small-scale water management structures were one of the most conspicuous remnants of past agriculture we recognized, but it was not initially clear how old they were, or what exactly they were used for. Archaeologists have long ignored small-scale irrigation structures, as it is frequently presumed it is impossible to accurately establish their age, but careful attention to geomorphology and new dating methods have begun to alleviate these challenges (Wilkinson 2003a) and formed an important part of our investigations (Harrower 2008b).

When we returned to Wadi Sana in 2004 our National Science Foundation support included funds not only to expand the scope of our investigations in human paleoecology but also a smaller NSF Dissertation Improvement Grant for targeted investigations of ancient water management. Studies of ancient transitions to agriculture have long been marked by debates between materialist explanations that premise environmental conditions, and idealist perspectives that emphasize social factors. I thus devised a plan of research that avoided advocating one or the other and was instead tailored to evaluate the explanatory efficacy of nature-focused versus culture-focused perspectives. We began with many more questions than answers. How many irrigation structures were distributed along Wadi Sana? How old were they? What were they used for, and were they strategically constructed according to water flow? I hypothesized that in such an arid environment the spatial distribution of ancient irrigation structures would be closely tied to environmental conditions including topography, potential water flow accumulation, and landforms reflecting close behavioral ties to environmental conditions. If irrigation was more predominantly shaped by social contingencies including managerial challenges, perceptions of landscapes, and land/water rights then I predicted irrigation structures would be less closely tied to environmental variables. Since spatial technologies are more readily capable of incorporating environmental data in comparison with social variables, I also planned ethnoarchaeological investigations of traditional small-scale irrigation to examine technological, logistical, and other social dimensions of small-scale water management.

Our fieldwork over the next two years (2004 and 2005) documented 174 irrigation structures and through careful attention to geomorphology, along with strategic test excavation and radiocarbon dating, we built a chronology for the appearance of irrigation. We discovered irrigation structures of two main types: (1) diversion channels that redirected flow on plateaus and rocky hill slopes, and (2) check dams that slowed flow along the sides of Wadi Sana or small tributaries. Although most are no longer active, springs along Wadi Sana would have offered water for domestic purposes, but no ancient wells, cisterns, or other water collection features were discovered. Test excavations were dug in five locations and indicated that irrigation began in the area no earlier than the mid-fifth millennium, and not later than the mid-fourth millennium BC (Harrower 2008a). This chronology was established through strategic radiocarbon dating of charcoal fragments in alluvial sediments (Harrower 2008b). We also attempted Optically Stimulated Luminescence (OSL), dating the last exposure to sunlight. Although this technique had previously been tried in Yemen (Balescu et al. 1998) and has successfully been used to date ancient canals in the American Southwest (Berger et al. 2004, 2009), our efforts met with little success and the dates (perhaps because sediments in the area lack sufficient quartz and feldspar grains) were contradictory and inconclusive. The project also searched and processed flotation samples from hearths and elliptical structures in numerous areas, but we never discovered direct evidence of domesticated crops or other plants that might have been irrigated. Although evidence from elsewhere in the region shows Levantine crops including wheat and barley were present in western Yemen by the late fourth millennium (Ekstrom and Edens 2003), it remains a possibility that the earliest irrigation in Wadi Sana watered wild plants using low-level food production strategies akin to those known in the American West including among the Owens Valley Paiute (see Chapter 3).

Particularly in light of continuing research over the past decade, our mapping and dating of early irrigation enables a more thorough evaluation of circumstances contributing to the beginnings of crop-rearing including climate change, demography, subsistence economics, social dynamics, and ideological factors. Interestingly, the earliest irrigation does bear a significant association with a major climatic shift toward aridity near 3200 BC. Investigations of local geomorphology led by Eric Oches delineate the local manifestation of this shift including terminal Pleistocene through early Holocene aggradation of alluvial gravel, sand, and silt along Wadi Sana with a pronounced shift to erosion and incision near the end of the fourth millennium. Indeed, of the thirty-nine radiocarbon assays embedded in alluvial sediments along Wadi Sana all but two yielded ages older than 3192 BC (Harrower 2006: table 8.1). As examined later in this chapter, geospatial analysis indicates this shift to incision was likely not only the result of aridity but also a function of greater inter- and intra-annual precipitation variability (Harrower et al. 2012). With vegetation cover declining, including both human and animal foods, the carrying capacity would have fallen. Based on the aforesaid rangeland analysis, the area may have been sustaining nearly as many cattle as possible and increased aridity would have resulted in significant demographic pressure. Cross-cultural analysis suggests irrigating solely to provide fodder for animals is unlikely (see Chapter 3); more probably residents of Wadi Sana began irrigating to grow food for themselves and fed the by-products, such as hay and straw, to their animals. We yet have little data about the type(s) and abundance of foods available that would help us evaluate the precise cost-benefit economics of different potential food choices (McCorriston 2006). However, edible wild plants would have included roots, tubers, seeds, and seed pods. A wild grain known as samḥ (*Mesembryanthemum forsskalei*) is ethnographically known to have been ground into flour and used to make porridge or added to wheat to make bread (Mandaville 2011: 105–27; Mustafa et al.1995). Accounts of samḥ as a food come almost exclusively from northern rather than southern Arabia, yet it remains possible future investigations in the south might discover archaeological remains of this or other gathered seeds. Ultimately, however, we require far more information from Holocene archaeological sites of the region to enable the types of dietary modeling advocated by proponents of Human Behavioral Ecology (e.g., Gremillion et al. 2014). As in many regions of the world, we unfortunately barely know what foods may have been available, let alone which ones people actually chose or how those choices shifted through time. Nevertheless, we do have good reason to believe that social transformation of territoriality and land/water rights played an important role in the adoption of irrigation. The late fourth millennium debut of irrigation is marked by the appearance of small circular cairn tombs across the Arabian Peninsula including along Wadi Sana and other drainages of the Hadramawt (McCorriston et al. 2011). These monuments are suggestive of increasing population densities and illustrate how nomads may have begun to express claims to land and water, reinforced through reference to ancestry, by building tombs overlooking valued water-rich areas amenable to irrigation.

Archaeologists can still only glean a relatively rudimentary apprehension of early Neolithic life in Southwest Arabia, yet comparisons with the American West can significantly inform our understanding of early water-use. Although distant in time and space, protohistoric Native American agropastoralism also provides insights into practices in ancient Arabia. In the U.S. Southwest the Navajo (Diné) began herding sheep and goats adopted from the Spanish at least by the early eighteenth century (Weisiger 2004). The Navajo, who referred to themselves as Diné but were known as Navajo (meaning people of cultivated fields in arroyos) to their Tewa neighbors, were long known as maize farmers. Amidst Spanish encroachments and conflicts with the Ute and Comanche, the Navajo adoption of livestock required transhumance to ensure water and forage but offered an enhanced defensive posture that allowed the Navajo to flee with their animals even if adversaries burned their crops. The Navajo built enclosures, expanded natural rock pools and dug shallow wells to capture water, drawing on detailed knowledge of terrain and seasonal moisture (Weisiger 2004: 262–63). From prehistoric times onward, water and water reservoirs took on deep symbolic meaning (Snead 2006) and these significations must have only intensified when provisioning animals. These histories echo agropastoralism in Arabia. In Hollywood movies and related literature the Navajo have often been depicted, like Arab nomads, as marauding raiders, but these portrayals belie long agricultural histories and are erroneously based on an comparatively short interval of conflict with Europeans that was not a long-term norm.

On a more technological level, many of the small-scale irrigation systems traditionally built by Native Americans of the American Southwest (Doolittle 2000) are very similar to those traditionally used in Yemen (Varisco 1996). Indeed, a range of irrigation techniques used in Yemen, including small-scale floodwater farming, diversion from springs, capturing hill-slope runoff, and terrace agriculture, bear close resemblance to systems found across the U.S.–Mexico Borderlands. Mabry and Doolittle (2008: 59) argue that different cultivation strategies were sequentially exploited in declining order of productive efficiency, with maize yields up to 2,350 kilograms/hectare (kg/ha) for floodwater systems to lows of 130 kg/ha for rainfed agriculture. Although comparable data on yields in Yemen is lacking, a related argument can be made that the most energy efficient and reliable techniques, such as flood and spring water diversion, appeared earliest with hill-slope runoff, terraces, and dry-land farming following later (Harrower 2006: 74–78). In a sense we might think of optimal foraging for water in which the easiest and most efficient cultivation strategies were exploited first and more labor intensive, less efficient technologies exploited later as the most attractive areas were sequentially occupied. Yet as water histories intertwined over millennia, strategies shifted to favor not only systems that were most efficient for households and small communities but also technologies that perpetuated particular social and political formations. Large-scale irrigation systems that harnessed water in otherwise inhospitable hyperarid areas were not a regional requirement of food production for large populations, but once constructed, massive waterworks were not only highly productive but were a public spectacle, and left disenthralled workers few nearby farming options if they chose not to participate in state systems.

The role of water in the emergence of new social relationships involves not only environmental conditions and the economics of water-use, but also their interface with water rights, allocations, politics, and ideologies. Particularly during drought, sufficient access to grazing lands and watering holes would have been crucial to ancient Arabian pastoralists. Among the Masai of southern Kenya and northern Tanzania, tradition instructs that anyone migrating with cattle can demand access to water, even sometimes in priority to local cattle (Fosbrooke 1948: 42). An analogous tradition in which travelers must be provided water for themselves and their animals quite famously prevails among Arabian Bedouin and is enshrined in the Quran (Naff 2009). And as Wilkinson (1983) described for Oman, historic territoriality often involved grazing or other periodic use-rights rather than ownership of the land itself. More generally, Islamic (*sharīa*) law describes circumstances where land and water can be owned or must be shared, and thus prescribes principles by which water claims should be negotiated. Indeed, one of the most basic, honored principles of Islamic law pertaining to water is the distinction between naturally flowing water bestowed by God that must be accessible to all and cannot be owned, versus water made available by people in wells, canals, or other improvements that can be privately controlled (Faruqui 2001; Lancaster and Lancaster 1999; Maktari 1971). Given that irrigators who invest substantial energies in capturing water need to protect their investment from encroachments of neighboring pastoralists and their herds, such private rights to captured water must have existed, I argue, as early as the beginnings of water management more than 5,000 years ago and would have played a crucial role in facilitating the early social viability of irrigation (Harrower 2008a).

Across the American West, histories of water rights and water law vividly exemplify the complexities of water politics in desert regions. In English common law, and for most of the eastern United States, water-use is guided by riparian rights doctrine. Riparian rights are conjoined to waterfront property so that all landholders can make reasonable local use of water as long as it does not impair the availability of water downstream. While riparian rights doctrine is reasonable and workable in temperate areas, it is ill suited to arid regions including most of the American West. Riparian rights generated enormous controversy as settlers scrambled to claim waterfront land depriving latecomers of water necessary for cattle and crops. Critics of riparian rights advocated the similarly problematic legal principle of prior appropriation "first in time, first in rights," which requires that those who used water first in time be accorded preferential rights to the quantities they originally utilized. Neither riparian rights nor prior appropriation offered an easy-fix to the vexing controversies surrounding claims to land and water. Riparian rights sent settlers clamoring to secure as much waterfront land as possible; while prior appropriation prompted the use of as much water as possible as quickly as possible, even if wasteful. In 1872, a pivotal Colorado court case pitted the two principles against one another and led the state to adopt prior appropriation, thereafter sometimes referred to as the Colorado doctrine. In California, the state constitution of 1849 centered on English common law and by default adopted riparian rights doctrine. Private monopolization of land and water, however, had begun to generate a ground-swell of discontent against riparian control and a series of court cases between wealthy land barons eventually led to a mixing of both riparian and prior appropriation that left little clarity and wide dissatisfaction. Legal wrangling over water doctrine in California since then has revolved predominantly around surface-water, and groundwater pumping remains almost entirely unfettered and unregulated. Analogous tragedy of the commons issues complicate water-use in contemporary Yemen where groundwater over-pumping has contributed to conflict and turmoil (Lichtenthäler 2003; Moore 2011). As further examined in Chapter 5, water-use complications are inevitably part of water politics in desert regions and frame the development and implementation of irrigation strategies and technologies.

*Spatial dimensions of water flow and irrigable areas along Wadi Sana*

Spatial analysis can substantially inform our understanding of how and why ancient pastoralists turned to irrigation in the late fourth millennium BC. In conjunction with the demographic, social, and ideological changes in play at the time, climatological and environmental conditions simultaneously shaped human livelihoods. Spatial patterning of ancient irrigation systems conveys a deep sense of how ancient irrigators understood local hydrology and modified their surroundings. Both local and regional climate records demonstrate a shift toward increased aridity at the close of the Holocene humid period near the end of the fourth millennium (Lézine 2009). As conditions became increasingly arid, human plant food and animal forage would have also become correspondingly scarce. Interannual rainfall variability in the tropics has a well-documented tendency to increase as mean annual precipitation declines (Dewar and Wallis 1999). Since rangeland productivity responds dramatically to precipitation changes, half the annual rain, for example, can lead to one quarter the available forage (Le Houérou and Hoste 1977). Decreased annual precipitation thus has the compound effect of higher variability, which can quickly result in overgrazing. Middle Wadi Sana was characterized by sheet flow, sedimentary infiltration, and vegetation absorption during the early Holocene, which shifted toward more sporadic and abrupt overland flows and wadi discharges during the middle Holocene. Instead of gradual accumulation of water-borne nutrient-bearing silts, erosive down-cutting began during the late fourth millennium, at nearly the same time as our earliest evidence for irrigation. Existing pastoral adaptations tailored to persistent or recurrent (e.g., seasonal) patterns in the availability and abundance of resources, such as marshy grasses, would have become increasingly tenuous and vulnerable. Geospatial hydrological modeling summarized in this chapter shows that irrigators selected low to moderate energy water flow areas to build small water management structures that fed fields commonly spanning less than a hectare. Geospatial analysis of Wadi Sana cross sections also illustrates how increased variability of precipitation, rather than solely a shift to aridity itself, contributed to the late fourth millennium transition from alluvial aggradation to degradation.

The tear-drop shaped Wadi Sana watershed covers 3,691 sq. km and flows northward into Wadi Hadramawt (Masila), which eventually drains into the Indian Ocean (Plate II). Throughout most of the watershed Umm er-Radhuma limestone is overlain by the lower Eocene Jeza limestone creating a deeply incised dendritic network of up to three successive limestone plateaus. These plateaus and the steep slopes leading up to them are either scree covered or bedrock and do not allow construction of soil-conserving terraces common in western Yemen. Precipitation falls predominantly during the summer monsoon when the Intertropical Convergence Zone (ITCZ) – an interface where subtropical and equatorial airs converge – moves to its most northerly position along the southern edge of the Arabian Peninsula. From west to east across Yemen, mean annual rainfall range from approximately 50 to 400 mm along the Tihama coast, 200 to 800 mm across the western highlands, 50 to 100 mm in the Ramlat as-Sab'atayn Desert, and from 50 to 150 mm across the eastern highlands of Hadramawt and Mahra (Bruggeman 1997: Annex I). Rainfall was far more plentiful during the early Holocene when the ITCZ extended further northward and began to decline near 6000 BC to more pronounced aridity by 3000 BC (Lézine et al. 2010: 427). An analogous pattern of early Holocene pluvial conditions followed by a late fourth millennium shift toward aridity accompanies the early appearance of crop agriculture in Southeast Arabia (Preston et al. 2012). While there is increasingly wide agreement that climatic changes played a role in the beginnings of agriculture in both regions, the social dynamics and interregional influences differ widely in Southwest versus Southeast Arabia (Cleuziou 2009).

In devising a plan to map and analyze the distribution of irrigation structures along Wadi Sana in 2004 and 2005 I quickly realized a relatively high-accuracy Digital Elevation Model (DEM) would be needed to analyze spatial patterning of water. Since the 90 m grid cells of SRTM data were far too coarse, I devised a strategy to extract our own higher (15 m) resolution DEM from the offset stereo bands (3n and 3b) of ASTER satellite imagery (using PCI Geomatics software). Just as humans' two offset eyes allow us to see objects in three dimensions, stereo air photos and satellite images can similarly represent the height and depth of topography. Creating a DEM requires precise geometric control, and in this case required collecting a series of high-accuracy GPS readings known as Ground Control Points (GCPs) at locations readily identifiable on ASTER imagery (such as road intersections and other prominent natural landmarks). These widely distributed GCPs covering much of the Wadi Sana watershed were then input into PCI Geomatics software to geometrically align the two stereo bands of two separate 60 × 60 km ASTER image scenes (Harrower 2006: 132–34). Collecting the sixty-four GCPs with a high-accuracy Trimble GPS receiver also offered far greater familiarly with the area and led to discovery of a number of important archaeological sites including the rediscovery of the Iron Age hill fort of Qalat Habshiya (see Chapter 5). Once the DEM was extracted it allowed a detailed GIS appraisal of irrigation structure locations and their background watershed-scale context.

Spatial patterning of irrigation structures along Wadi Sana reveals detailed understanding, advance planning, and careful design of ancient irrigation systems in the context of changing environments. As it would seem water shortfalls would be a pressing issue in the desert, I initially expected that irrigators (particularly when facing increased aridity) would have selected areas with the highest water flow, but mapping and modeling proved otherwise. Instead, ancient peoples of the Wadi Sana gained sophisticated understanding of local runoff and targeted areas with low to moderate energy water flows where water could be more easily managed in areas beyond the reach of powerfully dangerous flashfloods (Figure 4.3). Spatial technologies enabled comparison of water flow accumulation from our ASTER DEM for the entire Wadi Sana watershed with flow accumulation values for our sample of 174 irrigation structures (Harrower 2006, 2008a, 2010). Analysis of landforms using the ASTER satellite imagery landform layer described earlier also demonstrated associations between ancient irrigation structures and areas of alluvium most suited to cultivation (Harrower

# The beginnings of Southwest Arabian irrigation

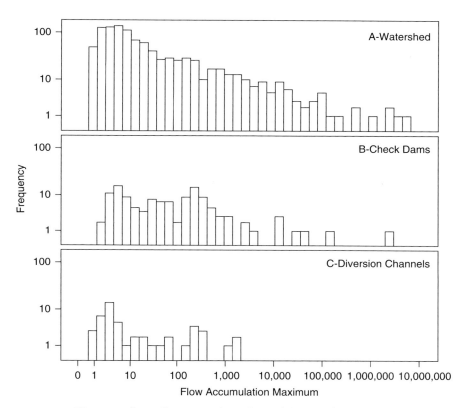

FIGURE 4.3. Histogram of water flow accumulation for Wadi Sana, Hadramawt (Yemen). GIS based water flow accumulation for the Wadi Sana watershed (top) is shown in comparison with values for check dams (middle) and diversion channels (bottom). Diversion channels are preferentially located in low flow areas while check dams are preferentially found in moderate flow locations. Differences shown are statistically significant at the 95 percent confidence level as demonstrated by Kolmogorov-Smirnov statistical testing (Harrower 2010).

2006, 2008a). Directions and potential intensities of runoff on low gradient rocky hill slopes are not obvious and would have needed to be judged through experience observing previous highly sporadic rainfall events. The dangers of heavy rain on rocky low-infiltration highlands nearly devoid of vegetation are starkly illustrated, for example, by devastating flooding of Hadramawt and Mahra in October 2008, which killed at least seventy-three people, leaving seventeen missing and 25,000 needing shelter, as well as destroying vast areas of agricultural land (Root and Papakos 2010). Early irrigators clearly needed to avoid areas with moderate to high-energy water flow. Large barrages that divert high volume water flows into canals would only appear far later, after thousands of years of experience with smaller scale irrigation.

Geospatial analysis alongside some basic principles of hydrology, fluvial geomorphology, and sediment transport can also assist in better understanding the transition from sedimentary aggradation to degradation in Wadi Sana that accompanied, and in part prompted, the earliest irrigation. In a simple sense, the balance between alluvial aggradation and degradation is governed by availability of sediment (sediment quantity and size) on one hand, and the ability of water to transport sediment (channel discharge and slope) on the other (Brooks et al. 2013: 243–65; Lane 1955; Rosgen 1996; Figure 4.4). Quite simply, as the amount of water in a channel increases and moves faster, it can carry more sediment of larger grain (clast) sizes. Conversely, as water volumes and flow velocities decrease, less sediment of smaller sizes can be transported. All other things being equal, more water will tend to lead to degradation and erosion, and less water will tend to lead to deposition and aggradation. For Wadi Sana, since we know that three of these four variables (sediment quantity, size, and channel slope) remained relatively stable through time, if we hold these variables constant less annual rainfall during the fourth millennium would (according to this equation) result in aggradation as reduced flows would be less capable and eroding and transporting sediment (Harrower et al. 2012). However, we know that the opposite occurred and Wadi Sana began down-cutting rather than aggrading near the end of the fourth millennium, which suggests something else must be left unaccounted for in this, admittedly simplified, model. The most probable explanation involves considering changes not only in the annual amount of precipitation but changes in the timing of precipitation and resultant runoff. As discussed earlier, it is likely not only that rainfall decreased but that inter- and intra-annual rainfall variability increased, and with less vegetation to absorb water, runoff would have become more sudden and sporadic, leading to more abrupt, punctuating floods (Harrower et al. 2012). Such conditions would have substantially altered the surroundings and grasslands on which early pastoralists relied, and it is probable that these newly erosive fluvial conditions contributed to new strategies, including experimentation with water diversion and irrigation. As increasingly sporadic water flows began to cut channels through valuable alluvial sediments it would have been increasingly crucial that water reach areas capable of sustaining grasses and/or crops. This need would have begun during the middle to late fourth millennium and became an increasingly acute problem over time. Today, very little

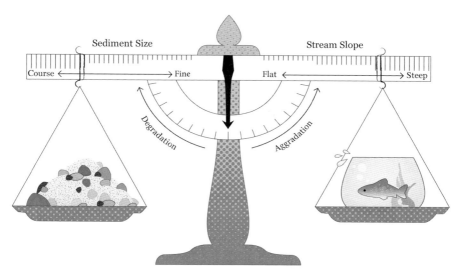

Sediment Load x Sediment Size ∝ Stream Slope x Stream Discharge

FIGURE 4.4. Lane's Balance of water flow and sediment transport. Sediment supply and sediment particle size on the left, balance with stream slope and stream discharge on the right (Lane 1955). All other things being equal, increases in water discharge and slope contribute to degradation and decreases in water discharge and slope contribute to aggradation (figure based on Rosgen 1996; see also Brooks et al. 2013: 243–65).

water reaches sediments along middle Wadi Sana and most channels contain almost exclusively gravel and cobbles with little potential to sustain vegetation.

## Agricultural origins, frontiers, and water in ancient Southwest Arabia

In summary, the beginnings of pastoralism and cultivation in Southwest Arabia and other archaeologically less explored regions offers considerable untapped potential to enhance understanding of transitions to agriculture worldwide. The archaeology of areas lacking the earliest agriculture has long been shaped by frontier perspectives, comparable to those that have long dominated views of the American West, in which agricultural populations grow, expand, demographically overwhelm, and colonize. Frontier formulations continue to be central to analysis of transitions to agriculture including, for example, in Europe (Rowley-Conwy 2011), South Asia (Fuller 2006), and Arabia (Drechsler 2007, 2009). However, framing the issue in terms of frontiers of dispersal underestimates the ingenuity of populations long portrayed as secondary and peripheral who are deemed recipients rather than originators of agriculture. Particularly when framed in comparative perspective, ancient Yemen and the ancient American Southwest illustrate and animate local expressions of agriculture as active social reconfiguration and reinvention rather migration, assimilation, or simple adoption of foreign plants and animals. The beginnings of pastoralism and irrigation in ancient Yemen depended not only on the appearance of agriculture in neighboring regions but more importantly on local factors including rugged arid-monsoon environments, the comparative cost-benefits of different potential food-acquisition strategies, perceptions of land/water rights and territoriality, alongside shifting conceptions of human relations with nature. Across these arid highlands, economic and social life were intertwined with water throughout histories that extend long before and long after plant and animal husbandry were supposedly invented or discovered.

Spatial dynamics and availabilities of water shaped histories from the very dawn of humans' appearance in Arabia. Fasad projectile points offer our earliest, albeit controversial, potential traces of interaction with Levantine populations. Yet, as lithic analysts have adamantly observed, Fasad points were produced using an entirely different reduction sequence than the Naviform cores used to manufacture similar looking points in the Levant. Fasad points, therefore, certainly cannot be considered *prima facie* evidence of an immigrant population. Moreover, since we have yet to establish whether groups that used Fasad points relied exclusively on wild game or occasionally on herded animals their appearance at most signifies wide regional interaction and perhaps stylistic emulation, not necessarily the spread of Neolithic lifeways. When cattle and caprine pastoralism does first definitively appear in Southwest Arabia during the early sixth millennium BC it is associated with a very different range of lithic technologies that are not derived from the Levant (Crassard et al. 2006). Changing notions of land and water-use accompanied early pastoralism and entailed shifts in patterns of mobility and territoriality. As populations of humans and animals expanded over time, pressures on water and grazing territories would have increased and GIS analysis suggests ritual gathering and sacrificial feasting at Shi'b Kheshiya would have involved aggregation of people from a wide area far beyond Wadi Sana. These gatherings would have built alliances, alleviated conflicts, and helped balance the demands and landscape impacts of desert pastoralism.

Local water histories and a shift toward aridity during the mid-fourth millennium BC played a substantial role in changing lifeways and the emergence of agriculture and irrigation. As grazing territories and wild food sources were progressively strained and depleted, even highly economical water exploitation strategies including targeting of water-rich areas like springs and seasonally flooded zones became precarious. As plant resources diminished, small-scale water management including hill-slope runoff, floodwater diversion and terracing became increasingly attractive, if not necessary, options. Even during drought, moves to lay claim to water resources did not initially, in eastern Yemen, result in sedentism (cf. Rosenberg 1998) but they did heighten competition and territoriality. Investments in water management, a form of landesque capital improvement, were linked to changing water rights tied to tomb building, mortuary landscapes, and ideologies of territoriality. While we will likely never know the precise nature of prehistoric water rights, it is highly probable some mode of exclusionary control allowed occasional open access while inhibiting freeloading in ways that contributed to long-standing rural land and water customs. Over succeeding millennia far more technologically complex systems that favored wide political alliances and promoted aggregation contributed to the political rhetoric and social logic of state formation.

CHAPTER 5

# Water histories of Southwest Arabian kingdoms (and the American West)

> *This rude platform is an altar, and on it we are here consecrating this water supply and dedicating this aqueduct to you and your children and your children's children – for all time. There it is. Take it.*
> William Mulholland at the opening of the
> Los Angeles-Owens Valley Aqueduct in 1913 (Ulin 2013: 32)

In both America and Arabia water was pivotal to histories of civilizations, and spatial heterogeneity (patterns and gradients of comparative abundance and great scarcity) were central to human geographies of both regions. As historians of the American West have cogently emphasized, public and private water exploitation was not only important economically but was also deeply significant in terms nationalism, identity, and sovereignty (Arax and Wartzman 2005; Hundley 2001; Worster 1985). Geographies of the Los Angeles-Owens Valley Aqueduct, with a great wealth of water just east of the Sierra Nevada Mountains and great scarcity to the west, set the stage for large-scale water diversion from inland mountains down toward the coast. Over the next 100 years, voluminous flows of the Colorado River, for example, have not only been channeled downhill but have even been pumped uphill over vast distances at enormous cost. It is perhaps most striking that many late-twentieth century waterworks of the American West were economically inadvisable in terms of total costs, which outweighed returns in food, flood control, and electricity, but were nevertheless perpetuated by benefits accrued to subset populations alongside great symbolic impact and political inertia (Wahl 1989; Wilson 2002). A comparable political pattern prevailed in ancient Yemen where construction of vast irrigation systems sustaining ancient state capitals at outlets of major watersheds transformed hyperarid deserts into lush bountiful oases. The spectacle of these massive waterworks beckoned nomads who became the indentured laborers and farm workers of early states. The ancient engineers who designed these systems must have gained considerable prestige, and the water managers who operated them would have been similarly indispensable. The Great Dam at Ma'rib, arguably the most important pre-Islamic monument in Arabia, was continually reconstructed over nearly 1,300 years even though most food production in Yemen began to shift by the end of the first millennium BC to highland areas where crops could be grown with rainfall. As examined in this chapter, inscriptions that attest to the many thousands of workers and massive quantities of food and drink supplied to rebuild Ma'rib Dam record investments that, like the costs of waterworks across the American West, would not have been warranted if rewards came solely in terms of agricultural production. Instead, (re)construction of the Ma'rib Dam was motivated not only by the need for food, but because it came to symbolize power, political ascendancy, and hegemony in the region. Experts in Ancient South Arabian (ASA) inscriptions still debate the meaning of the term *mukarrib*, a title that precedes yet overlaps with use of the more familiar term *malik* (king). Mukarrib, traditionally taken to mean unifier or federator of tribes (Beeston 1972), has more recently been reinterpreted by one scholar as an honorific meaning blessed (Drewes 2001), and the now outdated notion that the term mukarrib was exclusively used for preeminent kings who ruled over multiple kingdoms has been proven inaccurate (Avanzini 2010). What is not disputed, however, is that from the very outset of a literary tradition in the region mukarribs were frequently commissioning inscriptions emphasizing not only their prowess in war, but their capabilities in orchestrating irrigation systems. These referents to water were not only economic, but were also significant in marking identity, ideology, and religion, and proclaiming ties to cosmological authority through harnessing water in hyperarid deserts. For both America and Arabia, not only are views of histories inordinately shaped by our understandings of Western civilizations, but even more problematically, notions of economic efficiency and rationality (in this case with respect to water control) are drawn from mythical, chimerical conceptions of Western histories. Rather than water histories unfolding as forms of exploitive despotism, perfect social orderliness, or progressive economic efficiency, historical dynamics involve far more complex intermixtures of environmental, cultural, and political harmony, conflict, and turmoil.

The history of the American West helpfully animates the environmental, economic, political, and ideological interconnectivities of water. The rise and articulation of U.S. sovereignty across the West was in many ways driven by aspirations of homesteading, linked to government policies and major waterworks. As western states began to join the Union – California in 1850 and remaining areas over the half century thereafter – most water projects were initially private endeavors. The Homestead Act signed by Abraham Lincoln in 1862 allowed anyone who had not taken up arms against the United States to file an application for 160 acres; if they lived on the land and improved it, after five years they could own it. The implications for nation-building, sovereignty, and settlement of the West were enormous. Previously federal land was only available for sale at $1 per acre in parcels no less than 640 acres. Three prior homestead bills passed by the U.S. House of Representatives over the preceding decade had been defeated in the U.S. Senate due to the vigorous opposition of wealthy plantation farmers and factory owners, who feared competition and loss of cheap labor. Accelerating the process, The Desert Land Act of 1877 quadrupled the maximum homestead size from 160 to 640 acres, provided the land was irrigated within three years, further promoting colonization of land and exploitation of as much water as possible, as quickly as possible. Even with this expansion, limits on homestead acreage were almost never enforced. Married couples doubled their acreage, and many illegally paid stand-ins to claim land on their behalf. The Desert Land Act also removed the residency requirement, which required that homesteaders physically live on the land they claimed, so unscrupulous speculators quickly amassed tens of thousands of acres. By 1900, 62 percent of agricultural land in California was held by wealthy land holders in estates of more than a thousand acres (Hundley 2001: 89). As little as 160 acres with easy access to irrigation water (or water provided by government projects) could yield a windfall, yet those who held even thousands of desert acres without water often found such lands virtually worthless, meaning control of water was evermore important than control of land itself. As Kent Flannery commented on the ancient Near East ...

> It was not just that 100% of the food is produced on 10% of the land; it is the fact that in some cases 1% of the population owns the 1% of the land that produces 30% of the food. (Flannery 1969: 95)

Homesteading was thus ill-equipped to cure the vast inequities of the American East's slave-holding plantation farming across the West's highly heterogeneous landscapes where haves and have-nots were frequently determined by control and access to (often subsidized) water.

Ill-conceived irrigation schemes (spawned in part by the requirement that homesteaders improve their land) contributed to overuse, destructive flooding, and perpetual claims of shortage prompting calls for the government to intervene. In 1900 the poorly engineered Alamo Canal was built by the California Development Company to divert water for irrigation from the Colorado River through Mexico to California's Imperial Valley. The canal soon clogged with sediment, and in 1904 a breach was hastily cut into the bank of the Colorado to divert even more water. By 1905 the Colorado River had broken through and began carving its own path; eventually the entirety of its flow raged into the Imperial Valley. By the time the flooding was stopped in 1907 an enormous water body – the Salton Sea – had become California's largest lake and today remains a toxic, hypersaline environmental catastrophe. The fiasco highlighted the inability of private interests to safely grapple with the engineering expertise, costs, and management challenges of large water projects without rules or oversight. Amidst such challenges the United States Reclamation Service (eventually renamed the U.S. Bureau of Reclamation, USBR) was founded by President Theodore Roosevelt in 1902 inaugurating more than six decades of dramatic federal government transformation of western water resources. The intent was to help small farmers irrigate their land. The Reclamation Act stipulated that government supplied water could only be used to irrigate holdings no larger than 160 acres, but prohibitions against speculation and accumulation of inordinate amounts of land and water were routinely ignored.

The spark in USBR's impact began in 1928 with authorization of the Hoover Dam that environmentally and politically transformed the Colorado River and the history of the American West. The dam was devised and approved in conjunction with the 130-km All-American Canal that would move downstream water from the Colorado River to the Imperial Valley without entering Mexico. Together they were to regulate flow, prevent flooding, and more safely convey water for irrigation and domestic purposes, with electricity production added for cost recovery. Completed in 1935, the 726-foot high Hoover Dam was at the time the tallest dam and one of the largest human-made structures in the world. The dam is a monumental hallmark of American history that was funded by the federal government and built by six corporate contractors who completed the project on-budget in four years (just over half of the seven years originally scheduled) while creating thousands of important depression-era jobs. The $49 million dollar cost was, by the mid-1980s, entirely repaid to the U.S. Treasury through sales of electricity. The project still serves as an exemplar of successful government/corporate partnership, and the dam is now a major tourist attraction less than an hour drive from Las Vegas and receives nearly a million visitors every year. The enormous success of the

Hoover Dam created a powerful, self-perpetuating bureaucracy that sought increasing control of water; some even viewed any water that reached the ocean as a wasteful abrogation of dominion over nature (Worster 1985). Thousands of subsequent USBR projects along with competing efforts of the U.S. Army Corp of Engineers were augmented by state-funded endeavors, including the Central Valley Project (1933-onward) that moves enormous quantities of water from northern California down the San Joaquin Valley, and the Central Arizona Project (1968-onward) that pumps 22,000 gallons of water per second up over 2,000 feet from the Colorado River to Phoenix and eventually south to Tucson, Arizona. While many projects following on the Hoover Dam were meant to be paid for by water-user fees, these payments rarely materialized resulting in massive government subsidies for western agriculture that predominantly benefit(ed) large corporate landholders rather than homesteaders, small-holders, and households as originally planned. Even so, the Hoover Dam exemplifies the wide impacts of water control in environmentally, politically, and culturally directing the history of a region in ways that inform understanding of ancient and modern water histories worldwide.

## The elaboration of agriculture and irrigation in Bronze Age Yemen

In ancient Yemen, the prehistory of human water control plays out over a long interval from the fourth millennium BC origins of irrigation through the rise of massive state irrigation systems during the early first millennium BC. While clearly a very different cultural and historical context, Yemen is informatively juxtaposed against the far better known water histories of the American West and illustrates a comparable pattern of state control and political dominion over water in hyperarid parts of a nevertheless fertile region. Yemen is about 30 percent larger in area than California and like the American West is highly heterogeneous with broad alluvial lowlands along the Red Sea and Indian Ocean, rugged mountains up to 3,666 m (over 12,000 feet), and a vast interior Ramlat as-Sab'atayn Desert that is part of Arabia's Rub al-Khali (Empty Quarter). Irrigation is not inexorably necessary for crop-rearing in Yemen but nevertheless played, and continues to play, an important role in agriculture. While some low-lying areas receive less than 50 mm of precipitation per annum, the highest elevation parts of western Yemen receive as much as 800 mm with comparatively low evapotranspiration (Farquharson et al. 1996) offering conditions more than suitable for rainfed farming. Terrace agriculture and small-scale water

## The elaboration of agriculture and irrigation in Bronze Age Yemen

management have nevertheless played an important role in crop cultivation since its inception and serve to conserve soil, promote fertility, and offset the risk of water shortfalls (Rappold 2005; Wilkinson 1999). From their earliest appearance in the mid-fourth millennium, agricultural and irrigation technologies appear to have remained relatively small-scale over the succeeding thousand or more years. Based on local and global analogs (see Chapter 3), agricultural constructions were probably initially designed, constructed, and used by families and immediate kin groups, while decision making and dispute resolution operated by acephalous consensus building. As a primary preindustrial means of boosting agricultural production, large-scale irrigation began to emerge near the mid to late second millennium as increasing populations required greater food supplies, and mechanisms to prevent monopolization of water and food production deteriorated and intertwined with religion, pilgrimage, and frankincense trade.

By the early third millennium BC villages and towns often spanning a few hectares were established in the comparatively high rainfall western highlands of Yemen. Italian research in the 1980s in the Khawlan area southeast of Yemen's modern capital of Sana'a first documented the region's ceramic-bearing agricultural settlements, establishing that there was in fact an autochthonous Bronze Age in the region (De Maigret 1985, 1986, 1990, 2002). In nearby Dhamar Governate, University of Chicago survey documented more than fifty Bronze Age sites as large as 10–15 hectares (Edens 1999; Wilkinson 2003b). One of the best-known sites, the fortified hilltop town of Hammat al-Qa covered 5 hectares flanked by terraced fields and threshing floors (Edens et al. 2000). Analysis of the "semi-urban" architectural layout suggests Hammat al-Qa likely housed up to 500 people supported by a sophisticated pattern of crop cultivation on terraces with a wider surrounding sphere of grazing areas (Edens et al. 2000). While evidence from Yemen's Bronze Age remains somewhat limited, neither settlements nor burials indicate wide disparities of status as might be reflected in preferential access to food or luxury goods (Edens 2005). Although we have limited basis on which to infer political organization, this finding is similar to what we know of the third millennium in Oman and the United Arab Emirates, where agriculture and complex polities appear to have been marked by heterarchy and communality rather than political hierarchy (Cleuziou 2007; Harrower et al. 2014b).

On the alluvial lowlands near Yemen's modern port city of Aden, the expansion and elaboration of irrigation in the Bronze Age may have already involved diverting powerful floodwaters from relatively large catchments, a technique known as *sayl* irrigation. At the sites of Sabir and Ma'layba just upstream from Aden, settlement and irrigation date predominantly to the second and early first millennium BC; but the lowest layers of Ma'layba and associated paleosols intriguingly suggest even earlier occupation perhaps dated to the third millennium BC or before (Buffa 2002; Görsdorf and Vogt 2001; Vogt and Sedov 1998; Vogt et al. 2002). Since these sites are in an area that receives only 60mm of precipitation per annum, irrigation would have been crucial. Canals, that until recently were still visible as remnants, probably carried water from the 5,340 sq. km catchment of Wadi Tuban that outlets in the area or from associated springs (Farquharson et al. 1996; Vogt et al. 2002).

Research in areas immediately surrounding the eventual capitals of ancient kingdoms, particularly Ma'rib (Kingdom of Saba), has also yielded substantial evidence of irrigation as early as the third millennium BC. The Great Ma'rib Dam at the outlet of Wadi Dhana has been of understandably great interest to scholars for generations. In 1843 Joseph Arnaud mapped the impressive, monumental remnants of the north and south sluice gates of the dam (Arnaud 1874) and a great deal of important subsequent research on irrigation in the area has followed (Brunner 1983; 2000; Brunner and Haefner 1986; Francaviglia 2000, 2002; Hehmeyer 1989; Hehmeyer and Schmidt 1991; Schmidt 1988; Vogt et al. 2004). Considerable energies have been devoted to dating the beginnings of irrigation at Ma'rib. Brunner (1983) first estimated (based on alluvial sedimentation rates) that irrigation began at Ma'rib during the third millennium BC. Francaviglia (2000) retrieved fragments of charcoal from sediments near Ma'rib Dam that dated to as early as the mid-fourth millennium BC, which he used to argue that irrigation began in the area began by that time. More recent efforts retrieved even earlier radiocarbon dates from alluvial sediments at Ma'rib (e.g., 3786 +/− 94 cal BC) yet the authors more conservatively concluded irrigation appeared in the area by roughly 2500 BC (Kühn et al. 2010). Regardless, such disparities illustrate the difficulties of identifying the earliest irrigation around state capitals with extensive later histories of large-scale irrigation and massive quantities of alluvial overburden. Nevertheless, recent studies of both natural and anthropogenic sediments have greatly clarified the environmental history of the Ma'rib area showing that natural paleosol formation beyond the outlet of Wadi Dhana ceased after 6300 BC signifying a distinct shift toward aridity (Pietsch et al. 2012). Moisture-rich sediments were still being laid down by Wadi Dhana contributing to weak cambisol formation (Kühn et al. 2010) and early experiments with irrigation may have originated in such areas. Brunner (1997b) also reported indications of third millennium irrigation along Wadi Marha near

Hajar Yahirr, the eventual capital of the Kingdom of Awsan, albeit based on a single radiocarbon date. Gentelle was noticeably cautious in his studies of irrigation at Shabwa (Kingdom of Hadramawt) and along Wadi Bayhan (Kingdom of Qataban), but observed that stimulus of other regions alongside a long history of local experience likely both contributed to Yemen's impressive ancient irrigation systems (Gentelle 1991, 1998). Since the earliest radiocarbon dates from ancient city of Shabwa fall during the very early second millennium BC (Breton 2003) it is likely that substantial-scale irrigation was underway at least by that time. At the nearby head of Wadi Hadramawt the ancient town of Bi'r Hamad similarly shows evidence of irrigation and settlement as early as the last quarter of the second millennium BC (Sedov 1995).

These early developments undoubtedly contributed to the expertise that enabled construction of massive state irrigation systems during the late second millennium BC but evidence of irrigation for that period is exceedingly scant. The earliest state irrigation systems are obscured by many centuries of construction, reconstruction, and alluvial deposition and we lack inscriptions from the very earliest genesis of Southwest Arabian kingdoms to reveal how irrigation expanded from small-scale systems in the fourth and third millennia to large-scale systems in the second and early first millennia BC. A wider comparative realm of evidence, including ethnographic studies of irrigation and evidence from adjacent regions can substantially enhance interpretations of this pivotal interval.

In Bronze Age Oman, very different spatial patterning of water resources and cultural dynamics contributed to widely divergent water histories. Since Oman lacks the massive watersheds and corresponding intense floodwater discharges of Yemen, early human occupation concentrated instead at oasis nodes shaped by a diversity of geological factors (Luedeling and Buerkert 2008). Hafit tombs, similar to forms found across the Arabian Peninsula, began to appear around 3200 BC and established a striking visual presence across landscapes. By the mid-third millennium BC massive communal Umm an-Nar tombs and towers further expressed claims to water at oases. The famous *aflaj* irrigation systems that developed in Oman and the United Arab Emirates over subsequent millennia (Boucharlat 2003; Magee 2005) are arguably no less technologically complex than flashflood water systems in Yemen, but their social and environmental landscape contexts and ramifications are substantially different. In Yemen, disillusioned farm workers could, at least in theory, opt out of ancient state polities and farm independently in high rainfall highland areas. In Oman, early farmers had far fewer options outside the oases where water resources concentrate. Omani *aflaj* systems often flow relatively continuously and task requirements tend to promote equitable allocation and decentralized power. These circumstances probably limited population growth to areas with water and helped hold early leaders' authority in check, as continuously flowing water was more broadly available in comparison with sporadic flows that are more easily monopolized. In contrast, flashflood water systems of Yemen's ancient states favored massive constructions to divert powerful water discharges that required very different design skills alongside massive, intermittent aggregations of labor for construction and reconstruction, which thereby promoted political hierarchies.

## Intermediate-scale irrigation: A comparative perspective

In conjunction with cross-cultural evidence of irrigation worldwide, ethnographic evidence of intermediate-scale irrigation in Yemen greatly assists in clarifying water histories of ancient Southwest Arabian kingdoms. As ancient irrigation moved from exclusively small-scale practices to include intermediate and large-scale systems, logistical challenges contributed to social change, differentiation, and political complexity. In general, cross-cultural findings about irrigation management, which have identified elected water managers and water users associations as widely prevalent means of organizing intermediate-scale irrigation, quite closely coincide with what is known of irrigation in Yemen.

The descriptor "intermediate-scale" irrigation quite aptly describes systems larger than those often constructed independently by nuclear families yet smaller than those that involve centralized bureaucratic oversight. Indeed, a closer examination of the meaning of the term "scale" and the social logistics of irrigation systems is informative in interpreting archaeological remains. Scale can be defined as the total length of canals, time required for construction of waterworks, the size area irrigated, number of irrigators involved, or total number of people sustained by an irrigation system (Hunt 2007: 122–25; Mabry 1996). While there is a general tendency toward centralized management as scale increases, a wide range of studies have identified wide variability so that no fixed deterministic relationship holds between scale and centralization (Downing and Gibson 1974; Fernea 1970; Hunt 1988, 2007; Hunt and Hunt 1976; Kelly 1983; Lees 1994; Mabry 1996, 2000; Millon 1962; Mitchell 1973, 1976; Price 1994; Scarborough 1991). Circumstances that promote or necessitate increased agricultural production, such as drought or population growth, can often strain the capacities of households and nuclear families. Intensification, through greater production per unit area of land, or extensification, through expanding the area of land cultivated, are two primary options for boosting production. Extensification can involve large-scale irrigation schemes that supply water to a more expansive area or simple proliferation of independent small-scale systems over larger spans of terrain. Alternatively, intensification can entail new agricultural technologies, increased labor inputs, or increased water supply to the same area of land. Thresholds that divide acephalous household-scale, from community-level, and eventually bureaucratic management depend in complex ways on the wide variety of management activities required for any particular system or strategy. Organizational challenges and scalar stress emerge with as few as six people (Johnson 1982) and become increasingly problematic as scale increases. Beyond consensus-based management among an entire group or irrigators, copious ethnographic data points to appointed or elected managers and/or water users associations as widely prevalent management alternatives (Coward 1977; Hunt 1989). In drawing on a wide range of data analyzed in support of modern agricultural development, Uphoff (1986: 45–57) observed that systems that irrigate 40 hectares or less tend to been managed by consensus among irrigators, systems between 40 and 400 hectares often involve an appointed or elected manager, and systems larger than 400 hectares most frequently entail multiple levels of management.

In examining ancient irrigation, dividing activities involved in any particular system into a series of physical or logistical tasks offers helpful means of analyzing management and its consequences (Hunt 2007: 110–15; Uphoff 1986: 128–30). While ethnographers and those concerned with modern agricultural development have often focused on abstract tasks such as communication, decision-making, and conflict resolution (e.g., Coward 1977, 1979; Kelly 1983; Hunt 1988, 1989, 2007; Hunt and Hunt 1976; Uphoff 1986), archaeologists often lack direct evidence of these less tangible elements of management. Focusing, therefore, on physical logistics of tasks involved in any particular system, namely, design, construction, operation, and maintenance is, I argue, more practicable and revealing. These four logistical task stages can then lead to deeper consideration of more abstract ingredients, such as expertise, communication, coordination, and leadership that play important roles in operationalizing water control yet necessarily must remain subjects of greater conjecture in archaeological contexts. For example, small-scale systems such as those in Wadi Sana can readily be designed, constructed, operated, and managed at the household scale by one or a few people. The design, placement, and positioning of these systems would have required detailed knowledge

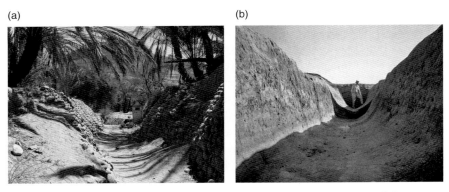

FIGURE 5.1. Irrigation canals of Wadi Daw'an, Hadramawt (Yemen), and the ancient Hohokam, near Phoenix, Arizona. A mainline canal of traditional intermediate-scale irrigation in Wadi Da'wan (left) beside an ancient Hohokam irrigation canal excavated at the site of Snaketown near Phoenix (right). Irrigation systems in these two areas widely differ – the former captures water from flashfloods and the latter from the perennially flowing Gila and Salt Rivers. However, constructions are of a similar scale and confronted comparable management challenges (photo on left by the author, photo on right reproduced with permission of Arizona State Museum).

of water flow potential, yet they could have been initially constructed in a few days or weeks even by one person. Such small-scale systems would have required frequent reconstruction seasonally or annually after rainfall. Operation would have involved planting, tending, and harvesting, and perhaps threshing, winnowing, and grinding grain depending on what was grown, but these activities are all readily accomplishable at the nuclear family scale. More expansive, intermediate-scale systems that irrigate areas greater than 40 hectares such as ethnographic systems in Wadi Daw'an Hadramawt (Plate IV and Figure 5.1) require a far more complex, labor and management demanding range of tasks. Moreover, as Hunt (2007: 117–22) emphasized, charter authority – the right to wield power over an irrigation system – is another particularly significant consideration. Early small-scale systems were probably chartered privately, with intermediate systems often overseen by irrigation communities, and larger systems chartered by bureaucracies and governments with more expansive authority.

The Hadramawt region of eastern Yemen is known for its impressive traditional irrigation systems that have long been of interest to historians and ethnographers. R. B. Serjeant's (1964, 1988) reporting on Yemeni irrigation systems, for instance, helpfully describes basic design and operational characteristics. Serjeant's work alongside related ethnographic studies of irrigation in western Yemen most notably those of Daniel Varisco (1983,

# Intermediate-scale irrigation: A comparative perspective

1996) set the foundations for dissertation investigations I conducted on indigenous small-scale irrigation mostly in Hadramawt in 2004 and 2005. With the gracious and invaluable support of Yemeni colleagues, we met irrigation farmers, inquired about crops, technical and organization aspects of irrigation, land and water rights, ownership, and the proceeds of irrigation. Since our initial focus was the very smallest household systems, it eventually became clear that continued study of larger scale systems was advisable. Wadi Daw'an, a tributary of Wadi Hadramawt, is one of the few places where traditional intermediate-scale floodwater irrigation survives in Yemen (Plate IV). Building on previous research, including Mikhail Rodionov's (1999) report on *khiyyl* irrigation managers and Baquhaizel et al.'s (1996) study of traditional irrigation in Hadramawt and Shabwa, I completed a short two-week interval of fieldwork in Wadi Daw'an in 2007. Irrigation in Wadi Daw'an involves long-standing social arrangements and traditions that promote equity and restrict opportunities to exploit positions of authority in water control (Al-Khanbashi and Badr 2000; Baquhaizel et al. 1996; Redkin 1995; Rodionov 1999). *Khiyyl* irrigation managers are elected by farmers with substantial land holdings to oversee irrigation along individual *sagi* canals that irrigate roughly 50–200 hectares. *Khiyyls* in some instances serve as head of water-users' committees known as a *lijna* whose members are similarly elected by landholders. *Khiyyls* are responsible for coordination of repairs and resolution of disputes and, since they serve at the behest of the community, they can be replaced if their service is deemed unsatisfactory. Although *khiyyls* sometimes co-opt labor mobilized for community repairs to improve their own land, they are not paid or rewarded at harvest. They serve to ensure practices conform to traditional norms of equity but their authority is subject to continual reevaluation and consent. Other titled positions, namely *a'adh* (surveyors) and *ra'ad* (canal operators), serve similarly important roles. *A'adhs* (also known as *mata'ir*) measure and layout fields in *matira* units (19.36 sq. m) with a stick (2–3 m long) known as a *fir* (see also Bujra 1971: 56; Serjeant 1964: 42). Their services are requested by those selling or renting land or to address disputes of control and ownership. *Ra'ad* canal operators are hired by landholders to open and close sluice gates during flashfloods, ensuring sufficient water is delivered when available and diverting excess back to wadis. *Ra'ad* are by far the most numerous as they are responsible for small parcels of land of up to approximately 5 hectares.

Ethnographic irrigation in Wadi Daw'an exemplifies the social challenges faced as irrigation systems surpass the capabilities of household-scale, acephalous management and illustrate how ancient leadership in irrigation offered a potential avenue to power as ancient irrigation systems increased in scale. The position of *khiyyl* sometimes traditionally passed from father to son but is not viewed as hereditary (Redkin 1995: 200–01). Instead, a reputation for fairness and impartiality were qualities sought in a *khiyyl*. These traits were similarly valued in *mugudam* tribal leaders, and for the position of *shaykh* in western Yemen (Dresch 1984), yet management of irrigation in Wadi Daw'an was purposefully independent of general political authority. The lack of compensation for services, and landholders' ability to immediately replace *khiyyl* managers if their services were deemed unsatisfactory, acts to help restrict *khiyyls*' ability to exploit their position for monetary or political gain. Such traditions are readily understandable as they work to maintain community control and equitable water allocation in contexts where managers with oversight of irrigation might otherwise abuse their authority.

Management details of prehistoric irrigation systems are more challenging to determine, yet a comparable intermediate-scale pattern of management most probably prevailed in a wide array of contexts, including, for example, among the ancient Hohokam. A uniquely impressive repertoire of material culture distinguishes the Hohokam, including distinct red-on-buff pottery, Great Houses used by elites, platform mounds, and ballcourts where a Mesoamerican-derived game was played with a rubber ball (Bayman 2001). The Hohokam redirected perennially flowing waters from the Gila and Salt Rivers near Phoenix, Arizona. They build head gates, junctions, reservoirs. and hundreds of kilometers of canals between AD 500 and 1450 (Masse 1981; Woodbury 1961) with some recent estimates suggesting (although probably not simultaneously) as much as 20,000 to 40,000 hectares was once irrigated (Fish and Fish 2012: 571). These remarkable systems were constructed, operated, and maintained with stone tools, digging sticks, and woven baskets and demonstrate considerable design expertise and aptitude in cooperative organization. Drawing on a wide array of literature and experience in studying irrigation management, Robert Hunt and colleagues reexamined potential management alternatives for Hohokam systems and concluded they most likely involved non-acephalous coordination, not as a centralized, bureaucratic system but rather as a form of community-chartered canal-level management (Hunt et al. 2005). This conclusion is further supported by analysis of Hohokam ceramics that suggests trade and therefore a semblance of social interconnectivity operated preferentially along canals rather than in a spherical pattern of straight-line distances (Abbott 2009; Abbott et al. 2006). Ancient intermediate-scale systems in other very different contexts, including ancient Yemen, would have

# Irrigation and the rise of Iron Age kingdoms

grappled with very similar logistical challenges that over time shaped and were shaped by social and political relations.

Collectively, ethnographic evidence and cross-cultural parallels (such as the Hohokam) hold important relevance for understanding the role of irrigation in the rise of Southwest Arabian complex polities. An intermediate-scale dynamic prevailed in ancient Yemen during the second millennium BC as irrigation moved from small, acephalous systems to increasingly large networks that irrigated hundreds (rather than tens) of hectares. Wadi Daw'an was also home to ancient irrigation systems (discussed later in this chapter) that watered at least 1,500 hectares surrounding the ancient Iron Age town of Raybun (Charbonnier 2012; Sedov 1996, 1997). These ancient irrigation works involved longer more permanently constructed canals, masonry sluice gates, and more regularly delineated field systems than their ethnographic counterparts. They superseded the design and labor capacities of acephalous management and likely involved more centralized oversight and planning. Ancient texts, which are first produced in substantial quantities in the region after approximately 800 BC, frequently reflect such logistical and managerial challenges. More technologically complex and more massive waterworks encouraged and fostered, if not required, more sophisticated design skills and systems of management. Given the importance of irrigation in the region, the lack (or breakdown) of mechanisms to prevent particular individuals or groups from gaining control of decision making and productive capacity undoubtedly contributed to hierarchical political power. Inscriptions help illustrate how large state-chartered (rather than solely private and community-chartered) irrigation systems played a role in ancient statecraft. State-controlled irrigation works were not a requirement of food production in the region; but through construction of massive irrigation works that entailed bureaucratic oversight, complex polities reinforced their indispensability and secured their own survival. Agency, in this formulation, is accorded not only to people, not only to objects, but to bureaucracies and polities, which operated not only as passive structures but took on a proactive, self-perpetuating aura of inevitability.

## Irrigation and the rise of Iron Age kingdoms

> The power and the richness of Arabia Felix did not derive from commercial activities, as the classical literature simplistically suggests, but originated rather in the fact that its people were skilled farmers, exceptionally gifted in creating and managing highly specialized irrigation systems. The

Marib dam is the most remarkable example of those skills. Only after this agricultural organisation succeeded in providing a complete social, economic and political integration of society did the South Arabians take advantage of commerce as a means for advancement. The commercial option could not have been afforded if the South Arabian population had not already possessed such a level of development as to be able to present themselves as important partners for exchange with the north. (De Maigret 1998: 223)

As a leading figure in demonstrating the indigenous character of early civilizations in Southwest Arabia, De Maigret's commentary reflects factors long known to have contributed to the rise of Southwest Arabia kingdoms – monumental irrigation systems and long-distance incense trade. While many decades of research and debate have centered on the relative impact of local versus foreign influences in origins of Southwest Arabia states, there is now copious evidence that complex polities emerged in a conglomerate pattern of both local cultural individuality and multiregional interrelationships. Experts in Yemen's Ancient South Arabian (ASA) writing system, still vigorously debate (based on more than 10,000 different texts known) the relative local versus foreign contributions to its development (Avanzini 2010; Nebes 2001). Ancient South Arabian was clearly inspired in part by early alphabetic writing of the eastern Mediterranean, yet the highly unique nature of ASA script and alphabet, which was used to represent a number of different South Arabian languages, indisputably attests to its local beginnings in Yemen (MacDonald 2010; Stein 2013). The establishment of a lucrative foreign market for frankincense and domestication of the camel were also clearly important late second millennium BC hallmarks of social and political change (Retsö 1991). Some like De Maigret argue that agriculture and irrigation were central (e.g. Brunner 2000; Mouton 2004), others emphasize the role of incense trade (Seland 2005), while still others take an intermediate view (Beeston 2005). Undoubtedly, irrigation, trade, writing, and religion were among the central factors that contributed to ancient state formation in Yemen, rather than attempting to adjudicate among them; the following section centers on the long-term role of water in the rise of ancient Southwest Arabian states as only one of several key ingredients in long-term histories of the region.

A wide range of archaeological, textual, ethnographic evidence contributes to understanding the role of water among Southwest Arabian states. By the second millennium BC, large settlements began to appear in lowland areas along the Ramlat as-Sab'atayn Desert fringe in areas that eventually became home to powerful irrigation-reliant states. Unlike the highlands

### Irrigation and the rise of Iron Age kingdoms

where water management was optional and supplemental, these hyper-arid areas required irrigation to grow crops, and would have only occasionally offered naturally watered areas for animal grazing when highland rains brought flashfloods. Some of the best evidence of settlements occupied by the late second millennium comes from the region surrounding Ma'rib including fortified sites of Yalā ad-Durayb (De Maigret and Robin 1989), Sirwah (Gerlach 2005), and Hajar ar-Rayhani (Glanzman 1994). Major settlements were similarly founded to the south, including at Hajar bin-Humeid in Wadi Bayhan, which later became one of the main centers of the Kingdom of Qatabān (Van Beek 1969). To the east, major settlements included Shabwa the capital of the Kingdom of Hadramawt (Breton 2003) and even further east Raybun in Wadi Daw'an (Sedov 1996), and Makaynun in Wadi Hadramawt (Mouton et al. 2011; Schiettecatte 2007). During this pivotal late second millennium BC period a literary tradition had begun to develop based, for example, on letters found etched into (and painted on) ceramics at Yalā ad-Durayb (Garbini 1992), Hajar bin Humeid (Van Beek 1956), and Raybun (Sedov 1996). However, epigraphic evidence this early is limited, and texts only begin to provide a wider repertoire of subject matter, including information on water and irrigation, during the first few centuries of the first millennium BC (MacDonald 2010; Stein 2013). Nevertheless, intermediate-scale *sayl* irrigation must have been crucial to sustenance of these desert towns and both challenges and opportunities in designing, constructing, operating, and maintaining irrigation systems contributed to social change. While they are less thoroughly documented than those of preceding periods, climatic oscillations during the late second millennium may have also resulted in intervals of aridity and drying of springs that necessitated increased reliance on irrigation (Lézine et al. 2010; Schiettecatte 2007).

As soon as a substantial textual record becomes available after the eighth–seventh century BC, water and irrigation are immediately significant topics, and inscriptions convey evidence of organizational arrangements and various claims of managerial, royal, and divine authority over water and agricultural land. Inscriptions frequently mention mukarribs, kings, and deities as authorizing, sponsoring, constructing, repairing, or conquering irrigation works and irrigated land. Inscriptions proclaiming the achievements of mukarribs and kings in irrigation at Ma'rib center on construction of the city's famous dam and extend over a long interval from 685 BC to AD 552 (Müller 1991; Robin 1988; Vogt et al. 2004). One of the region's most famous mukarribs – Karib'il Watar bin Damar'ali – ruled during the early seventh century BC, and his exploits are described in some of the longest ASA texts known (RES 3945 and 3946) that are carved into massive stone slabs in the Temple of Almaqah at Sirwah 40 km west of Ma'rib (Müller 1985; Nebes 1997). Epigraphers have long placed Karib'il Watar's rule near 685 BC, based on a foundation tablet of Assyrian King Sennacherib found at Assur, which mentions gifts from a King Karibili of Saba (Potts 2003). This assertion was further supported in 2005 through discovery of an even earlier inscription in excavations of the Temple of Almaqah at Sirwah that links the Sabaean Mukarrib Yita'amar Watar bin Yakrubmalik to Assyrian King Sargon II at 715 BC (Nebes 2007; Stein 2013). In terms of water, Karib'il Watar's Sirwah inscriptions are some of most informative as they highlight his exploits in: (1) conquering territories and cities in which he killed, imprisoned, and enslaved many thousands in different battles, controlling, seizing, and reconstructing canals, waterworks, and irrigated lands in honor of gods 'Athtar and Almaqah, and (2) constructing irrigation works at the mouth of Wadi Dhana that supplied the northern (*Abyan*) and southern (Yasrān) oases of Ma'rib – the first textual record of irrigation in the vicinity where the dam was eventually constructed (Müller 1991; RES 3946, lines 5 and 6). Karib'il Watar's temple inscriptions thus attest to the deep importance of irrigation in political authority and statecraft. The script not only concentrates on emphasizing his military prowess in subjugating surrounding cities but also his subsequent rightful ownership of water, waterworks, and agricultural land. In one passage of these lengthy inscriptions, after conquering the city of Nashshān he gave part of its irrigation system to King Nabat'alī of neighboring city of Kaminahū (Gajda and Maraqten 2010: RES 3945) a gift that highlights the importance of royal control over water and irrigation.

    The plethora of inscriptions directly carved onto, or related to, the Great Dam at Ma'rib illustrate the long-term symbolic and political importance of irrigation and the dam's significance as a monument of great regional renown. In its final configuration the dam spanned 620m between bedrock outcrops and was at least 16m high and 60m wide at its base (Brunner 2000). Rather than impounding water, it redirected flashfloods via two massive sluice gates at its northern and southern extremities (Plate I and Figure 1.1). These sluice gates connected to primary, secondary, and tertiary canals with an intricate series of canal buttressing and gateways to irrigate as much as 9,600 hectares (Brunner 1983, 2000; Brunner and Haefner 1986). The first textual record of a structure in something close to this final configuration (CIH 623 and 623a) dates to ca. 528 BC when the Mukarrib Sumhu'ali Yanuf bin Dhamar'ali proclaims in two identical inscriptions on stones of the dam to have carved away bedrock to construct the southern sluice

# Irrigation and the rise of Iron Age kingdoms

(Robin 1988). His son Yitha'amar Bayyin similarly recounts his accomplishment in cutting and constructing the southern sluice in a very similar pair of inscriptions (CIH 622 and 622a). These efforts are far surpassed nearly a millennium later near 449 AD when King Shurahbi'il Ya'fur organized two major reconstructions of the Ma'rib dam (CIH 540). The first involved 14,600 workers, 1,200 camels for transport, 217,000 measures of semolina, sorghum, wheat, barley, and dates, 1,302 head of cattle, 1,100 (?) sheep and 630 camel loads of drink. In a second reconstruction outlined in the same inscription he mobilized 20,000 people, 295,340 measures of grain, 1,363 cattle and sheep, 1,000 camels for transport, 670(?) camel loads of drink, and 42 amphorae of honey and butter (Nebes 2004; Robin 2013). Such massive quantities of labor and supplies clearly demonstrate the impressive leadership capacities of kings in marshalling the collective energies of a wide populace.

Among the other most notable texts relating to the Ma'rib dam are sixth century AD inscriptions (including two stelae) commemorating reconstruction orchestrated by Abraha of Aksum (Nebes 2004, 2005; Robin 1988; CIH 541, DAI GDN 2002–20; Ja 547). The Empire of Aksum (Ethiopia and Eritrea) began military interventions in Arabia during the third century AD with sporadic intervals of sovereignty (or claimed sovereignty) in the region over the next few hundred years (Hatke 2012). Aksum's conversion from South Arabian-inspired polytheism to Christianity in the mid-fourth century under King Ezana spawned even greater foreign intervention. In AD 518, Aksum's King Kaleb led a tumultuous interval of rule over Yemen that ended near AD 531 when one of his generals, Abraha, lead a revolt and proclaimed himself monarch (Hatke 2012). Abraha ruled until roughly 570 when the region fell to the Sasanians, but most significantly in terms of water histories Abraha went to considerable lengths to demonstrate his capabilities in large scale waterworks by rebuilding the Ma'rib dam. Three separate inscriptions in which Abraha is referred to as – King of Saba dhu-Raydan, Hadramawt and Yamnat and the Bedouin of highlands and lowlands – highlight his sovereignty in the region and achievements in rebuilding the dam. This royal title claims supremacy not only over Saba and Himyar (dhu-Raydan) but also Hadramawt and all surrounding lands. The longest inscription, the original Abraha stela (CIH 541), describes a fifty-eight-day reconstruction in which Abraha provisioned 50,806 measures of flour, 26,000 measures of dates, meat of 3,000 cattle, 7,200 small stock, 300 camel loads of wine, and 11,000 measures of date wine (Nebes 2005). Particularly, given that the capital and political center-point of the region had shifted many centuries before to the highland city of Zafar and then to Sana'a, Abraha's efforts to associate himself with the Ma'rib dam are even more significant in demonstrating the profound ideological importance of water control. It was not so much the dam's productive capacity, but its deep history, symbolic significance, and ability to rally tribes and *qayl* lords in a singularly cooperative endeavor that made the Great Ma'rib Dam so significant.

In addition to regal inscriptions, a far greater number of more mundane texts document roles and practices of lower-level dignitaries and managers involved with irrigation. These include construction texts commemorating building or repair of dams, wells, canals, and other waterworks, legal texts defining ownership of land or water, as well as personal correspondence on date-palm stalks with at least two examples related to water. A number of leadership positions with significance for irrigation can be identified, including *qayl* (a prince or lord) who among other responsibilities is known to have constructed fortifications, irrigation works, terraces, and planted crops on agricultural land (Müller 2010: 14–15, RES 3958; Prioletta 2009: 60–61). The position of *kabir* was held by a rotating hereditary representative of multiple clans (Ryckmans 1971) variably known to have had a leadership role in warfare (Retsö 2003: 553–55) and at least in some cases to have been in charge of irrigation (Loundine 1989: 94). Individuals selected for the position of *qdm* (leader, commander, manager, or supervisor) were similarly selected from Sabaean clans in rotation having, at times, oversight of water allocation. Texts from Wadi Jawf region written in stone and on date-palm stalks depict the activities of *qdm* irrigation managers, including allocating water and ensuring the functionality of irrigation systems with the blessing of divine and earthly authorities (Stein 2010). Two particularly revealing texts written on date-palm stalks convey instructions sent by absentee land/water owners to *qdm* managers authorizing them to permit release of water at particular times from particular canals (Stein 2010). Much like ethnographically known *khiyyl* irrigation managers in Wadi Daw'an, *qdm* managers supervised underling attendants who physically distributed the water that was leased or sold. However, as-of-yet we only have records of *qdm* managers for one region (Jawf) during the second to third centuries AD (Stein 2010). The position of *mdrr* is similarly thought to specifically relate to irrigation perhaps meaning "controller of irrigation" but details remain to be clarified (Mazzini and Porter 2009; Stein 2010). The institution of a "committee" or "council" that operated in conjunction with royal authority is also known in the early governance of ancient Southwest Arabia kingdoms. It is not entirely clear what responsibilities these councils had (Gajda and

Maraqten 2010) but according to some commentators they may have often involved oversight of irrigation (Breton 1999: 33).

In conjunction with practical elements of irrigation management, a divine role is often apparent in water-use both in agricultural and ritual contexts. Alfred Beeston (1949) long ago noted the importance of agricultural boundary-stone inscriptions, a subject matter that has garnered significant further attention. These inscriptions, often referred to as boundary stelae because of their prominence, have been found in irrigated areas where date palms, cereals, and other crops were grown, including at Ma'rib (Mazzini and Porter 2009) and Baraqish (Robin 1987). Boundary stelae also designated sacred pasture lands and invoked the divine in justifying penalties if animals encroached on controlled grazing areas (Beeston 1955; Frantsouzoff 2009). These various territorial stelae attest to well-developed legal traditions involving water control and land tenure overseen by sovereign central authorities and sustained in part by religious dominion. While the role of water in Southwest Arabian temple rituals remains somewhat opaque, we do know that in ancient Hadramawt cisterns and baths were made available and purification through ablution was required before participating in temple sacraments (Sedov 1994: 189, 2005: 67). In eastern Hadramawt, Mouton et al. (2011) have argued that the site of Makaynun was flanked by smaller villages, temples, sanctuaries, and cemeteries set within irrigated areas that formed a symbolic watered landscape. Collectively, such patterns point not only to the economic but to the deep representational and religious importance of water.

At the cusp of state formation peoples who settled in large towns along the desert margins required substantial irrigation systems to produce enough food to attract and sustain rapidly aggregating, urbanizing populations. The continuing enhancement and elaboration of floodwater irrigation systems attracted new inhabitants and bolstered the power and authority of those who devised and orchestrated them. Just as David Wengrow and colleagues (2014) have argued that the origins of Egyptian civilization originate in cattle pastoralism as early as the fifth millennium BC, ancient Southwest Arabian civilization can similarly be viewed as grounded in comparably early pastoralism and long-term meta-structures in Yemen (McCorriston 2011). Indeed, early pastoralists and agropastoralists were the foundational denizens of desert cities that were increasingly verdant, visual expressions of the success and influence of emergent complex polities. By the very early first millennium BC towns spanning 5 to 10 hectares were relatively common; with populations of hundreds if not thousands of people, food production along the desert would have required major diversions of runoff from highland watersheds. Pastoralists provided food, moved incense, and offered animals for sacrifice in state temples. More than any other, one animal – the camel – stands out as most significant to late second–early first millennium BC historical dynamics of Arabia (Magee 2014: 197–213). Camels, which were first domesticated during this interval, revolutionized transport and the rise of early cities along the margins of Yemen's Ramlat as-Sab'atayn Desert was in no small part a function of efforts to attract and provision camel caravans.

Mouton and Schiettecatte (2014: 255–78) argued that traditions of water-sharing were critical to complex polities of ancient Yemen, and that upstream portions of Yemen's watersheds would have been occupied first and downstream areas later. Water-sharing would have indeed been important in terms of watering of animals and grazing territories, including for camels that were traveling long distances with heavy loads. However, it is unlikely sharing of flashflood waters for irrigation was a major concern. Unlike temperate regions with perennially flowing rivers that are often characterized by conflicts between upstream and downstream water users, Yemen's drainages are marked by near absence of water most of the year punctuated by violent short-term flashfloods with far more water than can be diverted or utilized. Since water, when it becomes available, is vastly overabundant rather than scarce, upstream users rarely impinge on the water access of their downstream counterparts. There is therefore little reason to believe that upstream areas with far less accumulated runoff would be occupied first in an effort to ensure or monopolize access to water or preempt downstream use. Where floodwaters are concerned, the most central challenge was not *sharing* runoff water among residents of watershed but rather coordinating design, construction, and operation of systems that harness only a fraction of flashfloods while preventing oversupply of destructive high-velocity flows from entering headworks. Once partial flows had been captured, allocating water *within* (rather than between) irrigation systems would have involved careful coordination and apportionment (cf. Charbonnier 2014), but since charter authority over large-scale irrigation systems of desert kingdoms was held by *mukarribs* and kings, allocation is probably a more accurate term than sharing. As attested by residents of Wadi Daw'an, diversion of flashfloods must happen quickly, with careful group coordination to open and close sluice gates often in the middle of the night, optimally without injury or loss of life. At an early stage irrigation did not require bureaucratic coordination but the profound spatial heterogeneity of water did over time promote concentration of productive capacity in small progressively more valuable areas that favored differential power

# Irrigation and the rise of Iron Age kingdoms

and substantiated the ascendancy of the polities who constructed them. Indeed, sponsoring and holding charter authority over irrigation works was an important avenue to power for aspiring tribal leaders, *mukarribs*, and kings as they gained considerable prestige by orchestrating impressive collective endeavors and mobilizations of labor (Beeston 1972). Irrigation not only provided increasingly necessary, reliable food supplies but also instigated self-perpetuating reciprocating feedback involving concentrated agricultural production, population growth, political complexity, and religious ideologies centered, in part, on water.

Interestingly, substantial parallels and significant contrasts are to be found in water histories of the American West. In California, Native American populations racked by disease and violent disruption declined dramatically through the 1800s while non-Native populations rose from roughly 10,000 in 1846 to approximately 1.5 million by 1900, an undeniably massive and impactful inpouring of immigrants (Hundley 2001: 66). In contrast, urbanism and population increases that accompanied the rise of states in ancient Yemen appear to have been largely indigenous and autochthonous. Although parallels in ASA script point to connections with the Levant, we see no clear evidence for a dramatic influx of foreigners (Wilkinson 2009). Riparian rights and the prior appropriation "first in time, first in right" principle drove rapid colonization of the American West but created major challenges in devising equitable distributions of water among rapidly expanding populations. The political history of the Colorado River well exemplifies the difficulties of orchestrating flood control, irrigation, and electricity production among a wide diversity of private interests, local, state, and federal government agencies both upstream and downstream (Hundley 2009). The Colorado River Compact of 1922 – that set the stage for but did not explicitly mention the Hoover Dam – negotiated an agreement that divided flow evenly between four upper basin (Colorado, New Mexico, Utah, Wyoming) and three lower basin (California, Nevada, Arizona) states. As envisioned, each group of states was entitled to 7,500,000 acre feet of water annually and could then further negotiate and divide the allocated flow amongst themselves. The upper basin states agreed not to deplete the river below 7,500,000 acre feet to ensure sufficient downstream water access. However, as later studies have demonstrated, these figures were negotiated during a period of abnormally high flow (1905–1922) so that more water was allocated than the Colorado's long-term average annual flow actually provided. Even more troublingly, just as the Great Dam at Ma'rib over more than 1,000 years periodically required massive quantities of accumulated upstream sediment to be removed, the Hoover, Glen Canyon, and other dams have dramatically altered patterns of sediment transport so that immense quantities of eroded and redeposited sediment are infeasible to remove or replace and therefore nearly impossible to remediate (Schmidt 2010).

*Spatial dimensions of water flow and ancient Southwest Arabian kingdoms*

In conjunction with archaeological and epigraphic evidence, spatial analyses substantially clarify ancient Southwest Arabian water histories and illustrate how ancient polities exploited spatial heterogeneity of water resources. Brunner and Haefner's (1990) innovative study twenty-five years ago used satellite imagery to map Yemen's ancient oases. The more advanced spatial technologies now available, including more sophisticated software and digital models of terrain, offer an evermore vast array of opportunities to clarify ancient water-use and irrigation. Indeed, the hydrological and technological underpinnings of ancient large-scale irrigation systems are critically important to understanding how they influenced political complexity. Topography and precipitation are the two of the most central determinants of water availability that in turn shape agricultural potential and sociopolitical relations. Terrain and flow accumulation analyses, similar to methods used to examine small-scale irrigation systems in Chapter 4, also helpfully clarify regional-scale patterns of water-use among ancient Southwest Arabian kingdoms. Field studies of state irrigation systems over the past 170 years, from Joseph Arnaud's mapping of Ma'rib Dam in 1843, through more advanced investigations of the last few decades (Brunner 1983; Charbonnier 2009; Darles et al. 2013; Francaviglia 2000; Gentelle 1991; Hehmeyer and Schmidt 1991; Wilkinson 2006; Vogt 2004) inform the spatial analyses that follow. In conjunction with flow accumulation, I consider basic hydrological characteristics of ancient kingdoms' watersheds in comparison with each other and with watersheds of Yemen as a whole. In conjunction with catchment (watershed) size, spatial patterning of basic variables for catchments, namely elevation, slope, and annual precipitation (minimum, maximum, and mean) are considered and discussed. Spatial flow accumulation analysis shows that ancient state capitals, namely Qarnaw, Ma'rib, Timna, Hajar Yahirr, and Shabwa, exploited outlets of some of Yemen's largest watersheds (Plate II and Figure 5.2). Ancient capitals were exclusively located at the outlets of inward draining watersheds, rather than those draining into the Red Sea or Indian Ocean. Even though the watersheds of state capitals were not necessarily those

# Irrigation and the rise of Iron Age kingdoms

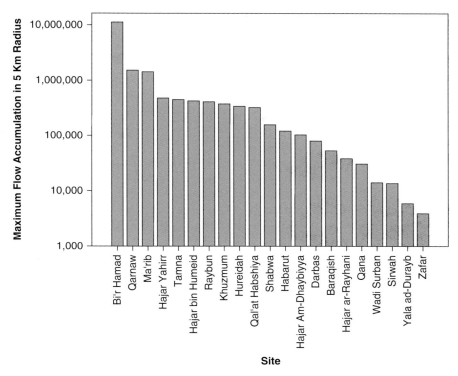

FIGURE 5.2. Histogram of maximum water flow accumulation within 5-km radius around a selection of major archaeological sites in Yemen. Most notably the early capital cities of Qarnaw, Ma'rib, Hajar Yahirr, and Tamna' were fed by some of the largest watersheds and thus exhibit some of the highest flow accumulation values.

with the highest annual flow volumes (Shahin 2007: chapter 7, table 1), they were marked by the some of the highest average elevations (offering cooler temperatures and lower evapotranspiration) and tend to be less steep (lower average slope) than their outward draining counterparts (Table 5.1). These hydrological characteristics afforded seasonally abundant, yet somewhat less dangerously powerful, water flows for inward in comparison with outward draining wadis. Indeed, nearly all the major catchments that drain into Yemen's Ramlat as-Sab'atayn Desert interior were occupied by major first millennium BC kingdoms (Plate II). Intriguingly, however, the same is not true of the major catchments that drain directly into the Red Sea and Indian Ocean, many of which were just as large or larger, yet none were home to major capital cities. By the end of the first millennium BC, in part due to the declining productivity of desert floodwater irrigation systems,

TABLE 5.1. *Major watersheds of Yemen and associated archaeological sites including ancient state capitals (in bold)*

| Name | Major Site | Area (sq km) | Elev. Min | Elev. Max | Elev. Mean | Slope Mean | Precip. Min | Precip. Max | Precip. Mean |
|---|---|---|---|---|---|---|---|---|---|
| Wadi Masila | – | 138,088 | 1 | 3649 | 1235 | 7 | 50 | 468 | 119 |
| Wadi Jawf-Hadramawt | **Shabwa** | 80,839 | 752 | 3486 | 1113 | 4 | 52 | 380 | 92 |
| Wadi al-Jawf | **Qarnaw** | 12,468 | 1092 | 3649 | 1999 | 7 | 97 | 468 | 206 |
| Wadi Dhana | **Ma'rib** | 11,598 | 1127 | 3507 | 2047 | 9 | 114 | 436 | 273 |
| Wadi Hajar | – | 9,199 | -19 | 2150 | 1109 | 10 | 27 | 165 | 83 |
| Wadi Mawr | – | 8,568 | -3 | 3372 | 1371 | 13 | 59 | 397 | 166 |
| Wadi Bana | – | 7,641 | 0 | 3231 | 1772 | 14 | 36 | 536 | 298 |
| Wadi Tuban | Ma'layba | 5,974 | -5 | 3198 | 1337 | 12 | 38 | 577 | 342 |
| Wadi Idm | Suna | 5,395 | 611 | 1698 | 1040 | 7 | 68 | 128 | 91 |
| Wadi Daw'an | Raybun | 4,788 | 721 | 1912 | 1279 | 7 | 61 | 150 | 98 |
| Wadi Siham | – | 4,615 | 1 | 3652 | 1375 | 14 | 56 | 457 | 245 |
| Wadi Zabid | Zabid | 4,576 | 5 | 3218 | 1463 | 15 | 132 | 538 | 367 |
| Wadi Sana | Sana | 3,926 | 504 | 1961 | 1032 | 8 | 73 | 163 | 98 |
| Wadi Marha | Hajar Yahirr | 3,796 | 962 | 2399 | 1541 | 10 | 78 | 271 | 151 |
| Wadi Bayhan | **Tamna'** | 3,597 | 1028 | 2394 | 1787 | 10 | 96 | 284 | 206 |
| Wadi Surdud | – | 3,218 | 0 | 3591 | 1254 | 15 | 56 | 459 | 200 |
| Wadi Rima | – | 3,100 | 4 | 2953 | 1403 | 16 | 118 | 476 | 314 |
| Wadi 'Amd | Hureidah | 3,046 | 716 | 1589 | 1261 | 5 | 60 | 114 | 91 |
| Wadi 'Atf | **Shabwa** | 1,257 | 820 | 1617 | 1304 | 8 | 57 | 113 | 89 |

*(watershed size, elevation values, and slope determined by GIS modeling using Shuttle Radar Topography Mission (SRTM) data, precipitation data from WorldClim Hijmans et al. 2005)*

## Irrigation and the rise of Iron Age kingdoms

the dominant political power shifted to the Kingdom of Himyar in Yemen's comparatively rainy western highlands.

One of Arabia's most famous ancient cities, the Sabaean state capital of Ma'rib grew to cover 110 hectares and serves as a premier example of a powerful polity's genesis through exploitation of fortuitous water geography that funneled runoff from the enormous Wadi Dhana watershed through a gap in bedrock only 350 meters wide. Archaeologists have long debated and sought to document the earliest irrigation at Ma'rib with most placing it during the third millennium BC (Brunner 2000; Francaviglia 2000; Pietsch et al. 2010). Yet even before irrigation systems were constructed, the area would have been exceptionally attractive to hunters-gatherers and eventually early herders and farmers as seasonal rains in the highlands would have naturally generated copious runoff. The potential profitability of diverting, capturing, or otherwise more fully exploiting this enormous natural windfall must have been almost immediately evident and eventually led to the rise of the region's most powerful empire.

The size of Ma'rib Dam's Wadi Dhana catchment has often been stated as 8,200 square kilometers (Darles et al. 2013: 11; Hehmeyer and Schmidt 1991: 40; Schaloske 1995: 15) or 8,300 square kilometers (Brunner 2000: 171) but this figure is most probably based on misreading of reports that divide the 11,500 square kilometer catchment into a 8,200 square kilometer runoff producing zone and a 3,300 square kilometer runoff absorbing zone (Uil and Dufour 1990: 23–46). As determined by GIS flow analysis with SRTM data, the Wadi Dhana catchment in fact spans 11,590 square kilometers (Harrower 2009: 64) a figure very close to previous estimates of 11,500 square kilometers (Uil and Dufour 1990: 23). To compare Wadi Dhana with other wadis of Yemen, inclusion of "runoff absorbing zones" that "only contribute to the runoff of the catchment after very heavy rains" (Uil and Dufour 1990: 40) is important (even if at times they might absorb rather than emit water) as they do topographically drain into Wadi Dhana and are properly included as part of the catchment. Other even larger estimates for the Wadi Dhana catchment of 13,240 square kilometers (Shahin 2007: 361) and 12,600 square kilometers (Farquharson et al. 1996: table 4) can similarly be disregarded as they include areas downstream of (or neighboring) the ancient Ma'rib Dam (see also van der Gun and Ahmed 1995).

Following on Saba, other early kingdoms, namely Ma'in, Qatabān, Awsan, and Hadramawt, similarly relied on floodwater irrigation using runoff from large inward-draining watersheds. More detailed understanding of hydrological underpinnings offers a variety of revealing insights, including that it was not only watershed size but other hydrological and social factors that were important. The city of Ma'rib today receives only 80 millimeters of precipitation per annum (Bruggeman 1997: Annex I.43) far below what is needed to sustain dense vegetation or rainfed agriculture. However, the Wadi Dhana watershed, which spans a vast swath of Yemen's western highlands, receives up to 360 millimeters per year at the city of Dhamar and a watershed average between roughly 163 millimeters (Farquharson et al. 1996) to 273 millimeters per year (Hijmans et al. 2005). The cooler temperatures of these high elevation areas lead to far less evapotranspiration so that precipitation to potential evapotranspiration ratios (P/PET) range from an annual average of 0.2 (arid) at Dhamar to 0.7 (subhumid) at Ibb (Bruggeman 1997). These characteristics understandably lead to sizable yet periodic runoff discharges. Even given the role of highland vegetation and soils in absorbing rainfall, mean annual runoff volume ($m^3$), increases with increases in mean annual rainfall for catchments across Yemen (Farquharson 1996: figure 6; Shahin 2007: 287). Correspondingly, the top five watersheds in terms of highest annual runoff volume, namely Wadi Rima, Wadi Surdud, Wadi Bana, Wadi Zabid, and Wadi Tuban, have some of the highest annual rainfall totals (Farquharson et al. 1996: table 4; Shahin 2007: chapter 7, table 1). However, these highest annual flow wadis all drain from the highlands to the Red Sea and Gulf of Aden, and notably were not among the power centers of Yemen's earliest civilizations. This may be due to an overabundance of high-energy flow generated by these outward draining watersheds, particularly given they tend to be of greater average slope (Table 5.1). Other environmental and social factors, such as the differential availability of irrigable sediments at wadi outlets, or the benefits that desert margin locations conferred in controlling incense trade and generating an ostentatious spectacle by transforming interior desert outlets into lush agricultural oases, likely also played key roles in state formation.

To the north of Saba, the ancient Kingdom of Ma'in arose in the area of copious highland runoff surrounding the confluence of Wadi al-Kharid and Wadi Madhâb where they together form the 12,536 square kilometer catchment of Wadi Jawf. Excavations and discoveries of early inscriptions over the past few decades have pushed the beginnings of the city states in the area to the early first millennium BC (De Maigret 2005; Gajda and Maraqten 2010; Schiettecatte 2010). This is considerably earlier than previously believed and further undermines the traditional notion that Saba was the solely preeminent power in the early history of the region. Schiettecatte (2010) has labeled early city-states of the Jawf "tribal cities" as they were politically organized according to, and often named after, tribes. Wadi

## Irrigation and the rise of Iron Age kingdoms

Jawf's catchment area is larger than Wadi Dhana's with a similar range of elevation values from 1,092 to 3,649 meters yet generates only marginally more annual runoff as it is comprised of areas receiving somewhat less precipitation (Table 5.1). The modern town of Al-Hazm (capital of Jawf Governate near ancient site of Qarnaw) receives only 66 millimeters of rainfall per year (Bruggeman 1997: I.53) while the southwest portion of the catchment at Sana'a receives 152 millimeters (Bruggeman 1997: I.24) and Sa'dah just beyond the northwest boundary of the catchment receives only 73 millimeters (Bruggeman 1997: I.26). Schiettecatte (2010) hypothesized that the areal retreat of floods led to the collapse of Jawf cites in a progressive pattern with settlements downstream abandoned earliest to those upstream abandoned comparatively later. He suggests this might be explained by dam and terrace building across the highlands of Wadi Jawf's watershed and the progressive silting up of the plain that rendered downstream irrigation systems inoperable. It seems unlikely terrace and dam construction across such a large (12,535 square kilometer) watershed could have substantially impacted sediment transport and, if anything, probably would have reduced the quantities of sediment arriving downstream. Patterns of sedimentary aggradation and degradation undoubtedly did contribute to denouement of desert cities but as Schiettecatte rightly notes these changes were accompanied by changing political dynamics that should not be discounted. Indeed, both the shift of political power from the desert margins to the highlands over the first few centuries AD and the late sixth century AD demise of Yemen's pre-Islamic kingdoms occurred across watersheds of very different sizes and configurations (e.g., Breton and Roux 2002; Vogt 2004). These concurrent changes indicate that a range of hydrological, geomorphological, economic, political, and religious factors were variably at play at comparable times in different places.

Immediately south of Saba, the Kingdom of Qatabān thrived in Wadi Bayhan from roughly the eighth century BC through second century AD. One of the best known ancient cities of the region, the capital city of Tamna' spans 26 hectares and stands up to 15 meters above the surrounding alluvium of Wadi Bayhan (De Maigret 2003). American investigations in the 1950s, although limited, revealed the city's south gate, a temple, and the nearby necropolis of Hayd ibn 'Aqil (Bowen 1958; Phillips 1955). More recent Italian-French excavations of Tamna' in the late 1990s and early 2000s reached the earliest layers so far documented at the site and retrieved radiocarbon dates as early as the eighth century BC with at least 5 meters of cultural deposits still below (De Maigret 2003, 2004). In association with temple architecture, they also discovered a monumental fountain built of white limestone fed by a well (De Maigret 2003: 136). In conjunction with irrigation systems of wide landscape impact, this fountain illustrates the deep symbolic and visual significance of water. Another relatively well-known, deeply stratified city, Hajar bin Humeid, which is located 13 kilometers upstream from Tamna' has also proved particularly revealing (Van Beek 1969). Although partially destroyed, Hajar bin Humeid measures a modest 3.96 hectares yet forms a prominent tell comprised of more than 15 meters of accumulated debris and archaeological remains (Van Beek 1997). American excavations in the 1950s, which included probing and obtaining a radiocarbon date from a basal layer of the site, were important in establishing occupation of the settlement as early as 1100 BC (Van Beek 1956).

Qatabān, like all ancient kingdoms of the desert margins other than Saba, lacked a singularly enormous dam like Ma'rib's and instead was supported by nevertheless impressive irrigation systems that diverted flow from major wadis. The Wadi Bayhan catchment spans 3,597 square kilometers with elevations from 1,028 meters to a high of 2,392 meters, substantially lower elevations than the catchments that sustained ancient Saba and Ma'in (Table 5.1). Today an average of only 84 millimeters of rainfall falls every year on the modern city of Bayhan (Bruggeman 1997: I.44) with Wadi Bayhan's catchment receiving an average 206 millimeters per year (Hijmans et al. 2005). While dating ancient irrigation is often challenging, after a relatively short interval of fieldwork with the AFSM team, Bowen (1958) generated a relatively detailed appraisal of large-scale irrigation including canals, sluices, and banked fields; he concluded irrigation in the area began during the second millennium BC. Using a combination of air photos and field survey he focused on a 1.2 kilometer-long section of ancient irrigation and described canals up to 40 meters wide that stretched more than 30 kilometers. Many decades later in the 1990s, French investigations of Wadi Bayhan and its tributaries continued examination of ancient Qatabān and its irrigation systems (Breton et al. 1998; Breton 2000). The vestiges of these systems, including irrigation-deposited alluvium many meters deep, still remain visible in air photos and as rectangular patterns of banked fields (Coque-Delhuille and Gentelle 1998). In addition to barrages built to divert water from flashfloods into canals, *naqab* systems in which a channel is carved out of the bedrock alongside wadis were also used (Gentelle 1998: 82; cf. Baquhaizel et al. 1996: 63 who documents the term *naqab* as a name for rock-cut cisterns).

Further southeast from Qatabān along the margins of the Ramlat as-Sab'atayn Desert, yet another powerful polity, the Kingdom of Awsan,

## Irrigation and the rise of Iron Age kingdoms

also vied for political influence across ancient Yemen and was sustained by major floodwater irrigation systems. Hajar Yahirr the probable capital of Awsan, whose location until relatively recently was uncertain, spans 16 hectares at the mouth of Wadi Marha (Becker 1999; Breton 1994). The city was surrounded by an outer wall constructed of mud-brick that would have originally stretched as much as 1700 meters (Breton 1994: 44). Most of what we know of irrigation in the area is from the reports of Ueli Brunner (1997a, 1997b) who described two enormous primary canals up to 100 meters wide on either side of Wadi Marha that were first fed 5 kilometers upstream, along with a canal that brought water 30 kilometers from neighboring Wadi Hammam. Irrigation began in the area at least as early as the third millennium BC and while many ancient fields and water control systems have been buried or destroyed, a vast oasis of at least 6,800 hectares was once irrigated (Brunner 1997b). Wadi Marha collects water from a 3,795 square kilometer area ranging in elevation from 968 meters to 2,399 meters that receives between 78 and 271 millimeters of rain per year. Interestingly these numbers are very close to those for the Kingdom of Qatabān (Table 5.1) one of the polities in competition and frequent conflict with Awsan. Upstream of Hajar Yahirr a number of large tells of roughly five hectares are distributed at the mouths of major tributaries of Wadi Marha where they relied on comparable sayl irrigation systems (Brunner 1997b). In a pattern quite similar to other major wadis of Yemen, ancient irrigated sediments standing up to 30 meters above the surrounding plain can be found along Wadi Marha and over time such areas often became stranded high ground that was extremely difficult to continue irrigating. This long term instability likely contributed to the eventual shift of political power to higher rainfall highland areas near the start of the Common Era. French investigations in Wadi Surbān (located between Wadi Bayhan and Wadi Marha) similarly documented extensive irrigation systems covering up to 3 square kilometers with canals more than 15 meters wide (Breton 2000; Darles 2000). Settlement in the area as early as the fourth millennium may have been supported by small-scale irrigation, and nearby remnants of architecture suggest larger scale irrigation systems along Wadi Surbān may date to the period of Iron Age kingdoms (Breton 2000). Since Wadi Surbān has a very small catchment of only 86 square kilometers based on SRTM imagery (even slightly smaller than the 100 square kilometers estimated by Darles 2000), it is intriguing that such a small catchment sustained irrigation.

Forty kilometers south of Hajar Yahirr (Plate II) ancient floodwater irrigation systems have also been documented in Wadi Dura, an interstitial area between western and eastern Yemen. Inscriptions pronounce repeated efforts to claim credit for building irrigation systems along Wadi Dura that broadly included dams, walls to defect and divert water, sluice-gate spillways, and channels carved into bedrock along drainages (Breton and Roux 2002). This intermediary area was a locus of political machinations and variably fell under the control of Awsan, Saba, Qataban, Hadramawt, and Himyar duly illustrating the oscillating fortunes of competing kingdoms vying for supremacy (Breton et al. 1998). The major mounded settlement and necropolis of Hajar am-Dhaybiyya yielded a rich assemblage of materials as well as numerous inscriptions (Breton and Bafaqih 1993; Breton et al. 1998). One major deflector weir near the site extends nearly 150 meters (with numerous others almost as long) and alluvium that stands as high as 12–15 meters above the surrounding wadi bed (Breton and Roux 2002). Inscriptions commemorating irrigation works often credit local leaders (rather than kings) with the blessing of various divinities (e.g., RES 3856; Avanzini 2004: 525–26). While considerably smaller than wadis of major capital cities, Wadi Dura above the site of Hajar Am-Dhaybiyya collects water from a nevertheless sizable 823 square kilometer area.

Roughly 60 kilometers to the northeast of Hajar Yahirr, Wadi Jirdān (oft controlled by the Kingdom of Hadramawt) has also yielded evidence of Iron Age irrigation systems. Although ancient settlements and irrigation in the area have long been known based mostly on air photos, more detailed on-the-ground recording was conducted by French-German survey of a projected pipeline route in 2006 (Brunner 2008; Crassard and Hitgen 2007). The two largest sites in Wadi Jirdān, Al-Binā and Al-Barīra, are fortified cities that roughly date to the first millennium BC (Doe 1971) and undoubtedly contributed to the roughly 500 hectares of ancient irrigation visible in satellite images of the area (Brunner and Haefner 1990). The French-German team also reported the newly discovered late first millennium BC settlement of Darbas which was similarly supported by the floodwaters of Wadi Jirdān, which drains a 643 square kilometer area above the site.

The Kingdom of Hadramawt – easternmost of ancient Yemen's ancient states – was ostensibly supplied by the smallest catchment among ancient desert kingdoms, but certainly was not correspondingly less influential. Wadi 'Atf drains an area of only 1,251 square kilometers ranging in elevation from 830 to 1,617 meters, which receives between 57 and 113 millimeters of average annual rainfall (Table 5.1). The kingdom's capital city of Shabwa was well known to classical scholars including Strabo and Pliny the Elder as pivotal to the frankincense trade; and the latter commentator reported that Shabwa contained sixty temples within its walls (Breton 1991: 59).

# Irrigation and the rise of Iron Age kingdoms

Particularly over past four decades, French, Russian, and American fieldwork has contributed to wider archaeological understanding of ancient Hadramawt (e.g., Breton 1999; McCorriston 2011; Sedov 2005). The kingdom is now known from inscriptions to have stretched to the east just past the modern city of Salalah (Oman) to the ancient port city of Sumhuram (Avanzini 2008). The small size of Wadi 'Atf's catchment might lead one to conclude water was less important to the location of Shabwa, yet it is critical to note that the city is also located near the head of Wadi Hadramawt which may have connected (or may connect underground) with Wadi Jawf and other drainages flowing into the Ramlat as-Saba'tayn. The possibility that the Jawf may have connected with Wadi Hadramawt during ancient periods of heightened rainfall, such as the early Holocene, was recognized some time ago through examination of satellite imagery (Cleuziou et al. 1992). Flow analysis with SRTM terrain data further supports this hypothesis and shows, according to topography, that a Jawf-Hadramawt system would form a massive watershed of up to 80,839 square kilometers that culminates near Shabwa. Following this topographic path even further, even though overland flow may have rarely (if ever) extended continuously on the surface, eventually leads from Wadi Hadramawt into Wadi Masila to form a 138,088 square kilometer mega-watershed that drains into the Indian Ocean. This terrain-defined drainage system would not have involved continuous flow along its length and would have been interrupted by shifting sand dunes, yet it may mark substantial quantities of subsurface water, and illustrates the scalar malleability of watersheds and catchments that can be defined at a very wide range of spatial scales.

Along Wadi Hadramawt-Masila and its tributaries, a range ancient settlements and vestiges of irrigation depict histories of water-use and political complexity. The most detailed appraisal of irrigation around the capital city of Shabwa consists of a report produced by the late Pierre Gentelle (1991) a geographer whose experience with ancient waterworks around the world enabled a helpful account after relatively short intervals of fieldwork in 1977 and 1980 assisted by historic air photos. Continued French investigations of the city of Shabwa have yielded a relatively detailed account of settlement beginning as early as the second millennium BC, after which occupations grew into a sizable metropolis with a central walled area of 15.5 hectares surrounded by outer wall encompassing 53.9 hectares (Breton 2003; Darles 2008). This substantial ancient settlement was centered within vast geometric patterns of banked fields covering nearly 2000 hectares (Darles 2008: 141) that were fed by canals into which water was deflected from wadi channels using diagonal weirs made of massive limestone blocks. Although dating these vast field systems proved challenging, Gentelle (1991) identified four phases of irrigation that included weirs, headworks, massive earthen canals, and sluice gates designed to regulate flow with some structures built using highly refined techniques and mortared masonry. Gentelle and colleagues also found fragments of inscriptions commemorating construction of irrigation works that further demonstrate the considerable social importance of water control.

In addition to the impressive irrigation works at Shabwa, water control systems have also been reported from a range of other Iron Age sites further downstream along Wadi Hadramawt. In their investigations in the 1930s, Caton-Thompson and Gardner (1939) reported on the geologic, sedimentary and irrigation history of Wadi 'Amd and Wadi Daw'an, particularly the former near the town of Hureidha. This area was subject to more lengthy archaeological investigations of Soviet (later Russian) Mission who focused in part on major settlements and temples including the site of Raybun in Wadi Daw'an (Sedov 1996, 2005). The watershed of Wadi Daw'an drains 4,791 square kilometers that extends from elevations of 721 to 1912 meters with rainfall of 61 to 150 millimeters per year (Table 5.1). Near its confluence with Wadi Hadramawt, the adjacent Wadi 'Amd joins Daw'an and adds another 3,043 square kilometers together capturing water flow from a very sizable portion of Hadramawt's southern highlands. Remnants of ancient irrigation mapped by the Russian team in Wadi Daw'an extend more than 10 kilometers covering more than 1500 hectares surrounding ancient Raybun (Sedov 1997). Using a collection of historic air photos taken by a French company in 1977–1978, Charbonnier (2012) expanded on previous Russian maps showing an even larger area was once irrigated. Irrigation in the area today is of a more modest extent, but as described earlier, ethnographic irrigation along Wadi Daw'an offers a wealth of insights helpful for understanding the development of increasingly sophisticated ancient irrigation technologies and their sociopolitical ramifications through time (Baquhaizel et al. 1996; Harrower 2009; Serjeant 1964). Undoubtedly one of the best recently documented sites, Makaynun has also been a focal point of French research and Mouton et al. (2011) helpfully emphasize the economic and symbolic role irrigation played in the establishment of this and other settlements.

## Irrigation, the Kingdom of Himyar, and the rise of highland power

For most of the first millennium BC ancient Saba vied for supremacy over other ancient kingdoms centered along the margins of the desert, then

## Irrigation, the Kingdom of Himyar, and the rise of highland power        145

during the late second century BC political power began to shift to the highlands where the Kingdom of Himyar with its capital at Zafar came to dominate the region (Yule 2013b). This historical shift marks an important turning point in water histories of ancient Yemen and demonstrates how there were options other than massive waterworks along the margins of the desert that could sustain large populations and complex polities. Nevertheless, the fact the Great Dam at Ma'rib remained politically important even after power shifted to the highlands illustrates the deep symbolic and ideological import of monumental waterworks in Southwest Arabian histories. While a range of factors combined to shift the gravitational center of political control from the lowlands to the highlands, two of the most critical variables in the rise of Southwest Arabia states, trade and agriculture, were again pivotal. By at least first century AD, if not earlier, seafaring along the Red Sea and Indian Ocean had advanced to become a major, reliable means of maritime commerce thereby circumventing at least some of the camel caravan traffic that relied on desert cities as staging points (Seland 2014). Highland areas closer to the Red Sea and Indian Ocean coastlines allowed closer oversight of maritime trade routes that could move incense to the Mediterranean more efficiently, and in larger quantities, than overland routes.

By the first few centuries AD nearly a millennia of large-scale irrigation agriculture along the desert margins had induced massive sedimentary changes that were difficult if not impossible to remedy. Highland areas offered the possibility of rainfed agriculture affording greater flexibility, less reliance on massive irrigation systems, and a deeper measure of autonomy from central authorities. As David Montgomery (2007) explored in his book *Dirt: The Erosion of Civilizations*, soil degradation is a vastly underappreciated global problem that contributed to the decline of numerous ancient civilizations. Such changes clearly played a major long term role in agricultural production across Southwest Arabia. Archaeologists working on irrigation in Yemen have frequently recognized that alluvial sediments many meters deep surround state capitals and were often the result of irrigation-based accumulation. These sediments, and rectangular patterns of ancient fields within them, have very helpfully been used to map the extent of ancient irrigation systems (e.g., Brunner 2000; Francaviglia 2000). While analyses have often focused on aggregation it is likely patterns of both aggregation and degradation played a role, as sediment accumulating in one area must necessarily have been eroded or derived from another. Indeed, by the first few centuries AD agriculturally valuable sediments had eroded and were impossible to replace in some locations, while in other places massive accumulations of irrigation-deposited alluvium had raised fields high above surrounding wadis making it increasingly difficult to redirect water to elevations high enough to reach them. Drawing a long history of investigations around Ma'rib (e.g., Brunner 1983), increasingly sophisticated geomorphological analysis and radiocarbon dating have helped unravel the natural and human-induced sedimentary history of the area (Kühn et al. 2010; Pietsch and Kuhn 2012; Pietsch et al. 2010). These studies show early Holocene pluvial period of paleosol formation until approximately 6300 BC (Pietsch and Kühn 2012) with the onset of natural alluvial deposition around 5000 BC (Pietsch et al. 2010) and the beginnings of irrigation during the third millennium BC (Kühn et al. 2010). Interestingly, these findings mirror results elsewhere in Yemen with the important difference that shifts between sedimentary aggregation and degradation are dependent, to a large degree, on local watershed conditions (Berger et al. 2012; Harrower et al. 2012). Soil salinity was troublesome issue elsewhere across the ancient Near East particularly in high water-table areas (Elgabaly 1977) including much of southern Mesopotamia (Altaweel and Watanabe 2012; Jacobsen and Adams 1958), but salinity may have been far less a problem in ancient Yemen. However, the spectrally distinct appearance of irrigated sediments around ancient desert cities (Plate I) may be in part the result of evaporates that could indicate heightened soil salinity (Brunner and Haefner 1990). Another perhaps more vexing challenge, tectonic activity also may have had significant impacts as structural alterations in upstream patterns of water flow could have contributed to the abandonment of irrigation systems in some areas including along Wadi Bayhan (Marcolongo and Bonacossi 1997).

In light of the substantive challenges of continued irrigation along the desert margins, archaeological and epigraphic investigations have yielded considerable evidence that the center-point of agricultural production and political power began to shift to the highlands during the first half of the first millennium AD. Drawing on a long history of expertise in water control engineering, numerous large agricultural constructions including dams and barrages that in some cases spanned entire valleys were built across Yemen's western highlands (Charbonnier 2009, 2011). Robin and colleagues reported a number of examples with foundation inscriptions that offer revealing details far beyond what can usually be surmised for ancient waterworks (Robin and Arbach 2009; Robin and Dridi 2004). Charbonnier and Schiettecatte (2013) helpfully offer a synthetic analysis of the at least sixty examples of highland dams identified since the 1970s including sixteen examples dated by foundation inscriptions which all fall

# Irrigation, the Kingdom of Himyar, and the rise of highland power

during the first century AD or later. As power shifted to the highlands, such constructions and associated texts illustrate the continued importance and prestige kings, *qayl* lords, and *kabir* tribal leaders gained in constructing irrigation works. Smaller-scale agriculture including rainfed, spring water, and terrace farming simultaneously offered many productive opportunities that continue into recent times (Varisco 1983). These strategies combined to provide a diverse and readily sustainable agricultural foundation far less reliant on the enormous state-chartered irrigation systems of Yemen's earliest desert kingdoms. However, the eventual collapse of massive desert systems including the Ma'rib Dam also served to undermine the landscape persona and ideological adhesive that bound early polities together.

By the third century AD, the Empire of Aksum, centered in what are today the northern highlands of Ethiopia, began to exert increasingly great influence in Yemen. Like the millennia before it, this span of history holds substantive insights for understanding water-use and irrigation. Decades of military conflict eventually led to the defeat of Aksumite forces in Yemen near the end of the third century, and the continuing dominance of Himyar (Hatke 2012). Aksumite king, Ezana's conversion to Christianity near 348 AD contributed to heightened aspirations to extend the empire's control into Arabia. In 518 AD King Kaleb of Aksum invaded Ethiopia and attempted to appoint a local Christian as ruler. A tumultuous interval of infighting followed that led an Aksumite general, Abraha, to cease power and proclaim himself monarch near 531 AD, and he ruled until the Sasanians of Persia conquered the region around 570 AD. Among Abraha's most notable achievements, he built a majestic church in Sana'a, the new capital of Himyar, which reportedly employed the skills of both Byzantine and Aksumite craftspeople and was adorned with lavish accoutrements and mosaics (Finster 2010). Even more significantly for the present analysis, he also organized reconstruction of the Great Dam at Ma'rib and commemorated this undertaking with two large stelae (Nebes 2004, 2005). The first stela (CIH 541) describes how after prevailing in a series of battles he received reports of the dam's collapse and marshaled tribes and *qayls* to restore the earth, stone facing, masonry, and plaster of the dam. As mentioned earlier in this chapter, this involved enormous quantities of provisions that sustained thousands of workers over fifty-eight days. The more recently discovered second stela (DAI GDN 2002–20), which also refers to Abraha as King of Saba, dhu Raydan, Hadramawt, Yamnat, and the Bedouin of the highlands and lowlands, recounts specific details and dimensions of the north sluice ('Awdān) which stood 19 meters (41 cubits) high on the foundations constructed by former King Shurahbi'il Ya'fur (Nebes 2004). Tracing back through agricultural histories of Yemen and Ethiopia helps illustrate why such reconstructions were so significant.

Dignitaries, engineers, and stonemasons of Aksum would have been far more familiar with the terrain and agricultural practices of highland Yemen than with the irrigation systems of Yemen's lowland desert margins, but Aksumite leaders in Arabia clearly came to recognize the deep symbolic importance of water control and Ma'rib's monumental dam. Archaeologists interested in pre-Aksumite and Aksumite societies traditionally postulated that large-scale irrigation technologies introduced from Yemen contributed to the initial rise of complex polities in Ethiopia (e.g., Butzer 1981; Michels 1988). This conclusion, however, is not substantiated by more recent investigations that show large-scale irrigation played a limited role (D'Andrea et al. 2008; Harrower and D'Andrea 2014; Sulas 2009). Some large-scale water management can indeed be found in the vicinity of pre-Aksumite and Aksumite settlements (Brunner 2005; Sulas 2009) but most cultivation throughout the core territories of Aksum was rainfed. Irrigation was predominantly used to supplement rainfall during times of drought and for high-value fruit and vegetable crops (Harrower and D'Andrea 2014). Like much of western Yemen, the highlands of northern Ethiopia and Eritrea are extensively terraced. This terracing, which commenced in Yemen during the fourth millennium BC, likely began in Ethiopia at least as early as the first millennium BC (Butzer 1981). Yet, there is little evidence peoples of Aksum ever engaged in irrigation on the scale of systems found in Yemen, nor specifically borrowed Southwest Arabian irrigation technologies.

Given the comparatively limited importance of irrigation to Aksum, why would Abraha exert such energies in organizing reconstruction of the Ma'rib Dam and go to such considerable lengths to emphasize his accomplishments in doing so? By the sixth century when Abraha claimed control of the region, political power in Yemen had for centuries focused in western highland areas. First establishing control of Yemen's highlands, Aksum may have even extended its reach as far as eastern Yemen where the fifth-sixth century Iron Age hill fort at head of Wadi Sana (Beeston 1962) is referred to by locals as Qal'at Habshiya, which roughly translates to mean castle or fort of the Ethiopians. Aksumite influence this far east is difficult to verify, and even sporadic military control does not necessarily demonstrate political control or legitimacy. However, like kings of Himyar before him, Abraha's claim to the title "King of Saba dhu-Raydan, Hadramawt ..." illustrates efforts to claim sovereignty over the region. This

# Irrigation, the Kingdom of Himyar, and the rise of highland power

titular continuity was similarly of long importance to kings of Himyar, as Norbert Nebes described ...

> In Mārib ... they [The kings of Himyar] continued the practice of placing their dedications in the central shrine of the main Sabean god Almaqah, to whom they were also addressed. The explanation for this is quite simply that Mārib had lost nothing of its significance as a political center symbolizing the centuries of Sabean rule. By placing their dedications at the Awām temple in Mārib, the Ḥimyarite kings were seeking to place themselves within this tradition and thereby to endow their rule with the necessary legitimacy. (Nebes 2010: 35)

Most notably in terms of water, the kings of Himyar not only recognized Ma'rib's historic religious importance, but also the deep importance of the Great Dam at Ma'rib. Himyarite king, Shurahbi'il Ya'fur's two consecutive reconstructions of the dam (AD 449) involved enormous exertions of labor and expenditures of resources involving as many as 20,000 people (CIH 540). Abraha's reconstruction similarly marshaled a massive labor force and cooperation of tribes to repair the Ma'rib Dam. Like Shurahbi'il Ya'fur before him, Abraha could then more substantively claim rightful heritance to leadership of the region. However, his reconstruction of the dam would unfortunately be one of the last. There were a number of less monumental irrigation works around Ma'rib during the fifth–sixth century AD such as the Al-Mabna Dam in Wadi Gufaina northwest of the main oasis (Schaloske 1995: 105–19) but these endeavors where only a fragment of the former grandeur of the Great Dam. Just as its construction marked the dawn of Yemen's pre-Islamic kingdoms, the final collapse of the Great Dam at Ma'rib between AD 575 and 600 (Vogt 2004) signified the demise of the region's pre-Islamic complex polities. The Holy Quran's eloquent description of the dam's final collapse quoted at the opening of this book demonstrates its deep and enduring importance as a symbol of the period often maligned as *Jahiliyya* "The Age of Ignorance." Notwithstanding the accomplishments of pre-Islamic civilizations, the sixth–early seventh century immediately before the rise of Islamic Empires was indeed a time of profound turmoil as Aksumites, Himyarites, and Sasanians successively controlled the region (Al-Ansary 1994). Even hundreds of years later during the tenth century, in recounting the grandeur of Ma'rib dam, Al-Hamdānī commented on its technical shortcomings (Faris 1938: 34). Accumulated sediments had ultimately raised and clogged the system in ways that were extremely difficult to remediate. Redesign and reconstruction, if it were possible, would have required an unprecedented undertaking of labor with a regional sense of common-purpose and leadership to orchestrate the work. While the loss of 10,000 hectares of agricultural land is unlikely to have had serious consequences in terms of regional food production (Darles et al. 2013: 10), the political failure to keep the dam operating signaled political disarray that foreshadowed the dramatic, charismatic rise of Islam.

## Water, complex polities, and spatial heterogeneity in ancient Southwest Arabia

Water interconnects a wide range of environmental, social, and political dynamics among histories of arid regions worldwide, including ancient Yemen and the American West. In his ambitious, voluminous review of world history Arnold Toynbee (1934) argued that civilizations arose to address challenges, and in arid regions such challenges often involved ensuring adequate and reliable food production. However, massive state orchestrated irrigation systems *were not agriculturally necessary* to provision ancient Yemen – rainfed cultivation and small-scale irrigation could have provided the food necessary to sustain ancient states. In essence, Yemen's earliest states exploited spatial heterogeneity to claim credit for harnessing water and creating verdant, visually striking oases that generated agricultural abundance. Historians have similarly argued that massive waterworks across the American West were as much about politics, colonization, and sovereignty as they were about food, which could very arguably be produced more effectively and equitably across the American East without government subsidized waterworks (Reisner 1986; Wahl 1989; Worster 1985). Agriculture encompasses roughly 80 percent of California's current water-use, with residential and industrial uses accounting for the remaining 20 percent (Christian-Smith et al. 2012). Recent drought threatens not so much urban populations, but the continuities and legacies of western agricultural production that have formed a critical element of western entrepreneurial identities and agribusiness. In ancient Yemen, irrigation's influences similarly emanated not only from greater productive capacity but from water's importance as a source of social magnetism and religiosity that drew together increasingly large aggregations of people around highly concentrated water sources. Large-scale irrigation works indentured farmers to states through largely state-contrived dependence on irrigation water across otherwise desiccated landscapes. Through ideologies that emphasized divine sponsorship of irrigation, mukarribs and later kings maintained and bolstered their legitimacy through construction of

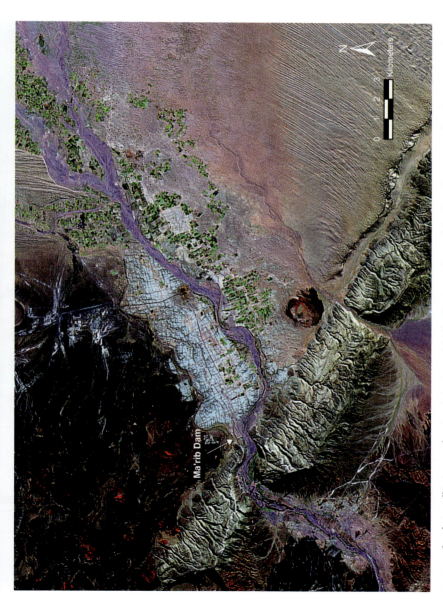

PLATE 1. Landsat satellite image of ancient irrigation at Ma'rib. The irrigated area of the Great Dam at Ma'rib is shown in a Landsat-5 image taken on March 18, 1985. The Landsat band 7-4-2 combination and image histogram equalization highlights the geometric patterns of ancient irrigated sediments shown in light blue as well as modern irrigated vegetation shown in green. The modern dam at Ma'rib built slightly upstream (bottom left in this image) was completed in 1986 and has contributed to a substantial irrigated area that to some extent obscures ancient systems (image by the author, analysis follows recommendations of Dr. Ronald Blom, NASA Jet Propulsion Laboratory).

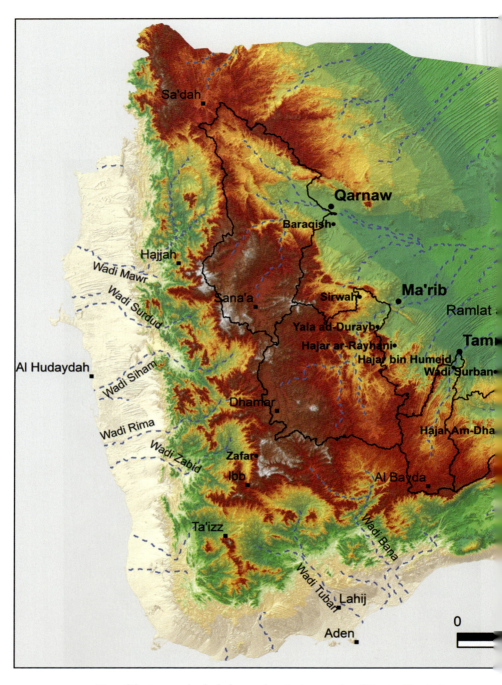

PLATE 11. Map of the topography, hydrology and ancient geography of Yemen. Terrain is based on NASA's Shuttle Radar Topography Mission (SRTM) data. Major wadis, and a selection of major watersheds including those of state capitals are shown. Kingdoms first emerged along the margins of the Ramlat as-Sab'atayn Desert during the early first millennium BC with capital cities of Qarnaw (Kingdom of Ma'in), Ma'rib (Kingdom of Saba), Tamna'

*(continued)*

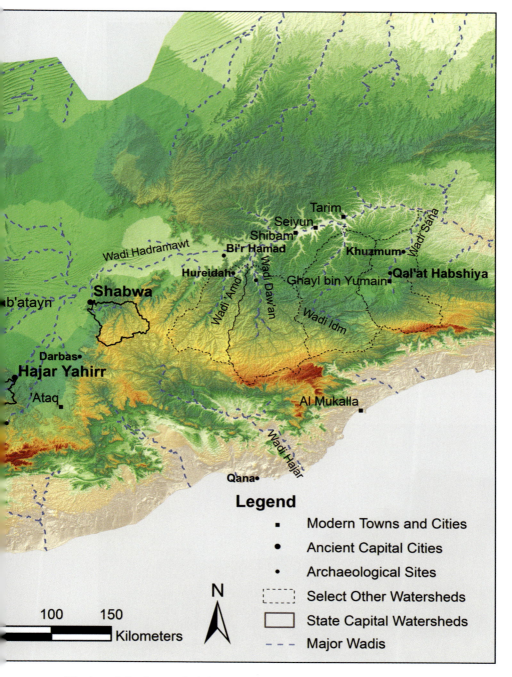

(Kingdom of Qatabān), and Shabwa (Kingdom of Hadramawt). Each of these cities were located at the outlet of major inward-draining watersheds and relied on massive flash floodwater irrigation systems. The center-point of political power later shifted to highland areas with far more rainfall during the early first millennium AD with the rise of the Kingdom of Himyar and its capital at Zafar (water flow modeling and image by the author).

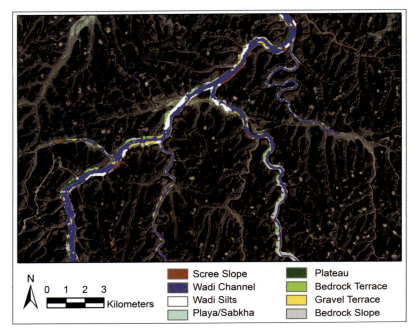

PLATE III. GIS model of ancient grazing areas along Wadi Sana, Hadramawt (Yemen). Drainages are buffered according to Strahler Stream Order (1st = 50 m, 2nd = 125 m, 3rd = 200 m, 4th = 275 m) so that landforms are shown in this plate only for areas that receive substantial water flow. Areas where substantial water flow combines with either Wadi Silts or Gravel Terrace landform classes are modeled as areas likely to have periodically sustained grasses suitable for cattle grazing.

PLATE IV. Intermediate-Scale Floodwater (sayl) Irrigation along Wadi Daw'an, Hadramawt (Yemen). Date-palms in the foreground, with cereals and fodder crops often grown beneath them, are irrigated by barrages and canals that divert water from periodic flash floods into earthen-banked fields.

massive irrigation systems including the renowned dam at Ma'rib that stood as an enduring symbol of state power. It is highly unlikely given the enormous costs of constructing and maintaining these systems that ancient Yemen's early waterworks were the most economically efficient means to produce the food necessary to supply urban populations. After nearly a thousand years of irrigation along the margins of the Ramlat as-Sab'atayn, desert state capitals eventually faced major sedimentary changes that induced nearly insurmountable reconstruction challenges. The Kingdom of Himyar rose to power in the highlands supported by some large dams, valleywide barrages and other impressive agricultural constructions, but most crops grown in the highlands were undoubtedly rainfed and roughly 75 percent of crops in Yemen today are grown without irrigation. Just as the Los Angeles Aqueduct and Hoover Dam and the many waterworks they inspired propelled colonization and sovereignty across the American West, massive irrigation works of Yemen's earliest kingdoms similarly transformed deserts into oases that pronounced the capabilities and legitimacy of early leaders and complex polities.

Juxtaposition of ancient Yemen and the American West illustrates not only the wide differences but some underlying commonalities between histories that outwardly seem entirely distinct and incomparable. In a recent paper Scarborough and Lucero (2010) examined the role of water among a selection of ancient complex societies of the tropics and concluded that unpredictable environments contributed to nonhierarchical patterns of sociopolitical organization. In other tropical regions, such as Yemen, Oman, and Ethiopia, trajectories of histories may have also been characterized by a measure of heterarchy (Harrower and D'Andrea 2014), yet histories unfolded very differently in different contexts and each region exhibits significant individualities and particularities, despite being neighbors. Studies of irrigation have over time alternated from emphasis on inequity and despotism (Wittfogel 1957) to depictions of harmony and communality (Lansing 1991, 2006); yet these two positive/negative polarities rarely describe the multifaceted complexities of water politics (Howe 2006). Earle and Doyel (2008) emphasized the importance of engineered landscapes of irrigation created by the Hohokam as means of staple finance, yet their analysis emphasizes economic and hierarchical dynamics of irrigation while overlooking the deep symbolic and ideological impacts of desert water control. Like the oases of ancient Arabia, Hohokam irrigation visually transformed the desert. It not only mattered who economically controlled, distributed, and consumed the food, but just as importantly the spectacle of bountiful agriculture amidst a sun-scorched desert that otherwise supplied only meager sustenance was deeply important politically and ideologically. Yemen's ancient desert irrigation systems are not necessarily a demonstration of prescient, insightful leadership and were not a function of any particular individual or elite group, nor were they part of a harmoniously sustainable system as they survived many hundreds of years yet eventually met a sudden, catastrophic end. Such impressive water systems not only demonstrate technological aptitude and economic capacity, but also the social and political malleability of spatial heterogeneity, scarcity, surplus, and the imperative of *perceived* prosperity in perpetuating polities. Water histories in different contexts undeniably followed their own unique course. For instance, in Southwest versus Southeast Arabia dynamics diverged substantially due in part to widely differing spatiotemporal patterning of water resources and the distinct north–south trade interconnections along the Red Sea and Persian Gulf. Further investigations of these and other lesser-known contexts have a great deal more to teach us about ancient and modern histories, and water challenges of the future.

CHAPTER 6

# Conclusion

Water histories, comparison, geopolitics, and spatial archaeology

> When archaeologists from some other planet sift through the bleached bones of our civilization, they may well conclude that our temples were dams. Imponderably massive, constructed with exquisite care, our dams will outlast anything else we have built – skyscrapers, cathedrals, bridges, even nuclear power plants.
>
> (Reisner 1986: 108)

Reisner's elaborate prose predicts the future significance of America's waterworks. It's impossible to confirm his speculations – predicting the future is exceedingly difficult – but retrodicting the past is somewhat less so. We do know that many hundreds of years after ancient kingdoms built massive irrigation works along Yemen's desert margins, medieval historians marveled at these impressive constructions. In the early tenth century Arab historian and geographer Al-Hamdānī reported on major waterworks of ancient South Arabia and vividly commented on the Ma'rib dam ...

> The aqueducts which carry the water from the Dam and distribute it among the villages still stand as though the builders had completed their construction only yesterday. I have also seen the structure of one of the two openings [of the Dam], through which the water flowed, still standing as strong as it has ever been. It will undergo no change until it be ordained by God. (Al-Hamdānī [ca. AD 945] translated by Faris 1938: 34)

Massive waterworks, whether revered as achievements of American engineering, or disparaged as the failed remnants of the pre-Islamic heathen past of Arabia, nevertheless shape contemporary cultures. Today, the Hoover Dam is somewhat unexpectedly a major tourist attraction visited by nearly a million people a year and is a symbolic apex of water control across the arid West. Freedom, individualism, ingenuity, hard work, self-reliance, religious reverence, even western frontier justice and cowboy diplomacy are deeply engrained center-points of American identity and culture linked to control of water. And like the Hoover Dam, the Great Dam at Ma'rib is a seminal monument and a pivotal historical reference point that contributes to Arab and Islamic culture and identity thereafter. Many very similar cultural values – self-sufficiency, autonomy, equity, charity, piety and valor – are linked to histories of water in Arabia. In both cases unique social logic, expressed very differently, turns in part on human mastery of water and conquest of deserts. The central themes of water histories and their archetypes – the American western frontier settler and the noble Arabian camel-riding nomad – structure and define understandings of ourselves and those we view as others. Deeper understanding of histories erodes these colloquial stereotypes to better reveal the complex range of commonalities among differences that situate us in front of the challenges of the present and the future. One of the key hallmarks of American water histories – that water shortage and subsidization of irrigation across the American West forgoes the great abundance of water in the American East – is mirrored in ancient Yemen. In both cases, it was less an absolute environmental need for irrigation than the rhetoric of water shortage and scarcity that came to socially and religiously justify state authority over water across deserts. Spatial heterogeneity and gradients of water availability, great abundance in some places and absence in others, propelled massive waterworks that made the polities that controlled them, for a time, indispensable. As combinations of political rhetoric and social logic, these societal configurations were self-perpetuating sometimes to the point of their own destruction.

**Water histories, contrastive juxtaposition, and spatial archaeology**

In working to understand the long-term role of water in ancient Yemen, and water's influences among civilizations generally, this book has utilized a number of approaches – water histories, contrastive juxtaposition, and spatial archaeology – which have broad utility beyond this particular study. Scholars have long recognized that water played a substantial role in trajectories of civilizations. Particularly given current challenges of water shortage in many regions of the world, analyzing the combined environmental, economic, social, political, cultural, and religious dynamics of water throughout histories can help more effectively and amicably address present and future water challenges. The ancient past rarely (if ever) offers technological quick-fix solutions to

# Water histories, contrastive juxtaposition, and spatial archaeology

contemporary water crises, but rather can helpfully reveal how interdigitization of geographies and politics frames the ways in which we view and use water.

Anthropology has long been marked by dichotomous interests in commonalities among human histories and cultures on one hand, alongside emphasis on human histories and cultures as unique, contingent, and exceptional on the other. Since both cross-cultural comparison and historical particularity are of deep importance in understanding histories and cultures, contrastive juxtaposition of two or a few cases holds great potential to advance research in ways that are of wide relevance to audiences beyond those who specialize in studies of the ancient past. In an era of increasingly plentiful information, single-authored, synthetic worldwide overviews that aim to distill the essence of histories in a multitude of regions are impractical. Multiauthored edited volumes that cover a topic or theme, such as water, in a variety of different regions or contexts are of great utility, but it is often challenging to build the consensus necessary for a well-honed, carefully specified argument among groups of scholars with necessarily diverse viewpoints. Pair-wise comparison has an illustrious history in anthropology (e.g., Adams 1966; Geertz 1968; Mead 1928; Sahlins 2004) and among the range of comparative approaches available to archaeologists (Smith 2011) contrasting two or three cases allows cross cultural comparison while weight is also given to historical and cultural contingency, particularity, and idiosyncracy. We need not aim solely to demonstrate likeness or similarity but instead to illuminate commonalities and differences among histories, such as those of America and Arabia, which are often marked by striking outward dissimilarities.

Archaeologists many decades ago recognized the importance of spatial perspectives in understanding the ancient past (e.g., Clarke 1977) and given the rapidly burgeoning recent impacts of spatial technologies, such as satellite imagery, GPS, and GIS software, renewed attention to the interface of spatial analysis and spatial theory is necessary to reconsider conventions of archaeological practice established over past decades. Advances lie not necessarily, or not solely, in more sophisticated technologies and statistical analyses, but more importantly in new ways to conceive of and theorize archaeological problems as inquiries into past human and physical geographies. This book has aimed to combine scientific applications of spatial technologies with humanistic analysis of spatiality, political rhetoric, social change in ways that, it is hoped, will be of utility to others, particularly with respect to understanding and analyzing comparative water histories.

## Water and ancient transitions to agriculture

Archaeologists long ago identified the basic factors that contributed to the world's earliest agriculture – ancient climates, environments, demographics, economics, culture, politics, and ideology. While deterministic, unicausal explanations focusing on one or a few of these variables are superficially appealing because of their seeming elegance and intelligibility, they do relatively little to explain the multifaceted complexities of early agricultural histories. Each of the aforementioned forces contributed in different ways in different contexts. The challenge ahead lies not so much in proving or disproving one or another deterministic hypothesis, but instead involves better resolving how various pieces of the puzzle fit together in different historical circumstances. Studies of agricultural origins often seek to explain very different phenomena at very different spatial scales, for example, the domestication and various biological changes in plants and animals, the human behaviors such as animal breeding and cultivation that induced domestication, and the beginnings of agricultural societies and polities. Some studies focus on the interactions of individuals and communities in villages, while others examine millennia-long demographic changes across continents. At least some of the conflict between different models and explanations for transitions to agriculture arises not only because they are fundamentally incompatible, but because different scholars often endeavor to explain spatiotemporally very different aspects of transitions to agriculture (Harrower et al. 2010). Similarly, the categories wild/domestic, forager/farmer, primary/secondary, origins/spread are sometimes helpful heuristic descriptors, yet their boundaries become fuzzy upon closer scrutiny. When viewed as mutually exclusive types that we seek to divide one from another, binary categories can often distract from broader, long-term understanding of human histories.

Ancient and historic agriculture in Yemen and the American West bear some illuminating similarities and critical differences. In both regions major drainage systems punctuated a diverse array of arid topography. Cultivation first took place in water-rich areas such as near springs, arroyos/wadis, and alluvial floodplains, and practices over time involved an increasingly wide range of locally tailored irrigation technologies. In both regions, the arrival of agriculture has often been depicted as a cascading migratory frontier of expansion in ways that discount the importance of preexisting populations. The dynamics of early agriculture were far more complex than portrayed by traditional unicausal models that posit a punctuating climate change, overpopulation, simple triumph of supposedly more economically efficient subsistence, or a determining socio-ideological change. In Yemen, a pronounced climatic shift to more arid conditions near 3500 BC accompanied by long-term population pressure contributed to beginnings of irrigation agriculture but these factors cannot be viewed as the sole determinants of change amidst similarly important social, political, and ideological transformations. Domesticates first appear across southern Arabia in conjunction with oscillating climates, long-term demographic pressure, new understandings of human relations with nature (including land, water, and territoriality) and changing cost/benefits of hunting, herding, gathering, and cultivating.

Dramatic social and economic changes accompanied and followed the sixth millennium BC adoption of cattle and caprine husbandry in Yemen. Although we scantly know the details of social interaction during Yemen's prehistory, the rapid seventeenth and eighteenth century AD adoption of horses among Native Americans across the American West demonstrates how rapidly and dramatically animal husbandry can alter peoples' lives and cultures. Throughout the two thousand or more years after domestic animals first appeared in Yemen, many people survived as forager-pastoralists who lacked opportunities to trade with settled farmers. Indeed, the conventional Near Eastern archetypal pattern of pastoral nomads interacting with farmers in villages inhibits understanding of Yemen's deeper past when such interactions were, based on present evidence, simply impossible as cultivation had yet to appear in the region. By the mid-fifth millennium forager-pastoralists built small circular structures in western Yemen (Fedele 2008, 2013), and in eastern Yemen similar platform structures and dolmen monuments built of massive stone slabs can be found sporadically dispersed along wadis (McCorriston et al. 2002, 2005, 2011; Steimer-Herbet et al. 2006). The long-term metastructural dynamics of cattle cult gatherings for sacrifice, rituals, and feasting maintained alliances crucial to regulating water use-rights and grazing territories and exerted deep social influences over succeeding millennia (McCorriston 2011; McCorriston et al. 2012).

The appearance of irrigation and terrace agriculture in Yemen during the mid-fourth millennium BC, like transitions to agriculture in other regions of the world, involved an interacting constellation of social, environmental, political, cultural, and ideological dynamics rather than a simplistically singular prime mover. When viewed from the vantage point of eastern Mediterranean archaeology, the appearance of domesticated plants in Yemen seems comparatively late; yet this transition occurred after a long interval in which forager-pastoralists would have been aware of peoples in other regions who grew crops, which speaks strongly against viewing agriculture as a discovery or an invention, as crops certainly did not appear in the region as soon as they were known. Rather than merely the introduction of crops from elsewhere, long-term population growth, mid-Holocene climatic variability, and changes in notions of human relations with nature, territoriality, mortuary practices, and land/water rights were all centrally important to transitions to agriculture across southern Arabia. The traditional notion that European-style rainfed agriculture is a primordial agricultural norm is contradicted by an increasingly wide range of evidence indicating that water-rich areas were specifically targeted from the very beginnings of cultivation in regions including the Levant (Finlayson et al. 2011) and southern Arabia (Harrower 2008a). Similarly, investigations of the earliest maize farming along the U.S.–Mexico borderlands show that targeting of water-rich areas and small-scale water management including terracing were important early strategies (Mabry 2002, 2005; Mabry and Doolittle 2008). Subsequent elaboration of water control across the American Southwest from small-scale floodwater farming and terraces to much larger Hohokam irrigation systems illustrates the ingenuity of locally derived design and management expertise, and demonstrates how many thousands of hectares can be irrigated without centralized state-level bureaucratic management (Hunt et al. 2005). The grand irrigation systems of ancient Yemen were not required to provide enough food for large populations, and these systems are not merely a consequence of civilization introduced from elsewhere. Instead, locally devised irrigation technologies were an integral component of state formation and political rhetoric as the growth of early kingdoms was interconnected with, and perpetuated by, spatially concentrated patterns of water-use across otherwise hyperarid desert margin areas.

## Water and the rise of ancient complex polities

In a contemporary era of information overload, archaeologists are among those facing a rapidly expanding plethora of data; and, on a topic as broad as ancient state formation, single-authored worldwide syntheses are increasingly impracticable and unlikely to yield compelling overarching explanations for such a diverse range of histories. Archaeologists are now tasked with analyzing and summarizing exponentially more information than scholars of previous generations – a challenge that will undoubtedly become progressively acute. Contrastive juxtaposition of two or three cases and analysis of specific themes such as water hold a promising future as means to examine similarities and differences among societies. The most critical variables, environment, demography, economics, culture, politics, and ideology have long reappeared in differing explanations, yet are manifest and interconnected in very different ways in different historical contexts.

Ancient Yemen offers a wide range of insights important to understanding ancient states and compels us to think about the past in substantially new ways. Rather than simply a secondary region on the receiving end of civilization, ancient people across southern Arabia selectively borrowed and reconfigured technologies, ideas, and styles of surrounding areas and combined them with unique locally devised practices, ideologies, and art. This long-term process of dynamic intermixing exemplifies patterns of local/global interaction well-suited to enhance understanding of many other contexts worldwide. The long-term metastructural social logic of gathering, sacrifice, and feast (McCorriston 2011) alongside the spectacle of vast agricultural oases in some of the region's lowest rainfall areas led nomadic populations to continually revisit early Southwest Arabian state capitals. As frankincense became an increasingly valuable luxury commodity in high demand throughout the eastern Mediterranean, domestication of camels offered an ideal means to transport large quantities across vast deserts (Fedele 2014). Geographies of water, in conjunction with religious rituals, warfare, and trade, shaped the interactive genesis of early Southwest Arabian kingdoms. The massive irrigation works along margins of Yemen's Ramlat as-Sab'atayn Desert that sustained ancient kingdoms were not the only way, nor necessarily the most efficient way, to produce enough food for large populations but they were critically important as a center-point of political rhetoric, social logic, and ideological magnetism that bound growing populations together in shared ideals and common enterprise. Such vibrant histories are ill-served by models that inflexibly divide polities into categories, primary/secondary types or restrict analysis to a single geographic culture area. Given that archaeologists are so often dealing with fragmentary remnants of material culture, the idiosyncratic types and preservational characteristics of evidence within regions (e.g., cursive inscriptions on date-palm stalks from Yemen) add evidence and understanding in some regions that is unavailable in others. Thinking past traditional categories and dichotomies opens up a far wider array of comparative perspectives and acknowledges that histories that span a wide diversity of spaces, times, and places can be mutually informative. Comparison need not aim to balance one case against another, nor aim solely to demonstrate likeness and similarity, but rather can help reveal fundamental underlying differences and commonalities via a wide range of sources, evidence, and methods.

The scholarly richness and popular recognizability of water histories of the American West significantly adds to understanding of complex polities in ancient Yemen and prompts new perspectives. Key figures, such as Abraham Lincoln, played crucial roles in water histories of the American West. However, as historians of the American West (and other regions) have long recognized, methodologies that concentrate on leaders, elites, and wars overlook the crucial roles of everyday people. Depicting aggrandizing ancient leaders, such as the seventh century BC mukarrib Karrib'il Watar, as despots who manipulated water for their own wealth, power and prestige to dictate the course of history unduly discounts the role of engineers, stonemasons, water managers, herders, farmers, fathers, mothers, sons, and daughters who labored to harness the water, produce, and cook the food that sustained ancient societies. Explanations that place elite control, hierarchy, and despotism at the forefront of histories, or alternatively portray local community organized water-use as unendingly sustainable and politically harmonious, require careful scrutiny. Such judgments readily depend on experiences and perspectives in the present and often tell us as much about ourselves and how we prefer to see the world as they do about histories. Counter-doctrinaire perspectives emphasized in this book acknowledge histories as shifting, aggregations of action, political rhetoric, and social logic perpetuated by people and polities that embroil a range of enthusiastic and reluctant participants.

For more than fifty years the hydraulic hypothesis has distracted studies of water among ancient civilizations; substantially new cross-cultural perspectives on irrigation and society are long overdue. A core argument of this book – that large state-managed irrigation systems were not necessarily required environmentally nor organizationally, but played a crucial social role in concentrating agricultural production in ways that rationalized and justified state authority and sovereignty – is well-suited to inform (and be further evaluated in) other regions. Robert McCormick Adams long rejected irrigation as the primary driving factor in the origins of Mesopotamian civilization and instead emphasized irrigation as a means later complex polities used to expand their influence (Adams 1960, 1974, 1981, 2006). Similarly, Tony Wilkinson viewed irrigation not as a prime mover in Mesopotamian state formation but as a mechanism by which later empires broadened their dominion (Wilkinson and Rayne 2010); and he emphasized "zones of uncertainty" where rainfed agriculture was tenuous and vulnerable (Wilkinson et al. 2014). If one extends these lines of thinking, which to some extent recognize political exploitation of water control and spatial variability, and expands them to further emphasize ideological/political rhetoric and social logic rather than direct state management of irrigation – early state authorities can be viewed not as unavoidably necessary to direct construction, operation, and managerial oversight of irrigation in southern Mesopotamia, but instead as essential to spectacle, magnetism, and presumptive ascendancy (Richardson 2012) of agricultural production that helped draw hinterland peoples toward the world's earliest cities. Similarly, in ancient Egypt early state authorities were not operationally indispensable to cultivation along the Nile but they clearly did politically and ideologically interject themselves, as evident through the rhetoric of art, into sanctifications of food production. One of the earliest depictions of Egyptian royal authority, the Scorpion mace head, for example, shows the pharaoh holding a hoe above water – perhaps opening and inaugurating an irrigation canal (Hendrickx and Förster 2010: 838). In essence, I argue, it is not so much the unavoidable need for state management of water control, but rather the spatial heterogeneity of water and the inculcation of fears and aspirations surrounding scarcity, crisis, and prosperity that funneled cultural and political exploitation of water, and the symbolism surrounding it, throughout histories.

## Xenophobia, water crises, and the War on Terror

Water richly exemplifies the importance and malleability of spatial perspectives in analyzing patterns in places, landscapes, and geographies that shape understandings of histories and interconnections through space and time with the present. Do East and West really define categorically different types of societies that were historically interlocked, and will perpetually remain, in conflict? Distinctions between Eastern and Western civilizations are foundational to contemporary understanding, yet are based more on politicized taken-for-granted rhetoric than on clear, rigorous, and widely agreed upon evaluations of the past. Endeavoring to determine where and when Western civilization first began and how it spread, predicates ones analysis on the existence of a contrasting Eastern type civilization(s) populated by inferior and adversarial others. As juxtaposition of American and Arabian water histories helps illustrate, outward differences often conceal commonalities; and it is not simply geographies of resources such as water and oil, nor solely political or religious differences that contribute to contemporary conflict but even more problematically misconstrual of the world's histories and correspondingly the future. Being an archaeologist is often a bit like being an emergency room doctor in slow motion; in considering the histories of ancient civilizations all of which eventually collapsed, one can easily envision future crises. But without the immediacy and finality of emergency medicine, recommending and instigating action is not only difficult, but is fraught with uncertainties and potentially deadly miscalculations with little real-world accountability. Stanford archaeologist Ian Morris (2010, 2014) finds a positive side to war and counterintuitively argues that violent conflict helps reorganize societies in ways that promote peace; but his arguments can easily be misappropriated to rationalize military interventions based on dubious readings of world history that are founded on dichotomous partitioning of the world into East and West. Conflicts across the Middle East today are concordantly shaped by fundamentalist, extremist rhetoric that portrays the West as the ultimate enemy; and our ability to counteract such portrayals requires more than solely economic, technological, or military prowess. For all the seemingly stark differences that divide and contribute to animosity and hostility, this book has compared and explored underlying patterning in what are outwardly very different histories. As comparative water histories help reveal, it is not solely disparities of resources or conflicting morals but a general lack of mutual understanding of cultures and histories that contributes to xenophobia and suspicions that inhibit dialog and promote conflict.

Current turmoil in Yemen and heralds a complex, uncertain future substantially related to water shortages (Fergusson 2015) that unfortunately, at least in the short term, seems likely to be decided through violence. Regrettably, Yemen is a critical recent battleground and has played an outsize role alongside Afghanistan and Iraq in the rise and perpetuation of Al Qaeda and ISIS (Johnsen 2013). As Houthi insurgents (sectarian rivals of Al Qaeda) took control of Yemen's capital Sana'a in 2014 one of their key practical demands was the return of diesel fuel subsidies, which played in part to farmers' anxieties and inability to secure water from rapidly depleting aquifers. While foreign actors do play a major role in shaping outcomes through weapons, the deep importance of political rhetoric (including with regard to water) supports the notion that Yemen's future also centrally depends on the competing ideas and ideologies that propel or alleviate conflict. The neighboring Sultanate of Oman is arguably as important as any other global power as it stands not only as an intermediary facilitating dialog between the United States and Iran, but also as a beacon of moderation against what Al-Qaeda and ISIS have long sought – an all-out war between the world's Jews, Christians, and Muslims. Archaeological research and protection of cultural heritage, in countries including but not limited to Oman, UAE, Turkey, and Jordan, holds important potential to help counteract East–West factionalization. As Luke and Kersel

(2012) cogently outlined, archaeological field projects, museums, tourism, and cultural heritage are critically important, yet broadly underestimated, tools of public diplomacy and peacemaking. These efforts not only play a role in diplomatic soft power in which we can advance particular agendas (Nye 2009), but alternatively and probably more importantly, humanistic research helps break down us/them barriers and works to better align the interests of disparate nationalities and constituencies. Indeed, mutual understandings are not only *a* basis for cooperation they are *the* basis for cooperation, and new means to terrorize and destroy can only be enduringly undermined through rigorous study and appreciation of the world's diverse historical, political, cultural, and social contexts.

A wide breadth of contemporary scholarship and media rightfully concentrates on looming water shortages and crises. Given what archaeology tells us of ancient societies' histories of collapse, public concern with environmental problems, such as water availability, is certainly warranted, but it is not only environmental challenges themselves but their political contexts that often shape the success or failure of proposed solutions. Given that millions in Yemen today lack basic access to sufficient food, water, and medical care, emergency relief is critically important. Longer-term solutions are similarly crucial. The foregoing analysis of ancient Yemen and the American West indicates that a good deal of skepticism and careful consideration of histories is warranted before adopting any particular course of long-term, institutional-scale action. Scarcity is relative, so areas naturally devoid of water may sometimes best stay that way while humans adjust not only in sustainable but also in resilient and equitable ways shaped by natural spatiotemporal availabilities. Ancient flash floodwater irrigation systems of Yemen's desert kingdoms were highly productive and sustainable for more than a thousand years but eventually collapsed due to both environmental factors – as they induced massive sedimentary changes – and political factors – which rendered polities incapable of reconstruction as farmers came to favor smaller-scale systems that were less reliant on state coordination. Current turmoil in Yemen has been fueled to a significant degree by misguided private and development projects' attempts to increase agricultural production by replacing traditional, sustainable, and resilient terrace farming systems with new technologies such as diesel pump-driven tube wells that have rapidly depleted aquifers (Lichtenthäler 2003; Moore 2011). Ancient water histories hold important lessons and ancient irrigation technologies have some utility in understanding potential strategies in the present, but ancient farming practices unfortunately are not a technological quick-fix that can replace practices floundering in the present. Western

Yemen's ancient terrace systems offer a highly sustainable alternative to groundwater pumping, but they are susceptible to erosion unless continually maintained, which has proven comparatively costly in a world of inexpensive (and often subsidized) internationally traded food. In some ways the predicted exhaustion of water supplies is a misrepresentation, since water almost never disappears entirely but instead becomes progressively more scarce and, for many, prohibitively expensive forcing migration and violent conflict. Although ignoring calls of crisis is foolhardy, deep understanding of past systems including their social and political contexts and ramifications far better equips judgments in the present and future, particularly since mistakes are often, like histories, irreversible.

Archaeologists are uniquely equipped to offer long-view historical perspectives and are exceptionally well qualified to help confront widely divergent understandings of histories, including in relation to water, that perpetuate continued hostilities. The most important crises we face are arguably not directly environmental, nor can be solved solely through economic power, technologies, or military force, but instead are social, political, and ideological. It is, of course, wise to look to science for solutions, but technologies alone cannot solve water crises and must be informed by considerations of political, cultural, and social contexts. Despite vast scientific acumen, water crises across the American West remain unresolved and controversial. The Colorado River Basin is referred to in a recent NASA-funded study as "the most overallocated river system in the world" (Castle et al. 2014:1) and even beyond the strikingly rapid recent depletion of Lake Powell and Lake Mead this study's findings indicate groundwater may be diminishing at an even more alarmingly rapid rate. The American West faces some of the very same water problems as Yemen and certainly cannot claim to have adequately devised (let alone implemented) long-term solutions. At the urging of international agencies, Yemen in 2002 passed its first national water legislation that among other things requires a permit to drill a well. Enforcement, however, proved difficult due to the political influence of tribes and deep reluctance of local water-users to abide by government restrictions (Caton 2013: 290–91). This law, at least in principle, even supersedes California's where the state's first legislative effort to regulate groundwater was only recently passed into law in 2014, during one of the worst droughts in the region's history. This law, however, does not actually regulate groundwater inasmuch as it requires that local water management agencies in each of California's twenty-two groundwater basins to begin devising sustainable management plans. Interestingly, this type of basin-centered local water management approach, while still complex and often controversial (Gleick et al. 2011), harkens back to John Wesley Powell's vision of watershed-focused management across the American West (Worster 2001) as well as the system of *lijna* water-users committees in Wadi Daw'an (Yemen) and numerous other contexts worldwide where traditional community water management thrived (Hunt 1989). We often have far more to learn from each other than we realize, and amicable international dialogue makes environmental problems, conflict, and war easier to avoid. While outwardly very different, the world's histories and cultures, including those of America and Arabia, are marked not only by wide differences but also substantial underlying commonalities. Better recognition of similarities and differences enables conciliatory dialogue. In the case of water, environmental, cultural, political, and religious understandings mix in complex ways to shape trajectories of history. Confronting and overturning narratives that paint dichotomous and divisive images of the past is among the central undertakings required to more peaceably shape the future. We can greatly benefit by thinking skeptically about the spatial patterns and categories by which we have long defined archaeological histories, and without discarding heuristic descriptors, recognizing the almost unavoidable political overtones and vantage points that shape identifications and explanations of ourselves and those we often misguidedly view as Others.

# Bibliography

Abbo, S., S. Lev-Yadun & A. Gopher, 2010. Agricultural Origins: Centers and Noncenters; A Near Eastern Reappraisal, *Critical Reviews in Plant Sciences* 29(5), 317–28.
    2012. Plant Domestication and Crop Evolution in the Near East: On Events and Processes, *Critical Reviews in Plant Sciences* 31(3), 241–57.
Abbott, D.R., 2009. Extensive and Long-Term Specialization: Hohokam Ceramic Production in the Phoenix Basin, Arizona, *American Antiquity* 74(3), 531–57.
Abbott, D.R., S.E. Ingram & B.G. Kober, 2006. Hohokam Exchange and Early Classic Period Organization in Central Arizona: Focal Villages or Linear Communities? *Journal of Field Archaeology* 31, 285–305.
Abu-Zahra, N., 1988. The Rain Rituals as Rites of Spiritual Passage, *International Journal of Middle East Studies* 20(4), 507–29.
Adams, R.M., 1960. Early Civilizations, Subsistence, and Environment, in *City Invincible: A Symposium on Urbanization and Cultural Development in the Ancient Near East*, eds. C.H. Kraeling & R.M. Adams. Chicago: University of Chicago Press, 269–95.
    1965. *Land Behind Baghdad: A History of Settlement on the Diyala Plains.* Chicago: University of Chicago Press.
    1966. *The Evolution of Urban Society: Early Mesopotamia and Prehispanic Mexico.* New York: Aldine-Atherton.
    1974. The Mesopotamian Social Landscape: A View from the Frontier, *Bulletin of the American Schools of Oriental Research* Supplemental Series No. 20, 1–20.
    1981. *Heartland of Cities: Surveys of Ancient Settlement and Land Use on the Central Floodplain of the Euphrates.* Chicago: The University of Chicago Press.
    2004. Understanding Early Civilizations: A Comparative Study, by Bruce G. Trigger (Book Review), *The International History Review* 26(2), 349–51.
    2006. Intensified Large-Scale Irrigation as an Aspect of Imperial Policy: Strategies of Statecraft on the Late Sassanian Mesopotamian Plain, in *Agricultural Strategies*, eds. J. Marcus & C. Stanish. Los Angeles: Cotsen Institute of Archaeology, 17–37.
    2012. Ancient Mesopotamian Urbanism and Blurred Disciplinary Boundaries, *Annual Review of Anthropology* 41, 1–20.

# Bibliography

Adams, R.M. & H.J. Nissen, 1972. *The Uruk Countryside*. Chicago: Chicago University Press.

Adams, W.M. & D.M. Anderson, 1988. Irrigation before Development: Indigenous and Induced Change in Agricultural Water Management in East Africa, *African Affairs* 87(349), 519–35.

Aitken, S.C. & M.-P. Kwan, 2009. GIS as Qualitative Research: Knowledge, Participatory Politics and Cartographies of Affect, in *The SAGE Handbook of Qualitative Geography*, eds. D. DeLyser, S. Herbert, S. Aitken, M.A. Crang & L. McDowell. London: SAGE, 287–304.

Al-Ansary, A.R., 1994. Arabia before Islam, in *History of Humanity Volume 3: From the Seventh Century BC to the Seventh Century AD*, eds. E. Condurachi, J. Herrman & E. Zurcher. Paris: UNESCO, 139–41.

Al-Ghulaibi, N.M.A., 2008. Traditional Water Harvesting on the Mountain Terraces of Yemen, in *What Makes Traditional Technologies Tick? A Review of Traditional Approaches for Water Management in Drylands*, eds. Z. Adeel, B. Schuster & H. Bigas. Hamilton, ON: United Nations University, 21–35.

Al-Hamdānī, Al-H. Ibn A., 1884–91 [945]. *Sifat Jazirat Al-Arab (Geographie Der Arabischen Halbinsel) Translated by D.H. Müller*, Leiden: Brill.

   1938 [945] *Al-Iklil (The Antiquities of South Arabia, Being a Translation from the Arabic with Linguistic, Geographic, and Historic Notes, of the Eighth Book)* Translated by N.A. Faris, Princeton, NJ: Princeton University Press.

Al-Khanbashi, S.U. & A.A. Badr, 2000. *Traditional Sayl Irrigation Systems in Do'an: Technologies, Laws, and Features (in Arabic)*. Mukalla, Yemen: Al-Manar.

Algaze, G., 2008. *Ancient Mesopotamia at the Dawn of Civilization*. Chicago: University of Chicago Press.

Allen, H., 1974. The Bagundji of Darling Basin: Cereal Gatherers in an Uncertain Environment, *World Archaeology* 5, 309–22.

Altaweel, M. & C.E. Watanabe, 2012. Assessing the Resilience of Irrigation Agriculture: Applying a Social-Ecological Model for Understanding the Mitigation of Salinization, *Journal of Archaeological Science* 39(4), 1160–71.

Amenta, A., M.M. Luiselli & M. No Sordi (eds.), 2005. *L'acqua nell'antico Egitto*. Rome: Bretschneider.

Ammerman, A.J. & L.L. Cavalli-Sforza, 1971. Measuring the Rate of Spread of Early Farming in Europe, *Man* 6(4), 674–88.

Andom, G. & M.K. Omer, 2003. Traditional cattle-husbandry systems in Eritrea: cattle–man relationships, *Journal of Arid Environments* 53(4), 545–56.

Anderson, K., 1993. Native Californians as Ancient and Contemporary Cultivators, in *Before the Wilderness: Environmental Management by Native Californians*, eds. T.C. Blackburn & K. Anderson. Menlo Park, CA: Ballena Press, 151–74.

Araus, J.L., A. Febrero, M. Catala, M. Molist & J. Votas, 1999. Crop Water Availability in Early Agriculture: Evidence from Carbon Isotope Discrimination of Seeds from a Tenth Millennium BP Site on the Euphrates, *Global Change Biology* 5, 201–12.

Arax, M. & R. Wartzman, 2005. *The King of California: J.G. Boswell and the Making of a Secret American Empire*. New York: Public Affairs.

# Bibliography

Arnaud, J.T., 1874. Plan de La Digue et de La Ville de Mareb, *Journal Asiatique* 7(3), 1–16.
Ascher, R., 1961. Analogy in Archaeological Interpretation, *Southwest Journal of Anthropology* 17, 317–25.
Ashmore, W., 2004. Social Archaeologies of Landscape, in *A Companion to Social Archaeology*, eds. L. Meskell & R.W. Preucel. London: Blackwell, 255–71.
Asouti, E. & D.Q. Fuller, 2013. A Contextual Approach to the Emergence of Agriculture in Southwest Asia, *Current Anthropology* 54(3), 299–345.
Avanzini, A., 2004. *Corpus of South Arabian Inscriptions I – III: Qatabanic, Marginal Qatabanic, Awsanite Inscriptions*. Pisa: Edizioni Plus, Università di Pisa.
  2008. The History of the Khor Rori Area: New Perspectives, in *A Port in Arabia Between Rome and the Indian Ocean (3rd C. BC to 5th C. AD)*, ed. A. Avanzini. Rome: L'erma di Bretschneider, 13–27.
  2010. A Reassessment of the Chronology of the First Millennium BC, *Aula Orientalis* 28, 181–92.
Bagg, A.M., 2012. Irrigation, in *A Companion to the Archaeology of the Ancient Near East*, ed. D.T. Potts. Hoboken, NJ: Wiley, 261–78.
Balescu, S., J.-F. Breton, Coque-Delhuille & M. Lamothe, 1998. La datation par luminescence des limons de crue: une nouvelle approche de l'etude chronologique de perimetres d'irrigation antiques du Sud-Yemen (Luminescence dating of flash flood deposits: a new approach for the chronological study of ancient irrigation, *Earth and Planetary Sciences* 327, 31–37.
Baquhaizel, S.A., I.A. Saeed & M.S. Bin Gouth, 1996. *Documentary Study on Models of Traditional Irrigation Systems and Methods of Water Harvesting in Hadramout and Shabwah Governates*. Sana'a, Yemen: Ministry of Water and the Environment.
Barber, B.R., 1995. *Jihad vs. McWorld: Terrorism's Challenge to Democracy*. New York, NY: Random House, Inc.
Barker, G., 2006. *The Agricultural Revolution in Prehistory: Why Did Foragers Become Farmers?* Oxford: Oxford University Press.
  2012. The Desert and the Sown: Nomad–Farmer Interactions in the Wadi Faynan, Southern Jordan, *Journal of Arid Environments* 86, 82–96.
Barker, G., D. Gilbertson & D. Mattingly, 2007. *Archaeology and Desertification: The Wadi Faynan Landscape Survey, Southern Jordan*. Oxford: Oxbow Books.
Barlow, M., 2007. *Blue Covenant: The Global Water Crisis and the Coming Battle for the Right to Water*. New York: The New Press.
  2014. *Blue Future: Protecting Water for People and the Planet Forever*. New York: The New Press.
Barlow, M. & T. Clarke, 2005. *Blue Gold: The Fight to Stop the Corporate Theft of the World's Water*. New York: The New Press.
Bar-Matthews, M. & A. Ayalon, 2003. Climatic Conditions in the Eastern Mediterranean during the Last Glacial (60-10 ky bp) and Their Relations to the Upper Palaeolithic in the Levant: Oxygen and Carbon Isotope Systematics of Cave Deposits, in *More Than Meets the Eye: Studies on Upper Palaeolithic Diversity in the Near East*, eds. A.N. Goring-Morris & A. Belfer-Cohen. Oxford: Oxbow Books, 13–18.

Barton, H., 2009. The Social Landscape of Rice within Vegecultural Systems in Borneo, *Current Anthropology* 50(5), 673–75.
Bar-Yosef, O., 1986. The Walls of Jericho: An Alternative Interpretation, *Current Anthropology* 27(2), 157–62.
  2011. Climatic Fluctuations and Early Farming in West and East Asia, *Current Anthropology* 52(S4), S175–S193.
  2013. The Origins of Agriculture in the Near East, *Backdirt: Annual Review of the Cotsen Institute of Archaeology at UCLA*, 46–53.
Bar-Yosef, O. & A. Khazanov (eds.), 1992. *Pastoralism in the Levant: Archaeological Materials in Anthropological Perspectives*. Madison, WI: Prehistory Press.
Başgöz, I., 2007. Rain Making Ceremonies in Iran, *Iranian Studies* 40(3), 385–403.
Bayman, J.M., 2001. The Hohokam of Southwest North America, *Journal of World Prehistory* 15(3), 257–311.
Bean, L.J. & H.W. Lawton, 1993. Some Explanations of the Rise of Cultural Complexity in Native California with Comments on Proto-Agriculture and Agriculture, in *Before the Wilderness: Environmental Management by Native Californians*, eds. T.C. Blackburn & K. Anderson. Menlo Park, CA: Ballena Press, 27–54.
Becker, H., J.W.E. Fassbinder & U. Brunner, 1999. The Discovery of the Royal Capital of Awsan at Hagar Yahirr, Wadi Markha, Yemen by Satellite Images, Aerial Photography, Field Walking and Magnetic Prospecting, in *Archaeological Prospection*, eds. J.W.E. Fassbinder & W.E. Irlinger. Munchen: Karl M. Lipp Verlag, 127–34.
Beeston, A.F.L., 1949. A Sabaean Boundary Formula, *Bulletin of the School of Oriental and African Studies* 13(1), 1–3.
  1955. The "Ta'lab Lord of Pastures" Texts, *Bulletin of the School of Oriental and African Studies* 17(1), 154–65.
  1962. Epigraphic and Archaeological Gleanings from South Arabia, *Oriens Antiqus* 1, 41–52.
  1972. Kingship in Ancient South Arabia, *Journal of Economic and Social History of the Orient* 15, 256–68.
  2005. The Arabian Aromatics Trade in Antiquity, *Proceedings of the Seminar for Arabian Studies* 53–64.
Bell, G.L., 1907. *The Desert and the Sown*. New York: E.P. Dutton and Company.
Bellwood, P., 2004. *First Farmers: The Origins of Agricultural Societies*. Oxford: Blackwell.
  2009. Rethinking the Origins of Agriculture: The Dispersals of Established Food-Producing Populations, *Current Anthropology* 50(5), 621–26.
  2013. *First Migrants: Ancient Migration in Global Perspective*. West Sussex, UK: Wiley Blackwell.
Benson, L.V., J.R. Stein & H.E. Taylor, 2009. Possible Sources of Archaeological Maize Found in Chaco Canyon and Aztec Ruin, New Mexico, *Journal of Archaeological Science* 36(2), 387–407.
Berger, G.W., T.K. Henderson, D. Banerjee & F.L. Nials, 2004. Photonic Dating of Prehistoric Irrigation Canals at Phoenix, Arizona, USA, *Geoarchaeology* 19(1), 1–19.

# Bibliography

Berger, G.W., S. Post & C. Wenker, 2009. Single and Multigrain Quartz-Luminescence Dating of Irrigation-Channel Features in Santa Fe, New Mexico, *Geoarchaeology* 24(4), 383–401.

Berger, J.-F., J.-P. Bravard, L. Purdue, A. Benoist, M. Mouton & F. Braemer, 2012. Rivers of the Hadramawt Watershed (Yemen) during the Holocene: Clues of Late Functioning, *Quaternary International* 266, 142–61.

Berking, J., B. Beckers & B. Schutt, 2010. Runoff in Two Semi-Arid Watersheds in a Geoarchaeological Context: A Case Study of Naga, Sudan and Resafa, Syria, *Geoarchaeology* 25(6), 815–36.

Bernbeck, R., 2012. The Political Dimension of Archaeological Practices, in *A Companion the Archaeology of the Ancient Near East*, ed. D.T. Potts. Hoboken, NJ: Wiley & Sons, 87–105.

Bernhardt, C.E., B.P. Horton & J. Stanley, 2012. Nile Delta Vegetation Response to Holocene Climate Variability, *Geology* 40(7), 615–18.

Bettinger, R., P. Richerson & R. Boyd, 2009. Constraints on the Development of Agriculture, *Current Anthropology* 50(5), 627–31.

Betts, A., 1989. The Solubba: Nomads Nonpastoral in Arabia, *Bulletin of the American Schools of Oriental Research* 274, 61–69.

Bhabha, H.K., 1994. *The Location of Culture*. New York: Routledge.

Binford, L.R., 1962. Archaeology as Anthropology, *American Antiquity* 28(2), 217–25.

1968. Methodological Considerations of the Archaeological Use of Ethnographic Data, in *Man the Hunter*, eds. R. Lee & I. DeVore. Chicago: Aldine Press, 268–73.

1972. Archaeological Reasoning and Smudge Pits Revisited, in *An Archaeological Perspective*, ed. L.R. Binford. New York: Seminar Press, 52–58.

1985. "Brand X" versus the Recommended Product, *American Antiquity* 50(3), 580–90.

2001. *Constructing Frames of Reference: An Analytical Method for Archaeological Theory Building Using Hunter-Gatherer and Environmental Data Sets*. Berkeley, CA: University of California Press.

Black, E., S. Mithen, B. Hoskins & R. Cornforth, 2010. Water and Society: Past, Present and Future, *Philosophical Transactions of the Royal Society A* 368(1931), 5107–10.

Blackburn, T. & K. Anderson, eds., 1993. *Before the Wilderness: Environmental Management by Native Californians*. Menlo Park, CA: Ballena Press.

Blake, E., 2004. Space, Spatiality, and Archaeology, in *A Companion to Social Archaeology*, eds. L. Meskell & R.W. Preucel. London: Blackwell, 230–54.

Boivin, N., D.Q. Fuller, R. Dennell, R. Allaby & M.D. Petraglia, 2013. Human Dispersal across Diverse Environments of Asia during the Upper Pleistocene, *Quaternary International* 300, 32–47.

Bolten, A., O. Bubenzer & F. Darius, 2006. A Digital Elevation Model as a Base for the Reconstruction of Holocene Land-Use Potential in Arid Regions, *Geoarchaeology* 21(7), 751–62.

Bongers, J., E. Arkush & M. Harrower, 2012. Landscapes of Death: GIS-based Analyses of Chullpas in the Western Lake Titicaca Basin, *Journal of Archaeological Science* 39(6), 1687–93.

Boucharlat, R., 2003. Iron Age Water-draining Galleries and the Iranian "Qanat," in *Archaeology of the United Arab Emirates*, eds. D.T. Potts, H. Al-Naboodah & P. Hellyer. Abu Dhabi, UAE: Trident Press, 162–72.

Bowen, R.L., 1958. Irrigation in Ancient Qataban (Beihan), in *Archaeological Discoveries in South Arabia*, eds. R.L. Bowen and F. P. Albright, Baltimore, MD: Johns Hopkins Press, 43–131.

Bowen, R.L. & F.P. Albright, 1958. *Archaeological Discoveries in South Arabia*. Baltimore, MD: Johns Hopkins University Press.

Boytner, R., L.S. Dodd & B.J. Parker (eds.), 2010. *Controlling the Past, Owning the Future: The Political Uses of Archaeology in the Middle East*. Tucson, AZ: University of Arizona Press.

Braemer, F., D. Genequand, C.D. Maridat, P.-M. Blanc, J.-M. Dentzer, D. Gazagne & P. Wech, 2009. Long-term Management of Water in the Central Levant: The Hawran Case (Syria), *World Archaeology* 41(1), 36–57.

Brass, M., 2013. Revisiting a Hoary Chestnut: The Nature of Early Cattle Domestication in North-East Africa, *Sahara* 24, 65–70.

Breman, H. & C.T. De Wit, 1983. Rangeland Productivity and Exploitation in the Sahel, *Science* 221(4618), 1341–47.

Breton, J.-F., 1991. Le site et la ville de Shabwa, *Syria* 68(1), 59–75.

1994. Hagar Yahirr, Capitale D'Awsan?, *Raydan* 6, 41–46.

1999. *Arabia Felix from the Time of the Queen of Sheba: Eighth Century B.C. to First Century A.D.* Notre Dame, ID: University of Notre Dame Press.

2000. The Wadi Surban (District of Bayhan, Yemen), *Proceedings of the Seminar for Arabian Studies* 30, 49–59.

2003. Preliminary Notes on the Development of Shabwa, *Proceedings of the Seminar for Arabian Studies* 33, 199–213.

Breton, J.-F. & A.A.-Q. Bafaqih, 1993. *Tresors Du Wadi Dura*. Paris: Institut Français du Proche-Orient.

2002. Le wadi Durâ': un modèle d'irrigation antique, *Chroniques Yéménites* 10.

Breton, J.-F., A.M. McMahon & D.A. Warburton, 1998. Two seasons at Hajar am-Dhaybiyya Yemen, *Arabian Archaeology and Epigraphy* 9(1), 90–111.

Brooks, K.N., P.F. Folliott & J.A. Magner, 2013. *Hydrology and the Management of Watersheds, 4th Edition*. Oxford, UK: Wiley-Blackwell.

Bruggeman, H.Y., 1997. *Agro-Climatic Resources of Yemen, Part 1*. Dhamar, Yemen: Ministry of Agriculture and Water Resources.

Brunner, U., 1983. *Die Erforschung de Antiken Oase Von Marib Mit Hilfe Geomorphologischer Untersuchungsmethoden*. Mainz: Verlag Philipp Von Zabern.

1997a. Geography and Human Settlements in Ancient Southern Arabia, *Arabian Archaeology and Epigraphy* 8(2), 190–202.

1997b. The History of Irrigation in Wadi Marhah, *Proceedings of the Seminar for Arabian Studies* 27, 75–85.

2000. The Great Dam and the Sabean Oasis of Ma'rib, *Irrigation and Drainage Systems* 14, 167–82.

2005. Water Management and Settlements in Ancient Eritrea. Water Management and Settlements in Ancient Eritrea, in *Afrikas Horn: Atken de Ersten Internationalen*. Weisbaden: Harrassowitz Verlag, 30–43.

# Bibliography

2008. Ancient Irrigation in Wadi Jirdan, Yemen, *Proceedings of the Seminar for Arabian Studies* 38, 75–87.

Brunner, U. & H. Haefner, 1986. The Successful Floodwater Farming System of the Sabeans: Yemen Arab Republic, *Applied Geography* 6, 77–86.

1990. Altsüdarabische Bewässerungsoasen, *Die Erde* 121, 135–52.

Bruno, M.C., 2009. Practice and History in the Transition to Food Production, *Current Anthropology* 50(5), 703–6.

Buffa, V., 2002. The Stratigraphic Sounding at Ma'layba, Lahj Province, Republic of Yemen, *Archaologische Berichte aus dem Yemen* 9, 1–14.

Bujra, A.S., 1971. *The Politics of Stratification: A Study of Political Change in a South Arabian Town*. Oxford: Clarendon Press.

Bulbeck, D., 2013. The Transition from Foraging to Farming in Prehistory and "Ethnography," *World Archaeology* 45(4), 557–73.

Burns, S.J., D. Fleitmann, A. Matter, J. Kramers & A. Al-Subbary, 2003. Indian Ocean Climate and Absolute Chronology over Dansgaard/Oeschger Events 9 to 13, *Science* 301, 1365–67.

Buskirk, W. & M.E. Opler, 1986. *The Western Apache: Living with the Land before 1950*. Norman: University of Oklahoma Press.

Butzer, K.W., 1976. *Early Hydraulic Civilization in Egypt*. Chicago: University of Chicago Press.

1981. Rise and Fall of Axum, Ethiopia: A Geo-Archaeological Interpretation, *American Antiquity* 46(3), 471–95.

1996. Irrigation, Raised Fields and State Management: Wittfogel Redux? (Book Review), *Antiquity* 70, 200–204.

Byrd, B.F., 2005. Reassessing the Emergence of Village Life in the Near East, *Journal of Archaeological Research* 13(3), 231–90.

Campbell, A.H., 1965. Elementary Food Production by the Australian Aborigines, *Mankind* 6(5), 206–11.

Castle, S.L., B.F. Thomas, J.T. Reager, M. Rodell, S.C. Swenson & J.S. Famiglietti, 2014. Groundwater Depletion during Drought Threatens Future Water Security of the Colorado River Basin, *Geophysical Research Letters* 41, 1–8.

Caton, S.C., 1990. *Peaks of Yemen I Summon: Poetry as Cultural Practice in a North Yemeni Tribe*. Berkeley, CA: University of California Press.

1999. *Lawrence of Arabia: A Film's Anthropology*. Berkeley, CA: University of California Press.

(ed.), 2013. *Yemen*. Santa Barbara, CA: ABC-CLIO.

Caton-Thompson, G., 1953. Some Palaeoliths from South Arabia, *Proceedings of the Prehistoric Society* 19(2), 189–218.

Caton-Thompson, G. & E.W. Gardner, 1939. Climate, Irrigation, and Early Man in the Hadhramaut, *The Geographical Journal* 93, 18–35.

Cattani, M. & S. Bökönyi, 2002. Ash-Shumah: An Early Holocene Settlement of Desert Hunters and Mangrove Foragers in the Yemeni Tihamah, in *Essays on the Late Prehistory of the Arabian Peninsula*, eds. S. Cleuziou, M. Tosi & J. Zarins. Roma: Instituto Italiano per l'Africa e l'Oriente, 3–53.

Charbonnier, J., 2009. Dams in the Western Mountains of Yemen: A Himyarite Model of Water Management, *Proceedings of the Seminar for Arabian Studies* 39, 81–94.

2011. The Distribution of Storage and Diversion Dams in the Western Mountains of South Arabia during the Himyarite Period, *Proceedings of the Seminar for Arabian Studies* 41, 35–46.

2012. Irrigation Systems from the Air: A Collection of Aerial Photographs from the Hadramawt and Wadi Bayhan Valleys, in *New Research in Archaeology and Epigraphy of South Arabia and Its Neighbors*. Moscow: The State Museum of Oriental Art, 155–64.

2014. In the Shadow of Palm Trees: Time Management and Water Allocation in the Oasis of Adam (Sultanate of Oman), *Proceedings of the Seminar for Arabian Studies* 44, 83–98.

Charbonnier, J. & J. Schiettecatte, 2013. Les Barrages de L'Arabie Méridionale Préislamique Architecture, Datation et Rapport au Pouvoir, in *Regards Croisés D'Orient et D'Occident: Les Barrages Dan L'Antiquité Tardive*, eds. C.J.R. François Baratte & et E. Rocca. Paris: Éditions de Boccard, 71–91.

Charles, M.P., C. Hoppé, G. Jones, A. Bogaard & J.G. Hodgson, 2003. Using Weed Functional Attributes for the Identification of Irrigation Regimes in Jordan, *Journal of Archaeological Science* 30(11), 1429–41.

Charpentier, V. & R. Crassard, 2013. Back to Fasad ... and the PPNB Controversy. Questioning a Levantine Origin for Arabian Early Holocene Projectile Points Technology, *Arabian archaeology and epigraphy* 36, 28–36.

Childe, V.G., 1952. *New Light on the Most Ancient East: The Oriental Prelude to European Prehistory*, 4th edition. New York, NY: W. W. Norton & Company.

Christaller, W., 1933. *Die Zentralen Orte in Süddeutschland*. Jena: Gustav Fischer.

Christian-Smith, J., H. Cooley & P.H. Gleick, 2012. Potential Water Savings Associated with Agricultural Water Efficiency Improvements: A Case Study of California, USA, *Water Policy* 14(2), 194.

Clark, V.A., 1976. Irrigation Terminology in Sabaean Inscriptions, *Abr-Nahrain* 16, 1–15.

Clarke, D.L., 1977. *Spatial Archaeology*. London: Academic Press.

Cleuziou, S., 1996. The Emergence of Oases and Towns in Eastern and Southern Arabia, in *The Prehistory of Asia and Oceania*, eds. G.E. Afanas'ev, S. Cleuziou, J.R. Lukacs & M. Tosi. Forli: UISPP, 159–65.

2007. Evolution toward Complexity in a Coastal Desert Environment: The Early Bronze Age in the Ja' alan, Sultanate of Oman, in *The Model-Based Archaeology of Socionatural Systems*, eds. T.A. Kohler & S.A. van der Leeuw (The Model-Based Archaeology of Socionatural Systems). Santa Fe, NM: School for Advanced Research, 209–27.

2009. Extracting Wealth from a Land of Starvation by Creating Social Complexity: A Dialogue between Archaeology and Climate?, *C.R. Geoscience* 341, 726–38.

Cleuziou, S., M-L. Inizan, B. Marcolongo, 1992. Le Peuplement pré-et protohistorique due système fluviatile fossile du Jawf-Hadramawt au Yémen (d'après l'interprétation d'images satellite, de photographies aériennes et de prospections). *Paléorient* 18(2): 5–29.

Cleuziou, S., & Tosi, M. 2007. In the Shadow of the Ancestors: The Prehistoric Foundations of the Early Arabian Civilization in Oman. Muscat: Sultanate of Oman, Ministry of Heritage and Culture.

# Bibliography

Close, A.E. & F. Wendorf, 1992. The Beginnings of Food Production in Eastern Sahara, in *Transitions to Agriculture in Prehistory*, eds. A.B. Gebauer & T.D. Price. Madison, WI: Prehistory Press.

Cohen, M.N., 2009. Introduction: Rethinking the Origins of Agriculture, *Current Anthropology* 50(5), 591–95.

Coleman, S. & P. von Hellermann (eds.), 2011. *Multi-Sited Ethnography: Problems and Possibilities in the Translocation of Research Methods.* New York: Routledge.

Cope, M.S. & S. Elwood (eds.), 2009. *Qualitative GIS: A Mixed Method Approach.* London: SAGE.

Coque-Delhuille, B. & P. Gentelle, 1998. Controlee des Perimetres d'Irrigation Antiques, in *Une Vallée Aride Du Yémen Antique: Le Wadi Bayhan*, eds. J.-F. Breton, J.C. Arramond, B. Coque-Delhuille & P. Gentelle. Paris: Editions Recherches sur les Civilisations, 87–94.

Coward, E.W., 1977. Irrigation Management Alternatives: Themes from Indigenous Irrigation Systems, *Agricultural Administration* 4, 223–37.

    1979. Principles of Social Organization in an Indigenous Irrigation System, *Human Organization* 38(1), 28–36.

Cowgill, G.L., 2004. Origins and Development of Urbanism: Archaeological Perspectives, *Annual Reviews of Anthropology* 33, 525–549.

Crassard, R., 2009a. Modalities and Characteristics of Human Occupations in Yemen during the Early/Mid-Holocene, *Comptes Rendus Geosciences* 341(8–9), 713–25.

    2009b. The Middle Paleolithic of Arabia: The View from the Hadramawt Region, Yemen, in *The Evolution of Human Populations in Arabia*, eds. M.D. Petraglia & J.I. Rose (Vertebrate Paleobiology and Paleoanthropology). Dordrecht: Springer Netherlands, 151–68.

Crassard, R. & P. Drechsler, 2013. Towards New Paradigms: Multiple Pathways for the Arabian Neolithic, *Arabian archaeology and epigraphy* 24, 3–8.

Crassard, R. & H. Hitgen, 2007. From Safer to Balhaf – Rescue Excavations along the Yemen LNG Pipeline Route, *Proceedings of the Seminar for Arabian Studies* 37, 1–17.

Crassard, R. & C. Thiébaut, 2011. Levallois points production from eastern Yemen and some comparisons with assemblages from East-Africa, Europe and the Levant, *Etudes et Recherches Archeologiques de l'Universite de Liege* 999, 1–14.

Crassard, R., J. McCorriston, E.A. Oches, A. Bin 'Aqil, J. Espagne & M. Sinnah, 2006. Manayzah, Early to Mid-Holocene Occupations in Wadi Sana (Hadramawt, Yemen), *Proceedings of the Seminar for Arabian Studies* 36, 151–73.

Crassard, R., M.D. Petraglia, N. Drake, P. Breeze, B. Gratuze, A. Alsharekh, M. Arbach, H.S. Groucutt, L. Khalidi, N. Michelsen, C.J. Robin & J. Schiettecatte, 2013a. Middle Palaeolithic and Neolithic Occupations around Mundafan Palaeolake, Saudi Arabia: Implications for Climate Change and Human Dispersals, *PloS one* 8(7), e69665.

Crassard, R., M.D. Petraglia, A.G. Parker, A. Parton, R.G. Roberts, Z. Jacobs, A. Alsharekh, A. Al-Omari, P. Breeze, N. Drake, H.S. Groucutt, R. Jennings, E. Régagnon & C. Shipton, 2013b. Beyond the Levant: First Evidence of a

Pre-Pottery Neolithic Incursion into the Nefud Desert, Saudi Arabia., *PloS one* 8(7), e68061.

Cremaschi, M. & F. Negrino, 2005. Evidence for an Abrupt Climatic Change at 8700 14C yr B.P. in Rockshelters and Caves of Gebel Qara (Dhofar-Oman): Palaeoenvironmental Implications, *Geoarchaeology* 20(6), 559–79.

Dahl, G. & G. Megersa, 1990. The Sources of Life: Boran Concepts of Wells and Water, in *From Water to World Making: African Models and Arid Lands*, ed. G. Palsson. Uppsala: The Scandinavian Institute of African Studies, 21–37.

D'Andrea, A.C., A. Manzo, M. Harrower & A. Hawkins, 2008. The Pre-Aksumite and Aksumite Settlement of Northeastern Tigrai, Ethiopia, *Journal of Field Archaeology* 33(2), 151–76.

Dansgaard, W., S.J. Johnsen, H.B. Clausen, D. Dahl-Jensen, N.S. Gundestrup, C.U. Hammer, C.S. Hvidberg, J.P. Steffensen, A.E. Sveinbjornsdottir, J. Jouzel & G. Bond, 1993. Evidence for General Instability of Past Climate from a 250-kyr Ice-Core Record, *Nature* 364, 218–20.

Darles, C., 2000. Les structures d'irrigation du Wadi Surban au Yemen, *Proceedings of the Seminar for Arabian Studies* 30, 87–97.

2008. Derniers résultats nouvelles datations et nouvelles données sur les fortifications de Shabwa (Hadramawt), *Proceedings of the Seminar for Arabian Studies* 38, 141–52.

Darles, C., C.J. Robin, J. Schiettecatte & A. de G. El-Masri, 2013. Contribution à une meilleure compréhension de l'Historie de la digue de Ma'rib au Yémen, in *Regards Croisés D'Orient et D'Occident: Les Barrages Dan L'Antiquité Tardive*, eds. F. Baratte, C.J. Robin & E. Rocca. Paris: Editions de Boccard, 9–70.

David, B. & J. Thomas, 2008. *Handbook of Landscape Archaeology*. Walnut Creek, CA: Left Coast Press.

Dawood, N.J. (ed.), 1969. *The Muqaddimah (An Introduction to History)* by A.Z. Ibn Khaldūn (1377), translated by F. Rosenthal, Princeton, NJ: Princeton University Press.

Deadman, W.M., 2012. Defining the Early Bronze Age Landscape: A Remote Sensing-based Analysis of Hafit Tomb Distribution in Wadi Andam, Sultanate of Oman, *Arabian Archaeology and Epigraphy* 23, 26–34.

De Chatel, F., 2007. *Water Sheikhs and Dam Builders: Stories of People and Water in the Middle East*. London: Transaction Publishers.

Delagnes, A., R. Crassard, P. Bertran & L. Sitzia, 2013. Cultural and Human Dynamics in Southern Arabia at the End of the Middle Paleolithic, *Quaternary International* 300, 234–43.

De Maigret, A., 1985. Archaeological Activities in the Yemen Arab Republic, 1985, *East and West* 35(1–3), 337–95.

1986. A Bronze Age for Southern Arabia, *East and West* 34(1–3), 75–106.

1990. *The Bronze Age Culture of Hawlan At-Tiyal and Al-Hada (Republic of Yemen)*. Rome: Ismeo.

1998. The Arab Nomadic People and the Cultural Interface between the "Fertile Crescent" and "Arabia Felix," *Arabian Archaeology and Epigraphy* 10(2), 220–24.

# Bibliography

2002. *Arabia Felix: An Exploration of the Archaeological History of Yemen.* London: Stacey International.

2003. Tamna', Ancient Capital of the Yemeni Desert. Information about the First Two Excavation Campaigns (1999, 2000), in *Arid Lands in Roman Times: Papers from the International Conference in Rome.* Firenze: All'insegna del giglio, 135–40.

2004. New Stratigraphical Data for the Ancient Chronology of Tamna, in *Scripta Yemenica*, eds. A.V. Sedov & M.B. Piotrovskii. Moskva: Vostochnaya Literatura, 242–56.

2005. *The Italian Archaeological Mission: An Appraisal of 25 Years Research (1980–2004).* Sana'a, Yemen: Yemeni-Italian Centre for Archaeological Research, Sana'a.

De Maigret, A. & C. Robin, 1989. Comptes Rendus de l'Académie des Inscriptions et Belles Lettres, in *Comptes Rendus de l'Académie Des Inscriptions et Belles Lettres*, 255–91.

Derricourt, R., 2005. Getting "Out of Africa": Sea Crossings, Land Crossings and Culture in the Hominin Migrations, *Journal of World Prehistory* 19(2), 119–32.

De Vries, D., P.W. Leslie & J.T. McCabe, 2006. Livestock Acquisitions Dynamics in Nomadic Pastoralist Herd Demography: A Case Study Among Ngisonyoka Herders of South Turkana, Kenya, *Human Ecology* 34(1), 1–25.

Dewar, R.E. & J.R. Wallis, 1999. Geographical Patterning of Interannual Rainfall Variability in the Tropics and Near Tropics: An L-Moments Approach, *Journal of Climate* 12, 3457–66.

Diamond, J., 1997. *Guns, Germs and Steel: The Fates of Human Societies.* New York: W.W. Norton and Co.

di Lernia, S., M.A. Tafuri, M. Gallinaro, F. Alhaique, M. Balasse, L. Cavorsi, P.D. Fullagar, A.M. Mercuri, A. Monaco, A. Perego & A. Zerboni, 2013. Inside the "African Cattle Complex": Animal Burials in the Holocene Central Sahara., *PloS one* 8(2), e56879.

Dingelstedt, V., 1916. Arabia and the Arabs, *Scottish Geographical Magazine* 22, 321–30.

Dixon, K.J., 2014. Historical Archaeologies of the American West, *Journal of Archaeological Research* 22, 177–228.

Doe, B., 1971. *Southern Arabia.* London: Thames and Hudson.

Doolittle, W.E., 2000. *Cultivated Landscapes of Native North America.* Oxford: Oxford University Press.

Dorshow, W.B., 2012. Modeling Agricultural Potential in Chaco Canyon during the Bonito Phase: A Predictive Geospatial Approach, *Journal of Archaeological Science* 39(7), 2098–2115.

Downing, T.E. & M. Gibson (eds.), 1974. *Irrigation's Impact on Society.* Tucson, AZ: The University of Arizona Press.

Drechsler, P., 2007. The Neolithic Dispersal into Arabia, *Proceedings of the Seminar for Arabian Studies* 37, 93–109.

2009. *The Dispersal of the Neolithic over the Arabian Peninsula.* Oxford: Archaeopress.

Drennan, R.D. & C.E. Peterson, 2004. Comparing Archaeological Settlement Systems with Rank-Size Graphs: A Measure of Shape and Statistical Confidence, *Journal of Archaeological Science* 31, 533–49.

2006. Patterned Variation in Prehistoric Chiefdoms, *Proceedings of the National Academy of Sciences* 103(11), 3960–67.

Dresch, P., 1984. The Position of Shaykhs Among the Northern Tribes of Yemen, *Man* 19(1), 31–49.

1986. The Significance of the Course Events Take in Segmentary Systems, *American Ethnologist* 13(2), 309–24.

1988. Segmentation: Its Roots in Arabia and its Flowering Elsewhere, *Cultural Anthropology* 3(1), 50–67.

1989. *Tribes, Government, and History in Yemen*. New York: Oxford University Press.

Dresch, P. & B. Haykel, 1995. Stereotypes and Political Styles: Islamists and Tribesfolk in Yemen, *International Journal of Middle East Studies* 27(4), 405–31.

Drewes, A.J., 2001. The Meaning of Sabaean MKRB, Facts and Fiction, *Semitica* 51, 93–125.

Dungan, J.L., J.N. Perry, M.R.T. Dale, P. Legendre, S. Citron-Pousty, M.-J. Fortin, A. Jakomulska, M. Miriti & M.S. Rosenberg, 2002. A Balanced View of Scale in Spatial Statistical Analysis, *Ecography* 25, 626–40.

Earle, T.K., 1980. Prehistoric Irrigation in the Hawaiian Islands: An Evaluation of Evolutionary Significance, *Archaeology and Physical Anthropology of Oceania* 15(1), 1–28.

Earle, T., 1997. *How Chiefs Come to Power*. Stanford, CA: Stanford University Press.

Earle, T. & D.E. Doyel, 2008. The Engineered Landscapes of Irrigation, in *Economies and the Transformation of Landscape*, eds. L. Cliggett & C.A. Pool. Lanham, MD: Altamira, 19–46.

Edens, C., 1999. The Bronze Age of Highland Yemen: Chronological and Spatial Variability of Pottery and Settlement, *Paleorient* 25(2), 105–28.

2005. Exploring Early Agriculture in the Highlands of Yemen, in *Sabaean Studies: Archaeological, Epigraphical, and Historical Studies in Honour of Yusuf Abdullah, Alessandro de Maigret, and Christian Robin on the Occasion of Their 60th Birthdays*, eds. A.M. Sholan, S. Antonini & M. Arbach. Naples and Sana'a: Sana'a University.

Edens, C. & T. Wilkinson, 1998. Southwest Arabia during the Holocene: Recent Archaeological Developments, *Journal of World Prehistory* 12(1), 55–119.

Edens, C., T.J. Wilkinson & G. Barratt, 2000. Hammat al-Qa and the Roots of Urbanism in Southwest Arabia, *Antiquity* 74, 854–62.

Egemi, O.A., 2000. Dryland Pastoralism among the Northern Bisharien of the Red Sea Hills, Sudan, in *Pastoralists and Environment: Experiences from the Greater Horn of Africa*, eds. L. Manger & A.G.M. Ahmed. Addis Ababa: Organization for Social Science Research in Eastern and Southern Africa, 113–26.

Ekstrom, H. & C. Edens, 2003. Prehistoric Agriculture in Highland Yemen: New Results from Dhamar, *Yemen Update: Bulletin of the American Institute for Yemeni Studies* 45, 23–35.

Elgabaly, M.M., 1977. Water in Arid Agriculture: Salinity and the Waterlogging in the Near-East Region, *Ambio* 6(1), 36–39.

# Bibliography

Emmons, D.M., 1971. *Garden in the Grasslands: Boomer Literature of the Great Plains*. Lincoln, NE: University of Nebraska Press.

Ertsen, M.W., 2010. Structuring properties of irrigation systems: Understanding relations between humans and hydraulics through modeling, *Water History* 2(2), 165–183.

Evans-Pritchard, E.E., 1940. *The Nuer: A Description of the Modes of Livelihood and Political Institutions of a Nilotic People*. Oxford: Clarendon Press.

1949. *The Sanusi of Cyrenacia*. Oxford: Oxford University Press.

Ewers, J., 1955. *The Horse in Blackfoot Indian Culture: With Comparative Material from Other Western Tribes*. Washington, D.C.: United States Government Printing Office.

Fagan, B., 2011. *Elixir: A History of Water and Humankind*. New York: Bloomsbury Press.

Fakhry, A., 1951. *An Archaeological Journey to Yemen (March-May 1947)*. Cairo: Government Press.

Falzon, M.-A. (ed.), 2009. *Multi-Sited Ethnography: Theory, Praxis and Locality in Contemporary Research*. Surrey, UK: Ashgate.

Faris, N.A., 1938. *The Antiquities of South Arabia, Being a Translation from the Arabic with Linguistic, Geographic, and Historic Notes, of the Eighth Book of Al-Hamdani's Al-Iklil*. Princeton, NJ: Princeton University Press.

Farquharson, F.A.K., D.T. Plinston & J.V Sutcliffe, 1996. Rainfall and Runoff in Yemen, *Hydrological Sciences Journal* 41(5), 797–811.

Faruqui, N.I., 2001. Islam and Water Management: Overview and Principles, in *Water Management in Islam*, eds. N.I. Faruqui, A.K. Biswas & M.J. Bino. Tokyo: United Nations University Press, 1–32.

Fedele, F., 2008. Wadi at-Tayyilah 3: a Neolithic and Pre-Neolithic occupation on the eastern Yemen Plateau, and its archaeofaunal information, *Proceedings of the Seminar for Arabian Studies* 38, 153–72.

2013. Neolithic Settlement of the Eastern Yemen Plateau: An Exploration of Locational Choice and Land Use, *Arabian Archaeology and Epigraphy* 24, 44–50.

Fedele, F.G., 2014. Camels, Donkeys and Caravan Trade: An Emerging Context from Baraqish, Ancient Yathill (Wadi al-Jawf, Yemen), *Anthropozoologica* 49(2), 25–42.

Feinman, G., 2011. *Comparative Frames for a Diachronic Analysis of Complex Societies: Next Steps*, in *Comparative Archaeology of Complex Societies*, ed. M.E. Smith. Cambridge: Cambridge University Press, 21–43.

Feldman, M., 2010. Object Agency? Spatial Perspective, Social Relations, and the Stele of Hammurabi, in *Agency and Identity in the Ancient Near East*, eds. S. Steadman & J. Ross. London: Equinox, 149–65.

Fergusson, J., 2015. Yemen is Tearing Itself Apart Over Water, *Newsweek*. (January 20, 2015).

Fernea, R., 1970. *Shaykh and Effendi: Changing Patterns of Authority among the El Shabana of Southern Iraq*. Cambridge, MA: Harvard University Press.

Ferrill, J.W., 1980. The Marginal Lands of Australia and the American West: Some Comparisons in their Perceptions and Settlement, in *The Process of Rural Transformation: Eastern Europe, Latin America and Australia*, eds. I. Volgyes, R.E. Lonsdale & W.P. Avery. Oxford: Pergamon Press, 68–85.

Ferrio, J.P., J.L. Araus, R. Buxó, J. Voltas & J. Bort, 2005. Water Management Practices and Climate in Ancient Agriculture: Inferences from the Stable Isotope Composition of Archaeobotanical Remains, *Vegetation History and Archaeobotany* 14, 510–17.

Field, J.S., M.D. Petraglia & M.M. Lahr, 2007. The Southern Dispersal Hypothesis and the South Asian Archaeological Record: Examination of Dispersal Routes through GIS Analysis, *Journal of Anthropological Archaeology* 26, 88–108.

Finlayson, B., J. Lovell, S. Smith & S.J. Mithen, 2011. The Archaeology of Water Management in the Jordan Valley from the Epipalaeolithic to the Nabataean, 21,000 BP (19,000 BC) to AD 106, in *Water, Life and Civilization: Climate, Environment and Society in the Jordan Valley*, eds. S.J. Mithen & E. Black. Cambridge: Cambridge University Press, 191–216.

Finlayson, C., 2013. The Water Optimisation Hypothesis and the Human Occupation of the Mid-Latitude Belt in the Pleistocene, *Quaternary International* 300, 22–31.

Finster, B., 2010. Arabia in Late Antiquity: An Outline of the Cultural Situation in the Peninsula at the Time of Muhammad, in *The Qur'an in Context: Historical and Literary Investigations into the Qur'anic Milieu*, eds. A. Neuwirth, N. Sinai & M. Marx. Boston, MA: Brill, 61–114.

Fish, S.K. & P.R. Fish, 2012. Hohokam Society and Water Management, in *Oxford Handbook of the Archaeology of Ritual and Religion*, ed. T.R. Pauketat. Oxford: Oxford University Press, 571–84.

Fish, S.K., P.R. Fish & M.E. Villalpando, 2007. *Trincheras Sites in Time, Space, and Society*. Tucson, AZ: University of Arizona Press.

Fishman, C., 2012. *The Big Thirst: The Secret Life and Turbulent Future of Water*. New York: Free Press.

Flannery, K., 1969. Origins and Ecological Effects of Early Domestication in Iran and the Near East, in *The Domestication and Exploitation of Plants and Animals*, eds. P. Ucko & G.W. Dimbleby. Chicago, IL: Aldine, 73–100.

1973. Archaeology With a Capital 'S', in *Research and Theory in Current Archaeology*, ed. C.L. Redman. New York: John Wiley and Sons, 47–58.

Flannery, K. & J. Marcus, 1996. Cognitive Archaeology, in *Contemporary Archaeology in Theory*, eds. R.W. Preucel & I. Hodder. Oxford, UK: Blackwell, 350–63.

2012. *The Creation of Inequality: How Our Prehistoric Ancestors Set the Stage for Monarchy, Slavery, and Empire*. Cambridge, MA: Harvard University Press.

Fleitmann, D., S.J. Burns, M. Mudelsee, U. Neff, J. Kramers, A. Mangini & A. Matter, 2003. Holocene Forcing of the Indian Monsoon Recorded in a Stalagmite from Southern Oman, *Science* 300, 1737–39.

Fletcher, R., D. Penny, D. Evans, C. Pottier, M. Barbetti, M. Kummu & T. Lustig, 2008. The Water Management Network of Angkor, Cambodia, *Antiquity* 82, 658–70.

Flohr, P., G. Muldner & E. Jenkins, 2011. Carbon Stable Isotope Analysis of Cereal Remains as a Way to Reconstruct Water Availability: Preliminary Results, *Water History* 3, 121–44.

Fogelin, L., 2007. Inference to the Best Explanation: A Common and Effective Form of Archaeological Reasoning, *American Antiquity* 72(4), 603–25.

## Bibliography

Fosbrooke, H.A., 1948. *An Administrative Survey of the Masai Social System*. Dar-es-Salaam, Tanzania: Tanganyika Notes and Records.

Frachetti, M.D., 2012. Multiregional Emergence of Mobile Pastoralism and Non-uniform Institutional Complexity across Eurasia, *Current Anthropology* 53(1), 2–38.

Francaviglia, V.M., 2000. Dating the Ancient Dam of Ma'rib (Yemen), *Journal of Archaeological Science* 27, 645–53.

2002. Some Remarks on the Irrigation Systems of Ancient Yemen, in *Essays on the Late Prehistory of the Arabian Peninsula*, eds. S. Cleuziou, M. Tosi & J. Zarins. Roma: Instituto Italiano per L'Africa e l'Oriente, 111–44.

Frantsouzoff, S.A., 2009. The Status of Sacred Pastures according to Sabaic Inscriptions, *Proceedings of the Seminar for Arabian Studies* 39, 155–61.

Fujii, S., 2007. Wadi Abu Tulayha and Wadi Ruweishid as-Sharqi: An Investigation of PPNB Barrage Systems in the Jafr Basin, *Neo-Lithics* 2/07, 6–16.

Fuller, D.Q., 2006. Agricultural Origins and Frontiers in South Asia: A Working Synthesis, *Journal of World Prehistory* 20, 1–86.

Fuller, D.Q., R.G. Allaby & C. Stevens, 2010. Domestication as Innovation: The Entanglement of Techniques, Technology and Chance in the Domestication of Cereal Crops, *World Archaeology* 42(1), 13–28.

Fuller, D.Q., G. Willcox & R.G. Allaby, 2011. Cultivation and Domestication Had Multiple Origins: Arguments against the Core Area Hypothesis for the Origins of Agriculture in the Near East, *World Archaeology* 43(4), 628–52.

2012. Early Agricultural Pathways: Moving outside the "Core Area" Hypothesis in Southwest Asia, *Journal of Experimental Botany* 63(2), 617–33.

Fuller, D.Q., T. Denham, M. Arroyo-kalin, L. Lucas, C.J. Stevens, L. Qin & R.G. Allaby, 2014. Convergent Evolution and Parallelism in Plant Domestication Revealed by an Expanding Archaeological Record, *Proceedings of the National Academy of Sciences* 111(17), 6147–52.

Gajda, I. & M. Maraqten, 2010. A South Arabian Dedicatory Inscription from the Kingdom of Kaminahu, *Semitica et Classica* 3, 235–39.

Galili, E. & Y. Nir, 1993. The Submerged Pre-Pottery Neolithic Water Well of Atlit-Yam, Northern Israel, and its Palaeoenvironmental Implications, *The Holocene* 3, 265–70.

Garbini, G., 1992. Le iscrizioni su ceramica da ad-Durayb-Yalâ, Yemen, *Studi archeologici, storici e filologici sull'Arabia meridionale* 1, 79–92.

Garcia, A., 2013. GIS-based Methodology for Palaeolithic Site Location Preferences Analysis. A Case Study from Late Palaeolithic Cantabria (Northern Iberian Peninsula), *Journal of Archaeological Science* 40(1), 217–26.

Garfinkel, Y., A. Vered & O. Bar-Yosef, 2006. The Domestication of Water: The Neolithic Well at Sha'ar Hagolan, Jordan Valley, Israel, *Antiquity* 80, 686–96.

Gebel, H.G.K. & S. Fujii, 2010. The Domestication of Water: A Short Introduction, *Neo-Lithics* 2, 3–4.

Geertz, C., 1968 *Islam Observed: Religious Development in Morocco and Indonesia*. Chicago: University of Chicago Press.

1972. The Wet and the Dry: Traditional Irrigation in Bali and Morocco, *Human Ecology* 1(1), 23–39.

Gentelle, P., 1991. Les Irrigations Antiques a Shabwa, *Syria* 68, 5–54.

1998. La nature et l'irrigation, in *Une Vallée Aride Du Yémen Antique: Le Wadi Bayhan*, eds. J.-F. Breton, J.C. Arramond, B. Coque-Delhuille & P. Gentelle. Paris: Editions Recherche et Civilizations, 75–85.

Gerlach, I., 2005. Sirwah: New Research at the Sabaean City and Oasis, in *Caravan Kingdoms: Yemen and the Ancient Incense Trade*, ed. A. Gunter. Washington, D.C.: Smithsonian.

Giddens, A., 1984. *The Constitution of Society: Outline of the Theory of Structuration*. Cambridge, UK: Polity Press.

Gilbert, A.S., 1983. On the Origins of Specialized Nomadic in Western Pastoralism Iran, *World Archaeology* 15(1), 105–19.

Gillings, M., 1995. Flood Dynamics and Settlement in the Tisza Valley of North-east Hungary: GIS and the Upper Tisza Project, in *Archaeology and Geographical Information Systems: A European Perspective*, eds. G.R. Lock & Z. Stancic. London: Taylor and Francis, 67–84.

2012. Landscape Phenomenology, GIS and the Role of Affordance, *Journal of Archaeological Method and Theory* 19, 601–11.

Gillmore, G.K., R.A.E. Coningham, H. Fazeli, R.L. Young, M. Magshoudi, C.M. Batt & G. Rushworth, 2009. Irrigation on the Tehran Plain, Iran: Tepe Pardis — The Site of a Possible Neolithic Irrigation Feature?, *Catena* 78(3), 285–300.

Glanzman, W.D., 1994. *Toward a Classification and Chronology of Pottery from HR3 (Hajar Ar-Rayhani), Wadi Al-Jubah, Republic of Yemen, PhD Dissertation*. Philadelphia, PA: University of Pennsylvania.

Glaser, E., 1913. *Edward Glaser's Reise Nach Marib*, eds. D.H. von Muller and N. Rhodokanakis. Vienna: Alfred Holder, 1913.

Gleick, P.H., 1994. Water, War and Peace in the Middle East, *Environment: Science and Policy for Sustainable Development* 36(3), 6–42.

2014a. *The World's Water Volume 8: The Biennial Report on Freshwater Resources*. Washington, D.C.: Island Press.

2014b. The Syrian Conflict and the Role of Water, in *The World's Water Volume 8" The Biennial Report on Freshwater Resources*, ed. P.H. Gleick. Washington, D.C.: Island Press, 147–52.

Gleick, P.H., J. Christian-Smith & H. Cooley, 2011. Water-Use Efficiency and Productivity: Rethinking the Basin Approach, *Water International* 36(7), 784–98.

Glennon, R., 2010. *Unquenchable: America's Water Crisis and What to Do About It*. Washington, D.C.: Island Press.

Goring-Morris, N. & L.K. Horwitz, 2007. Funerals and Feasts during the Pre-Pottery Neolithic B of the Near East, 81, 902–19.

Gorsdorf, J. & B. Vogt, 2001. Excavations at Ma'Layba and Sabir, Republic of Yemen: Radiocarbon Datings in the Period 1900 to 800 cal BC, *Radiocarbon* 43(3), 1353–61.

Gremillion, K.J. & D.R. Piperno, 2009. Human Behavioral Ecology, Phenotypic (Developmental) Plasticity, and Agricultural Origins, *Current Anthropology* 50(5), 615–19.

Gremillion, K.J., L. Barton & D.R. Piperno, 2014. Particularism and the Retreat from Theory in the Archaeology of Agricultural Origins, *Proceedings of the National Academy of Sciences of the United States of America* 111(17), 6171–77.

# Bibliography

Grossman, J.R. (ed.), 1994. *The Frontier in American Culture*. Berkeley, CA: University of California Press.

Hackenberg, R.A., 1962. Economic Alternatives in Arid Lands: A Case Study of the Pima and Papago Indians, *Ethnology* 1(2), 186–96.

Haggett, P., 1966. *Locational Analysis in Human Geography*. New York: St. Martin's Press.

Haines, F., 1938a. Where Did the Plains Indians Get their Horses?, *American Anthropologist* 40(1), 112–17.

1938b. The Northward Spread of Horses among the Plains Indians, *American Anthropologist* 40(3), 429–37.

Al-Hakimi, A. & F. Pelat (eds.), 2003. *Indigenous Knowledge and Sustainable Agriculture in Yemen*. Sana'a, Yemen: Center Francais d'Archeologie et de Sciences Sociales de Sana'a.

Hall, S.A., 2010. Early Maize Pollen from Chaco Canyon, New Mexico, USA, *Palynology* 34(1), 125–37.

Haraway, D.J., 1991. Situated Knowledges: The Science Question in Feminism and the Privilege of Partial Perspective, in *Simians, Cyborgs, and Women: The Reinvention of Nature*, ed. D.J. Haraway. New York: Routledge, 183–202.

Hard, R.J., J.E. Zapata, B.I.Z. Moses & J.R. Roney, 1999. Terrace Construction in Northern Chihuahua, Mexico: 1150 B.C. and Modern Experiments, *Journal of Field Archaeology* 26, 129–46.

Hard, R.J. & J.R. Roney, 2007. Cerros de Trincheras in Northwestern Chihuahua: The Arguments for Defense, in *Trincheras Sites in Time, Space, and Society*, eds. S.K. Fish, P.R. Fish & M.E. Villalpando. Tucson, AZ: University of Arizona Press, 11–52.

Hard, R.J., K.R. Adams, J.R. Roney, K.M. Schmidt & G.J. Fritz, 2008. The Emergence of Maize Farming in Northwest Mexico, in *Case Studies in Environmental Archaeology*, eds. E. Reitz, S.J. Scudder & C.M. Scarry. New York: Springer, 315–33.

Harlan, J.R., 1971. Agricultural Origins: Centers and Noncenters, *Science* 29, 468–74.

Harris, D.R., 1989. An Evolutionary Continuum of People-Plant Interaction, in *Foraging and Farming: The Evolution of Plant Exploitation*, eds. D.R. Harris & G.C. Hillman. London: Unwin Hyman, 11–26.

Harrower, M.J., 2006. *Environmental versus Social Parameters, Landscape, and the Origins of Irrigation in Southwest Arabia (Yemen), PhD Dissertation*. Columbus, Ohio: The Ohio State University.

2008a. Hydrology, Ideology, and the Origins of Irrigation in Ancient Southwest Arabia (Yemen), *Current Anthropology* 49(3), 497–510.

2008b. Mapping and Dating Incipient Irrigation in Wadi Sana, Hadramawt (Yemen), *Proceedings of the Seminar for Arabian Studies* 38, 187–202.

2009. Is the Hydraulic Hypothesis Dead yet? Irrigation and Social Change in Ancient Yemen, *World Archaeology* 41(1), 58–72.

2010. Geographic Information Systems (GIS) Hydrological Modeling in Archaeology: An Example from the Origins of Irrigation in Southwest Arabia (Yemen), *Journal of Archaeological Science* 37(7), 1447–52.

Harrower, M.J. & A.C. D'Andrea, 2014. Landscapes of State Formation: Geospatial Analysis of Aksumite Settlement Patterns (Ethiopia), *African Archaeological Review* 31(3): 513–541.

Harrower, M., J. McCorriston & A.C. D'Andrea, 2010. General/Specific, Local/Global: Comparing the Beginnings of Agriculture in the Horn of Africa (Ethiopia/Eritrea) and Southwest Arabia (Yemen), *American Antiquity* 75(3), 452–72.

Harrower, M., J. McCorriston & E.A. Oches, 2002. Mapping the Roots of Agriculture in Southern Arabia: The Application of Satellite Remote Sensing, Global Positioning System and Geographic Information System Technologies, *Archaeological Prospection* 9, 35–42.

Harrower, M., E.A. Oches & J. McCorriston, 2012. Hydro-Geospatial Analysis of Ancient Pastoral/Agro-Pastoral Landscapes along Wadi Sana (Yemen), *Journal of Arid Environments* 86, 131–38.

Harrower, M., J. Schuetter, J. McCorriston, P. Goel & M. Senn, 2013. *Survey, Automated Detection, and Spatial Distribution Analysis of Cairn Tombs in Ancient Southern Arabia*, in, eds. D.C. Comer & M.J. Harrower. New York: Springer, 249–59.

Harrower, M., M. Senn & J. McCorriston, 2014a. Tombs, Triliths and Oases: Spatial Analysis of The Arabian Human Social Dynamics Project (AHSD) Archaeological Survey 2009–2010, *Journal of Oman studies* 18, 145–151.

Harrower, M.J., K.M.O. Meara, J.J. Basile, C.J. Hickman, J.L. Swerida, I.A. Dumitru, J.L. Bongers, C.J. Bailey & E. Fieldhouse, 2014b. If a Picture Is Worth a Thousand Words... 3D Modelling of a Bronze Age Tower in Oman, *World Archaeology* 46(1), 43–62.

Hassan, F., 1997. The Dynamics of a Riverine Civilization: A Geoarchaeological Perspective on the Nile Valley, Egypt, *World Archaeology* 29(1), 51–74.

Hatke, G., 2012. Holy Land and Sacred History: A View from Early Ethiopia, in *Visions of Community in the Post-Roman World: The West, Byzantium and the Islamic World, 300–1100*, eds. W. Pohl, C. Gantner & R. Payne. Surrey: Ashgate, 259–75.

Hayden, B., 2003. Were Luxury Foods the First Domesticates? Ethnoarchaeological Perspectives from Southeast Asia, *World Archaeology* 34(3), 458–69.

2009. The Proof Is in the Pudding: Feasting and the Origins of Domestication, *Current Anthropology* 50(5), 597–601.

Headland, T.N. & L.A. Reid, 1989. Hunter-Gatherers and Their Neighbors from to the Prehistory Present, *Current Anthropology* 30(1), 43–66.

Hehmeyer, I., 1989. Irrigation Farming in the Ancient Oasis of Marib, *Proceedings of the Seminar for Arabian Studies* 19, 33–44.

2008. Water and Sign Magic in al-Jabin, Yemen, *The American Journal of Islamic Social Sciences* 25(3), 82–96.

Hehmeyer, I. & J. Schmidt, 1991. *Antike Technologie-Die Sabaische Wasserwirtschaft von Marib*. Mainz: Verlag Philipp Von Zabern.

Heine, R.A., C.L. Lant & R.R. Sengupta, 2004. Development and Comparison of Approaches for Automated Mapping of Stream Channel Networks, *Annals of the Association of American Geographers* 94(3), 477–90.

Helbaek, H., 1960. Ecological Effects of Irrigation in Ancient Mesopotamia, *Iraq* 22, 186–96.

# Bibliography

Hendrickx, S. and F. Forster, 2010. Early Dynastic Art and Iconography, in *A Companion to Ancient Egypt*, ed. A.B. Lloyd, London: Wiley Blackwell, 826–852.

Henton, E., J. McCorriston, L. Martin & E.A. Oches, 2014. Seasonal Aggregation and Ritual Slaughter: Isotopic and Dental Microwear Evidence for Cattle Herder Mobility in the Arabian Neolithic, *Journal of Anthropological Archaeology* 33, 119–31.

Hijmans, R.J., S.E. Cameron, J.L. Parra, P.G. Jones & A. Jarvis, 2005. Very High Resolution Interpolated Climate Surfaces for Global Land Areas, *International Journal of Climatology* 25(15), 1965–78.

Hildebrandt, A., M. Al Aufi, M. Amerjeed, M. Shammas & E.A.B. Eltahir, 2007. Ecohydrology of a Seasonal Cloud Forest in Dhofar: 1. Field Experiment, 43, 1–13.

Ho, E., 2006. *The Graves of Tarim: Genealogy and Mobility across the Indian Ocean.* Berkeley, CA: California University Press.

Hodder, I., 1986. *Reading the Past: Current Approaches to Interpretation in Archaeology.* Cambridge: Cambridge University Press.

2007. Catalhoyuk in the Context of the Middle Eastern Neolithic, *Annual Reviews of Anthropology* 36, 105–20.

2011. The Role of Religion in the Neolithic of the Middle East and Anatolia with Particular Reference to Catalhoyuk, *Paleorient* 37, 111–22.

Honeychurch, W., 2014. Alternative Complexities: The Archaeology of Pastoral Nomadic States, *Journal of Archaeological Research* 22, 277–326.

Howe, L., 2006. Perfect Order: Recognizing Complexity in Bali (Book Review). *Anthropological Quarterly* 79(4), 777–782.

Hoyland, R.G., 2001. *Arabia and the Arabs: From the Bronze Age to the Coming of Islam.* New York: Routledge.

Hritz, C., 2010. Tracing Settlement Patterns and Channel Systems in Southern Mesopotamia Using Remote Sensing, *Journal of Field Archaeology* 35(2), 184–203.

Hritz, C. & T.J. Wilkinson, 2006. Using Shuttle Radar Topography to Map Ancient Water Channels in Mesopotamia, *Antiquity* 80, 415–24.

Hull, E.J., 2011. *High-Value Target: Countering Al-Qaeda in Yemen.* Washington, D.C.: Potomac Books.

Hundley, N., 2001. *The Great Thirst: Californians and Water: A History*, Revised Edition. Berkeley, CA: University of California Press.

2009. *Water and the West: The Colorado River Compact and the Politics of Water in the American West*, 2nd Edition. Berkeley, CA: University of California Press.

Hunt, R.C., 1988. Size and the Structure of Authority in Canal Irrigation Systems, *Journal of Anthropological Research* 44(4), 335–55.

1989. Appropriate Social Organization? Water User Associations in Bureaucratic Canal Irrigation Systems, *Human Organization* 48(1), 79–90.

2007. *Beyond Relativism: Comparability in Cultural Anthropology.* Lanham, MD: Altamira Press.

Hunt, R.C. & E. Hunt, 1976. Canal Irrigation and Local Social Organization, *Current Anthropology* 17(3), 389–411.

Hunt, R.C., D. Guillet, D.R. Abbott, J. Bayman, P.R. Fish, S.K. Fish, K. Kintigh & J.A. Neely, 2005. Plausible Ethnographic Analogies for the Social Organization of Hohokam Canal Irrigation, *American Antiquity* 70(3), 433–56.

Huntington, S.P., 1996. *The Clash of Civilizations and the Remaking of World Order*. New York: Touchstone.

Huot, J.-L., 1989. 'Ubaidian Village of Lower Mesopotamia: Permanence and Evolution from 'Ubaid o to "Ubaid 4 as seen from Tell el"Oueili, in *Upon This Foundation: The 'Ubaid Reconsidered*, eds. E.F. Henrickson & I. Thuesen. Copenhagen: Museum Tusculanum Press, 19–42.

Inizan, M.L., 1980. Sur les industries a lames de Qatar., *Paleorient* 6, 233–36.

Inizan, M.-L., 1988. *Préhistorie À Qatar, Mission Archéologique Française À Qatar*. Paris: Editions Recherche sur les Civilizations.

Inizan, M.-L., A.-M. Lezine, B. Marcolongo, J.-F. Saliege, C. Robert & F. Werth, 1997. Paleolacs et Peuplements Holocenes due Yemen: Le Ramlat As-Sabat'ayn, *Paleorient* 23(2), 137–49.

Iriarte, J., 2009. Narrowing the Gap: Exploring the Diversity of Early Food-Production Economies in the Americas, *Current Anthropology* 50(5), 677–80.

Jacobsen, T. & R.M. Adams, 1958. Salt and Silt in Ancient Mesopotamian Agriculture, *Science* 128(3334), 1251–58.

Jackson, J.B., 1951. The Need of Being Versed in Country Things, *Landscape* 1, 1–5.

— 1980. *The Necessity for Ruins: And Other Topics*. Amherst, MA: The University of Massachusetts Press.

Janzen, J., 1986. *Nomads in the Sultanate of Oman: Tradition and Development in Dhofar*. Boulder, CO: Westview Press.

— 2000. The Destruction of Resources among the Mountain Nomads of Dhofar, in *The Transformation of Nomadic Society in the Arab East*, eds. M. Mundy & B. Musllam. Cambridge: Cambridge University Press, 160–76.

Johnson, G.A., 1972. A Test of the Utility of Central Place Theory in Archaeology, in *Man, Settlement, and Urbanism*, eds. P.J. Ucko, R. Tringham & G.W. Dimbleby. London: Duckworth, 769–85.

— 1977. Aspects of Regional Analysis in Archaeology, *Annual Reviews of Anthropology* 6, 479–508.

— 1980. Rank-Size Convexity and Systems Integration: A View from Archaeology, *Economic Geography* 56(3), 234–47.

— 1982. Organizational Structure and Scalar Stress, in *Theory and Explanation in Archaeology: The Southampton Conference*, eds. C. Renfrew, M.J. Rowlands & B.A. Segraves. New York: Academic Press, 389–421.

Johnson, G.D., 2012. *The Last Refuge: Yemen, Al-Qaeda, and America's War in Arabia*. New York, NY: W. W. Norton & Company.

Jones, E.E., 2006. Using Viewshed Analysis to Explore Settlement Choice: A Case Study of the Onondaga Iroquois, *American Antiquity* 71(3), 523–38.

Jones, G., M. Charles, A. Bogaard, J.G. Hodgson & C. Palmer, 2005. The Functional Ecology of Present-Day Arable Weed Floras and Its Applicability for the Identification of Past Crop Husbandry, *Vegetation History and Archaeobotany* 14, 493–504.

Jones, G., M. Charles, A. Bogaard & J. Hodgson, 2010. Crops and Weeds: The Role of Weed Functional Ecology in the Identification of Crop Husbandry Methods, *Journal of Archaeological Science* 37(1), 70–77.

# Bibliography

Kahrl, W.L., 1983. *Water and Power: The Conflict over Los Angeles Water Supply in the Owens Valley*. Berkeley, CA: University of California Press.

Kapel, H., 1967. *Atlas of Stone Age Cultures of Qatar*. Aarhus: JASP.

Kelly, R.L., 1995. *The Foraging Spectrum: Diversity in Hunter-Gatherer Lifeways*. Washington, D.C.: Smithsonian Institution Press.

Kelly, W.W., 1983. Concepts in the Anthropological Study of Irrigation, *American Anthropologist* 85(4), 880–86.

Kemp, B.M., A. González-oliver, R.S. Malhi, C. Monroe & K. Britt, 2010. Evaluating the Farming / Language Dispersal Hypothesis with Genetic Variation Exhibited by Populations in the Southwest and Mesoamerica, *Proceedings of the National Academy of Sciences* 107(15), 6759–64.

Kennett, D. & B. Winterhalder, 2006. *Behavioral Ecology and the Transition to Agriculture*. Berkeley, CA: University of California Press.

Kirch, P. V, 1994. *The Wet and the Dry: Irrigation and Agricultural Intensification in Polynesia*. Chicago, IL: University of Chicago Press.

Kirkbride, D., 1974. Umm Dabaghiyah: A Trading Outpost?, *Iraq* 36(1), 85–92.

Kliot, N., 1993. *Water Resources and Conflict in the Middle East*. London: Routledge.

Knysh, A., 1997. The Cult of Saints and Religious Reformism in Hadhramaut, in *Hadhrami Traders, Scholars and Statesmen in the Indian Ocean, 1750's–1960's*, eds. U. Freitag & W. Clarence-Smith. Leiden, The Netherlands: E.J. Brill, 199–216.

Kroeber, A.L., 1935. *Walapai Ethnography*. Sante Fe, NM: Memoirs of the American Anthropological Association.

Kuijt, I., 2009. What Do We Really Know about Food Storage, Surplus, and Feasting in Preagricultural Communities?, *Current Anthropology* 50(5), 641–44.

Kuijt, I., B. Finlayson & J. Mackay, 2007. Pottery Neolithic Landscape Modification at Dhra ', *Antiquity* 81, 106–18.

Kühn, P., D. Pietsch & I. Gerlach, 2010. Archaeopedological Analyses around a Neolithic Hearth and the Beginning of Sabaean Irrigation in the Oasis of Ma'rib (Ramlat as-Sab'atayn, Yemen), *Journal of Archaeological Science* 37, 1305–10.

Kvamme, K., 1985. Determining Empirical Relationships between the Natural Environment and Prehistoric Site Locations, in *For Concordance in Archaeological Analysis*, ed. C. Carr. Arkansas: Westport Publishers, 208–39.

2006. There and Back Again: Revisiting Archaeological Locational Modeling, in *GIS and Archaeological Site Location Modeling*, eds. M.W. Mehrer & K.L. Wescott. Boca Raton, FL: CRC Press, 4–34.

Larson, G., D.R. Piperno, R.G. Allaby, M.D. Purugganan & L. Andersson, 2014. Current Perspectives and the Future of Domestication Studies, *PNAS – Proceedings of the National Academy of Sciences of the United States of America* 111(17), 6139–46.

Latz, P., 2004. *Bushfires and Bushtucker: Aboriginal Plant Use Central Australia*. Alice Springs, NT: IAD Press.

Lawton, H.W. et al., 1976. Agriculture among the Paiute of Owens Valley, *Journal of California Anthropology* 3(1), 13–50.

Lees, S.H., 1994. Irrigation and Society, *Journal of Archaeological Research* 2(4), 361–78.

Lees, S.H. & D. Bates, 1974. Origins of Specialized Nomadic Pastoralism: A Systemic Model, *American Antiquity* 39(2), 187–93.

Lefebvre, H., 1974. *La Production de L'espace*. Paris: Anthropos.

Lancaster, W. & F. Lancaster, 1999. *People, Land and Water in the Arab Middle East: Environments and Landscapes in the Bilad Ash-Sham*. Amsterdam, The Netherlands: Harwood Academic Publishers.

Lane, E.W., 1955. The Importance of Fluvial Morphology in Hydraulic Engineering, *Proceedings American Society of Civil Engineers* 81(745).

Lansing, J.S., 2006. *Perfect Order: Recognizing Complexity in Bali*. Princeton, NJ: Princeton University Press.

Lansing, S., 1991. *Priests and Programmers: Technologies of Power in the Engineered Landscape of Bali*. Princeton, NJ: Princeton University Press.

Le Houérou, H.N., 1980. The Rangelands of the Sahel, *Journal of Range Management* 33(1), 41–46.

Le Houérou, H.N. & C.H. Hoste, 1977. Rangeland Production and Annual Rainfall Relations in the Mediterranean Basin and in the African Sahelo-Sudanian Zone, *Journal of Range Management* 30(3), 181–89.

Le Houérou, H.N., R.L. Bingham & W. Skerbek, 1988. Relationship between the Variability of Primary Production and the Variability of Annual Precipitation in World Arid Lands, *Journal of Arid Environments* 15, 1–18.

Levy, T.E., 1983. The Emergence of Specialized Pastoralism in the Southern Levant, *World Archaeology* 15(1), 15–36.

Lézine, A.-M., 2009. Timing of Vegetation Changes at the End of the Holocene Humid Period in Desert Areas at the Northern Edge of the Atlantic and Indian Monsoon Systems, *Comptes Rendus Geoscience* 341(8–9), 750–59.

Lézine, A.-M., C. Robert, S. Cleuziou, M.-L. Inizan, F. Braemer, J.-F. Saliege, F. Sylvestre, J.-J. Tiercelin, R. Crassard, S. Mery, V. Charpentier, T. Steimer-Herbet, A.M. Lézine, C. Robert, S. Cleuziou, M.L. Inizan, F. Braemer, J.F. Saliège, F. Sylvestre, J.J. Tiercelin, R. Crassard, S. Méry, V. Charpentier & T. Steimer-Herbet, 2010. Climate Change and Human Occupation in the Southern Arabian Lowlands during the Last Deglaciation and the Holocene, *Global and Planetary Change* 72, 412–28.

Libecap, G.D. 2007. *Owens Valley Revisted: A Reassessment of the West's First Great Water Transfer*. Stanford: Stanford University Press.

Lichtenthäler, G., 2003. *Political Ecology and the Role of Water: Environment, Society and Economy in Northern Yemen*. Aldershot, UK: Ashgate.

Limbert, M.E., 2001. The Senses of Water in an Omani Town, *Social Text* 19(3), 35–55.

Limbert, M., 2010. *In the Time of Oil: Piety, Memory and Social Life in an Omani Town*. Stanford: Stanford University Press.

Limerick, P.N., 1987. *The Legacy of Conquest: The Unbroken Past of the American West*. New York: Norton.

Linseele, V., 2010. Did Specialized Pastoralism Develop Differently in Africa than in the Near East? An Example from the West African Sahel, *Journal of World Prehistory* 23(2), 43–77.

Llobera, M., 2012. Life on a Pixel: Challenges in the Development of Digital Methods Within an "Interpretive" Landscape Archaeological Framework, *Journal of Archaeological Method and Theory* 19, 495–509.

Logan, A.L., C.A. Hastorf & D.M. Pearsall, 2012. "Let's Drink Together": Early Ceremonial Use of Maize in the Titicaca Basin, *American Antiquity* 23(3), 235–58.

Loundine, A.G., 1989. Les Inscriptions du Jabal al-'Amud et le Conseil des Anciens de Saba, *Proceedings of the Seminar for Arabian Studies* 19, 93–97.

Lucero, L.J., 1999. Water Control and Maya Politics in the Southern Maya Lowlands, in *Complex Polities in the Ancient Tropical World*, eds. L.J. Lucero & E.A. Bacus, Archaeological Papers of the American Anthropological Association 9, 34–49.

2003. The Politics of Ritual: The Emergence of Classic Maya Rulers, *Current Anthropology* 44(4), 523–58.

2006. *Water and Ritual: The Rise and Fall of Classic Maya Rulers*. Austin, TX: University of Texas Press.

Lucero, L.J. & B.W. Fash (eds.), 2006. *Precolumbian Water Management: Ideology, Ritual, and Power*. Tucson, AZ: University of Arizona Press.

Luedeling, E. & A. Buerkert, 2008. Typology of Oases in Northern Oman Based on Landsat and SRTM Imagery and Geological Survey Data, *Remote Sensing of Environment* 112(3), 1181–95.

Luke, C. & M. Kersel, 2012. *U.S. Cultural Diplomacy and Archaeology: Soft Power, Hard Heritage*. New York, NY: Routledge.

Mabry, J.B. (ed.), 1996. *Canals and Communities: Small-Scale Irrigation Systems*. Tucson: University of Arizona Press.

2000. Wittfogel Was Half Right: The Ethnology of Consensual and Nonconsensual Hierarchies in Irrigation Management, in *Hierarchies in Action*, ed. M. W. Diehl. Carbondale, IL: Southern Illinois University Press, 284–94.

2002. The Role of Irrigation in the Transition to Agriculture and Sedentism in the Southwest, in *Traditions, Transitions, and Technologies Themes in Southwestern Archaeology: Proceedings of the 2000 Southwest Symposium*, ed. S. Schlanger. Boulder, CO: University Press of Colorado, 178–99.

2005. Changing Knowledge and Ideas about the First Farmers in Southeastern Arizona, in *The Late Archaic Across the Borderlands: From Foraging to Farming*, ed. B.J. Vierra. Austin, TX: University of Texas Press, 41–83.

Mabry, J.B. & W.E. Doolittle, 2008. Modeling the Early Agricultural Frontier in the Desert Borderlands, in *Archaeology without Borders: Contacts, Commerce, and Change in the U.S. Southwest and Northwestern Mexico*, eds. M.E. McBrinn & L.D. Webster. Boulder, CO: University Press of Colorado, 55–70.

Mabry, J.B., J.P. Carpenter & G. Sanchez, 2008. Archaeological Models of Early Uto-Aztecan Prehistory in the Arizona-Sonora Borderlands, in *Archaeology without Borders: Contact, Commerce, and Change in the US Southwest and Northwestern Mexico*. Boulder, CO: University Press of Colorado, 155–83.

Macdonald, M.C.A., 2010. Ancient Arabia and the Written Word, *Proceedings of the Seminar for Arabian Studies* 40, 5–27.

Mackintosh-Smith, T., 2002. *The Travels of Ibn Battutah*. London: Picador.

Madella, M., M.K. Jones, P. Echlin, A. Powers-Jones & M. Moore, 2009. Plant Water Availability and Analytical Microscopy of Phytoliths: Implications for Ancient Irrigation in Arid Zones, *Quaternary International* 193, 32–40.

Magee, P., 2005. The Chronology and Environmental Background of Iron Age Settlement in Southeastern Iran and the Question of the Origin of the Qanat Irrigation System, *Iranica Antiqua* 40, 217–31.

2014. *The Archaeology of Prehistoric Arabia: Adaptation and Social Formation from the Neolithic to the Iron Age.* Cambridge: Cambridge University Press.

Maher, L.A., E.B. Banning & M. Chazan, 2011. Oasis or Mirage? Assessing the Role of Abrupt Climate Change in the Prehistory of the Southern Levant, *Cambridge Archaeological Journal* 21(1), 1–29.

Maidment, D.R., 2002. *ArcHydro: GIS for Water Resources.* Redlands, CA: ESRI Press.

Makarewicz, C.A., 2013. A Pastoralist Manifesto: Breaking Stereotypes and Re-Conceptualizing Pastoralism in the Near Eastern Neolithic, *Levant* 45(2), 159–74.

Makdisi, S., 2014. *Making England Western: Occidentalism, Race and Imperial Culture.* Chicago: University of Chicago Press.

Maktari, A.M.A., 1971. *Water Rights and Irrigation Practices in Lahj; a Study of the Application of Customary and Shari`ah Law in South-West Arabia.* Cambridge: Cambridge University Press.

Mandaville, J.P., 2011. *Bedouin Ethnobotany: Plant Concepts and Uses in a Desert Pastoral World.* Tucson, AZ: University of Arizona Press.

Marcolongo, B. & D.M. Bonacossi, 1997. L'abandon du systeme d'irrigation qatabanite dans la vallee du wadi Bayhan (Yemen): analyse geo-archeologique (Abandonment of the Qatabanian irrigation system in the Wadi Bayhan valley (Yemen): a geoarchaeological analysis, *Earth and Planetary Sciences* 325, 79–86.

Marcus, G.E., 1995. Ethnography in/of the World System: The Emergence of Multi-Sited Ethnography, *Annual Review of Anthropology* 24, 95–117.

1999. What is at Stake – And is Not – In the Idea and Practice of Multi-sited Ethnography, *Canberra Anthropology* 22(2), 6–14.

2009. Multi-Sited Ethnography: Notes and Queries, in *Multi-Sited Ethnography: Theory, Praxis and Locality in Contemporary Research*, ed. M.-A. Falzon. Surrey, UK: Ashgate, 181–96.

Marcus, G.E. & M.M.J. Fischer, 1986. *Anthropology as Cultural Critique: An Experimental Moment in the Human Sciences.* Chicago, IL: University of Chicago Press.

Marcus, J., 2008. The Archaeological Evidence for Social Evolution, *Annual Reviews of Anthropology* 37, 251–66.

Marcus, J. & C. Stanish (eds.), 2006. *Agricultural Strategies.* Los Angeles, CA: Cotsen Institute of Archaeology, University of California.

Margariti, R.E., 2007. *Aden and the Indian Ocean Trade.* Chapel Hill, NC: University of North Carolina Press.

Marshall, F. & E. Hildebrand, 2002. Cattle before Crops: The Beginnings of Food Production in Africa, *Journal of World Prehistory* 16(2), 99–143.

Marston, S.A., J.P. Jones & K. Woodward, 2005. Human Geography without Scale, *Transactions of the Institute of British Geographers* 30(4), 416–32.

Martin, L., J. McCorriston & R. Crassard, 2009. Early Arabian Pastoralism at Manayzah in Wadi Sana, Hadramawt, *Proceedings of the Seminar for Arabian Studies* 39, 285–96.

Masse, W.B., 1981. Prehistoric Irrigation Systems in the Salt River Valley, Arizona, *Science* 214(4519), 408–15.

## Bibliography

Mays, L.W., 2010. Water Technology in Ancient Egypt, in *Ancient Water Technologies*, ed. L.W. Mays. New York: Springer, 53–65.

Mazzini, G. & A. Porter, 2009. Steal BM 102600=CIH 611 in the British Museum: Water Regulation between Two Bordering Estates, *Proceedings of the Seminar for Arabian Studies* 39, 283–94.

McClure, H.A., 1976. Radiocarbon Chronology of Late Quaternary Lakes in the Arabian Desert, *Nature* 263, 755–56.

1988. Late Quaternary Palaeogeography and Landscape Evolution of the Rub' Al Khali, in *Araby the Blest: Studies in Arabian Archaeology*, ed. D.T. Potts. Chicago, IL: University of Chicago Press, 9–13.

McCorriston, J., 2006. Breaking the Rain Barrier and the Tropical Spread of Near Eastern Agriculture into Southern Arabia, in *Behavioral Ecology and the Transition to Agriculture*, eds. D. Kennett & B. Winterhalder. Berkeley: University of California Press, 217–36.

2011. *Pilgrimage and Household in the Ancient Near East*. Cambridge: Cambridge University Press.

2013. Pastoralism and Pilgrimage: Ibn Khaldun's Bayt -State Model and the Rise of Arabian Kingdoms, *Current Anthropology* 54(5), 607–41.

McCorriston, J. & L. Martin, 2009. Southern Arabia's Early Pastoral Population History: Some Recent Evidence, in *The Evolution of Human Populations in Arabia: Paleoenvironments, Prehistory and Genetics*, eds. M.D. Petraglia & J. Rose. Dordrecht, Netherlands: Springer, 237–50.

McCorriston, J., E.A. Oches, D.E. Walkter & K.L. Cole, 2002. Holocene Paleoecology and Prehistory in Highland Southern Arabia, *Paléorient* 28(1), 61–88.

McCorriston, J., M.J. Harrower, E.A. Oches & A. Bin 'Aqil, 2005. Foraging Economies and Population in the Middle Holocene Highlands of Southern Yemen, *Proceedings of the Seminar for Arabian Studies* 35, 143–54.

McCorriston, J., T. Steimer-herbet, J. Kemang, M. Harrower & K. Williams, 2011. Gazetteer of Small-Scale Monuments in Prehistoric Hadramawt, Yemen: A Radiocarbon Chronology from the RASA-AHSD Project Research 1996–2008, 22, 1–22.

McCorriston, J., M. Harrower, L. Martin & E. Oches, 2012. Cattle Cults of the Arabian Neolithic and Early Territorial Societies, *American Anthropologist* 114(1), 45–63.

McGee, W.J., 1895. The Beginning of Agriculture, *American Anthropologist* 8, 350–75.

Mead, M., 1928. *Coming of Age in Samoa*. New York: Harper Collins.

Merrill, W.L., R.J. Hard, J.B. Mabry, G.J. Fritz, K.R. Adams, J.R. Roney & A.C. MacWilliams, 2009. The Diffusion of Maize to the Southwestern United States and Its Impact, *Proceedings of the National Academy of Sciences of the United States of America* 106(50), 21019–26.

Merrill, W.L., R.J. Hard, J.B. Mabry, G.J. Fritz, K.R. Adams, J.R. Roney & A.C. MacWilliams, 2010. Reply to Hill and Brown: Maize and Uto-Aztecan Cultural History, *Proceedings of the National Academy of Sciences* 107(11), 35–36.

Meskell, L. (ed.), 1998. *Archaeology Under Fire: Nationalism, Politics and Heritage in the Eastern Mediterranean and Middle East*. London: Routledge.

Meskell, L., 2012. The Social Life of Heritage, in *Archaeological Theory Today, Second Edition*, ed. I. Hodder. Cambridge: Polity Press, 229–49.

Michels, J.W., 1988. The Axumite Kingdom: A Settlement Archaeology Perspective, in *Proceedings of the Ninth International Congress of Ethiopian Studies*, ed. A.A. Gromyko. Moscow: Nauka Publishers, 173–83.

Miller, C., 2009. *Water in the 21st Century West: A High Country News Reader*. Portland, OR: Oregan State University Press.

Miller, R., 1980. Water Use in Syria and Palestine from the Neolithic to the Bronze Age, *World Archaeology* 11(3), 331–41.

Millon, R., 1962. Variations in Social Responses to the Practice of Irrigation Agriculture, in *Civilizations in Desert Lands*, ed. R.B. Woodbury. Utah: Department of Anthropology, University of Utah.

Mitchell, W.P., 1973. The Hydraulic Hypothesis: A Reappraisal, *Current Anthropology* 14(5), 532–34.

1976. Irrigation and Community in the Central Peruvian Highlands, *American Anthropologist* 78(1), 25–44.

Mithen, S., 2010. The Domestication of Water: Water Management in the Ancient World and Its Prehistoric Origins in the Jordan Valley., *Philosophical Transactions of the Royal Society A* 368(1931), 5249–74.

2012. *Thirst: Water and Power in the Ancient World*. Cambridge, MA: Harvard University Press.

Mithen, S.J. & E. Black (eds.), 2011. *Water, Life and Civilization: Climate, Environment and Society in the Jordan Valley*. Cambridge: Cambridge University Press.

Mithen, S.J., E. Jenkins, K. Jamjoum, S. Nuimat, S. Nortcliff & B. Finlayson, 2008. Experimental Crop Growing in Jordan to Develop Methodology for the Identification of Ancient Crop Irrigation, *World Archaeology* 40(1), 7–25.

Montgomery, D.R., 2007. *Dirt: The Erosion of Civilization*. Berkeley, CA: University of California Press.

Moore, A., 2008. Rethinking scale as a geographical category: from analysis to practice, *Progress in Human Geography* 32(2), 203–25.

Moore, A.M.T., G.C. Hillman & A.J. Legge, 2000. *Village on the Euphrates: From Foraging to Farming at Abu Hureyra*. Oxford: Oxford University Press.

Moore, S., 2011. Parchedness, Politics, and Power: The State Hydraulic in Yemen, *Political Ecology* 18, 38–50.

Morgan, W.T.W., 1974. The South Turkana Expedition: Scientific Papers X. Sorghum Gardens in South Turkana: Cultivation among a Nomadic Pastoral People, *The Geographical Journal* 140(1), 80–93.

Morris, I., 2010. *Why the West Rules – For Now*. New York, NY: Farrar, Straus and Giroux.

2014. *War! What Is It Good For? Conflict and the Progress of Civilization from Primates to Robots*. New York, NY: Farrar, Straus and Giroux.

Mouton, M., 2004. Irrigation et Formation de la Societe Antique dan les Basses-Terres du Yemen: un essai de modele, *Syria* 81, 81–104.

2009. L'eau en partage: territorialité, réseaux d'irrigation et formation des sociétés antiques dans les basses-terres du Yémen, in *Stratégies D'acquisition de L'eau et Société Au Moyen-Orient Depuis l'Antiquité*. Paris: Institut français du Proche-Orient, 79–95.

Mouton, M. & J. Schiettecatte, 2014. *In the Desert Margins: The Settlement Process in Ancient South and East Arabia*. Rome: L'erma di Bretschneider.

# Bibliography

Mouton, M., A. Benoist & J. Schiettecatte, 2011. Makaynûn and Its Territory: The Formation of an Urban Centre during the South Arabian Period in the Hadramawt, *Arabian Archaeology and Epigraphy* 22, 155–65.

Mulholland, C., 2002. *William Mulholland and the Rise of Los Angeles.* Berkeley, CA: University of California Press.

Müller, D.H., 1884. *Geographie Der Arabischen Halbinsel (Translation of Sifat Jazirat Al-Arab by Al-Hamdānī, Al-Hasan Ibn Ahmad).* Leiden: E.J. Brill.

Müller, W.W., 1985. Altsüdarabische und frühnordarabische Inschriften, in *Historisch-Chronologische Texte. Rechts- Und Wirtschaftsurkunden: Texte Aus Der Umwelt Des Alten Testaments*, ed. O. Kaiser. Gütersloh: Gütersloher Verlags-Haus, 651–68.

   1991. Ma'rib, in *Encyclopaedia of Islam, Second Edition*, ed. H.A.R. Gibb. Leiden: Brill.

   2010. *Sabäische Inschriften Nach Ären Datiert. Bibliographie, Texte Und Glossar.* Wiesbaden: Harrassowitz Verlag.

Murakami, M., 1995. *Managing Water for Peace in the Middle East: Alternative Strategies.* Tokyo: United Nations University Press.

Murdoch, D.H., 2001. *The American West: The Invention of a Myth.* Reno, NV: University of Nevada Press.

Mustafa, A.I., M.S. Al-Jassir, M.A. Nawawy & S.E. Ahmed, 1995. Studies on Samh Seeds (Mesembryanthemum forsskalei Hochst) Growing in Saudi Arabia: 3. Utilization of Samh Seeds in Bakery Products, *Plant Foods for Human Nutrition* 48, 279–86.

Nabhan, G.P., 1979. The Ecology of Floodwater Farming in Arid South-Western North America, *Agro-Ecosystems* 5, 245–55.

   1986a. Papago Indian Desert Agriculture and Water Control in the Sonoran Desert, 1697–1934, *Applied Geography* 6, 43–59.

   1986b. 'Ak-ciñ 'Arroyo Mouth' and the Environmental Setting of the Papago Indian Fields in the Sonoran Desert, *Applied Geography* 6, 61–75.

Naff, T., 2009. Islamic Law and the Politics of Water, in *The Evolution of the Law and Politics of Water*, eds. J.W. Dellapenna & J. Gupta. New York: Springer, 37–52.

Nebes, N., 1997. Karib'îl Watâr, premier unificateur du Yémen, in *Yémen, Au Pays de La Reine de Saba. Exposition Présentée à l'Institut Du Monde Arabe Du 25 Octobre 1997 Au 28 Février 1998*, eds. C.J. Robin & B. Vogt. Paris: Flammarion, Institut du Monde Arabe, 95–97.

   2001. Zur Genese der altsudarabischen Kultur: Eine Arbeitshypothese, in *Migration Und Kulturaltransfer: Der Wandel Vorder Und Zentralasiatischen Kulturen Im Umbruch*, eds. R. Eichmann & H. Parzinger. Berlin: Akten des Internationalen Kolloquiums, 427–35.

   2004. A New Abraha Inscription from the Great Dam of Marib, *Proceedings of the Seminar for Arabian Studies* 34, 221–30.

   2005. Sabäische Texte, in *Staatsverträge, Herrscherinschriften Und Andere Dokumente Zur Politischen Geschichte. Texte Aus Der Umwelt Des Alten Testaments*, eds. F. Breyer & M. Lichtenstein. Gütersloh: Gütersloher Verlagshaus, 331–67.

   2007. Ita'amar der Sabaer: Zur Datierung der Monumentalinschrift des Yita'amar Watar aus Sirwah, *Arabian Archaeology and Epigraphy* 18, 25–33.

2010. The Martyrs of Najran and the End of the Himyar: On the Political History of South Arabia in the Early Sixth Century, in *The Qur'an in Context: Historical and Literary Investigations into the Qur'anic Milieu*, eds. A. Neuwirth, N. Sinai & M. Marx. Leiden: Brill, 27–60.

Nye, J.S., 2009. *Soft Power: The Means to Success in World Politics*. New York: Public Affairs.

Oates, D. & J. Oates, 1976. Early Irrigation Agriculture in Mesopotamia, in *Problems in Economic and Social Archaeology*, eds. G. Sieveking & I.H. Longworth. London: Duckworth, 109–35.

O'Connell, J.F. & K. Hawkes, 1981. Alyawara Plant Use and Optimal Foraging Theory, in *Hunter-Gatherer Foraging Strategies: Ethnographic and Archaeological Analyses*, eds. B. Winterhalder & E.A. Smith. Chicago, IL: University of Chicago Press, 99–125.

Connell, J.F.O., P.K. Latz, P. Barnett & J.F. O'Connell, 1983. Traditional and Modern Plant Use Among the Alyawara of Central Australia, *Economic Botany* 37(1), 80–119.

O'Donovan, M., 2002. *New Perspectives on Site Function and Scale of Cerro de Trincheras, Sonora, Mexico: The 1991 Surface Survey*. Tucson, AZ: Arizona State Museum, University of Arizona.

Oestigaard, T., 2011. Water, in *Oxford Handbook of the Archaeology of Ritual and Religion*. Oxford: Oxford University Press, 38–51.

Opler, M.E. & C.R. Kraut, 1996. *An Apache Life-Way: The Economic, Social, and Religious Institutions of the Chiricahua Indians*. Lincoln, NE: University of Nebraska Press.

Orlove, B. & S. Caton, 2010. Water and Sustainability Anthropological Approaches and Prospects, *Annual Reviews of Anthropology* 39, 401–15.

Ortloff, C.R., 2009. *Water Engineering in the Ancient World: Archaeological and Climate Perspectives on Societies of Ancient South America, the Middle East, and Sout-East Asia*. Oxford: Oxford University Press.

Pagden, A., 2009. *Worlds at War: The 2,500-Year Struggle Between East and West*. New York, NY: Random House, Inc.

Pál, N., 2013. Lateral Vision: Juxtaposition as a Method, *Ethnography* 14(3), 369–83.

Parker, A.G., A.S. Goudie, S. Stokes, J.W. White, M.J. Hodson, M. Manning & D. Kennet, 2006. A Record of Holocene Climate Change from Lake Geochemical Analyses in Southeastern Arabia, *Quaternary Research* 66, 465–76.

Parkinson, W.A., (ed.) 2002. *The Archaeology of Tribal Societies*. Ann Arbor, MI: International Monographs in Prehistory.

Pauketat, T., 2007. *Chiefdoms and Other Archaeological Delusions*. Lanham, MD: Altamira Press.

Paynter, R., 2000. Historical Archaeology and the Post-Columbian World of North America, *Journal of Archaeological Research* 8(3), 169–217.

Pearce, F., 2006. *When the Rivers Run Dry: Water – The Defining Crisis of the Twenty-First Century*. Boston, MA: Beacon Press.

Peltenburg, E., S. Colledge, P. Croft, A. Jackson, C. McCartney & M.A. Murray, 2000. Agro-Pastoralist Colonization of Cyprus in the 10th Millennium BP: Initial Assessments, *Antiquity* 74(286), 844–53.

Petraglia, M.D., 2003. The Lower Paleolithic of the Arabian Peninsula: Occupations, Adaptations, and Dispersals, *Journal of World Prehistory* 17(2), 141–79.

Phillips, W., 1955. *Qataban and Sheba: Exploring the Ancient Kingdoms on the Biblical Spice Routes of Arabia*. New York: Harcourt Brace and Company.

Phillipps, R., S. Holdaway, W. Wendrich & R. Cappers, 2012. Mid-Holocene Occupation of Egypt and Global Climatic Change, *Quaternary International* 251, 64–76.

Pietsch, D. & P. Kühn, 2012. Early Holocene Paleosols at the Southwestern Ramlat As-Sab 'atayn Desert Margin: New Climate Proxies for Southern Arabia, *Palaeogeography, Palaeoclimatology, Palaeoecology*.

Pietsch, D. & L. Mabit, 2012. Geoderma Terrace Soils in the Yemen Highlands: Using Physical, Chemical and Radiometric Data to Assess Their Suitability for Agriculture and Their Vulnerability to Degradation, *Geoderma* 185–186, 48–60.

Pietsch, D., P. Kühn, T. Scholten, U. Brunner, H. Hitgen & I. Gerlach, 2010. Holocene Soils and Sediments around Ma'rib Oasis, Yemen: Further Sabaean Treasures?, *The Holocene* 20(5), 785–99.

Pinder, D., I. Shimada & D. Gregory, 1979. The Nearest-Neighbor Statistic: Archaeological Application and New Developments, *American Antiquity* 44(3), 430–45.

Pirenne, J., 1971. Une Legislation Hydrologique en Arabie du Sud Antique, in *Hommages a Andre Dupont-Sommer*, eds. A. Caquot & M. Philonenco. Paris.

   1977. *La Maîtrise de L'eau En Arabie Du Sud Antique: Six Types de Monuments Techniques*. Paris: Imprimerie Nationale.

Por, D.F., 2004. The Levantine Waterway, Riparian Archaeology, Paleolimnology, and Conservation, in *Human Paleoecology in the Levantine Corridor*, eds. N. Goren-Inbar & J.D. Speth. Oxford: Oxbow Books, 5–20.

Postgate, J.N. & M.A. Powell, 1988. *Irrigation and Cultivation in Mesopotamia, Part I*. Cambridge, UK: Sumerian Agriculture Group.

   1990. *Irrigation and Cultivation in Mesopotamia, Part II*. Cambridge, UK: Sumerian Agriculture Group.

Potts, D.T., 1990. *The Arabian Gulf in Antiquity, Volume 1: From Prehistory to the Fall of the Achaemenid Empire*. Oxford: Clarendon Press.

   2003. The Mukarrib and his Beads: Karib'il Watar's Assyrian Diplomacy in the Early 7th Century BC, *Isimu* 6, 197–206.

   2012. *In the Land of the Emirates: The Archaeology and History of the UAE*. Abu Dhabi: Trident Press.

Pournelle, J., 2003. The Littoral Foundations of the Uruk State: Using Satellite Photography toward a New Understanding of 5th/4th Millennium BCE Landscapes in the Warka Survey Area, Iraq, in *Chalcolithic and Early Bronze Age Hydrostrategies*, ed. D. Gheorghiu. Oxford: British Archaeological Reports, 5–23.

   2007. From KLM to Corona: Using Satellite Photography toward a New Understanding of 5th/4th Millennium BC Landscapes in Southern Mesopotamia, in *Settlement and Society: Ecology, Urbanism, Trade and*

*Technology in Ancient Mesopotamia*, ed. E. Stone. Los Angeles, CA: Cotsen Institute of Archaeology, UCLA, 29–62.

Preston, G.W., a. G. Parker, H. Walkington, M.J. Leng & M.J. Hodson, 2012. From Nomadic Herder-Hunters to Sedentary Farmers: The Relationship between Climate Change and Ancient Subsistence Strategies in South-eastern Arabia, *Journal of Arid Environments* 86, 122–30.

Price, D.H., 1994. Wittfogel's Neglected Hydraulic/Hydroagricultural Distinction, *Journal of Anthropological Research* 50, 187–204.

Prickett, M.E., 1985. *Man, Land and Water: Settlement Distribution and the Development of Irrigation Agriculture in the Upper Rud-I Gushk Drainage, Southeastern Iran*, Harvard University.

Prioletta, A., 2009. Baynun in Ancient Time: The Site and Inscriptions, in *Art and Technique in Yemen: The Bronzes from the Museum of Baynun*. Piza: La Limonaia, 57–66.

Rambeau, C., B. Finlayson, S. Smith, S. Black, R. Inglis & S. Robinson, 2011. Palaeoenvironmental Reconstruction at Beidha, Southern Jordan (c. 18,000–8,500 BP): Implications for Human Occupation during the Natufian and Pre-Pottery Neolithic, in *Water, Life and Civilization: Climate, Environment and Society in the Jordan Valley*. Cambridge: Cambridge University Press, 245–68.

Rappold, G.D., 2005. Precipitation Analysis and Agricultural Water Availability in the Southern Highlands of Yemen, *Hydrological Processes* 19, 2437–49.

Redkin, O., 1995. The Dialect of Hadramawt, *St. Petersburg Journal of Oriental Studies* 7, 193–203.

Redmond, E.M. & C.S. Spencer, 2012. Chiefdoms at the Threshold: The Competitive Origins of the Primary State, *Journal of Anthropological Archaeology* 31, 22–37.

Reisner, M., 1986. *Cadillac Desert: The American West and Its Disappearing Water*. New York, NY: Penguin.

Renfrew, C., I. Todd & R. Tringham, 1974. Beyond a Subsistence Economy: The Evolution of Social Organization in Prehistoric Europe, *Bulletin of the American Schools of Oriental Research Supplementary Studies* No. 20, 69–95.

Retsö, J., 1991. The Domestication of the Camel and the Establishment of the Frankincense Road from South Arabia, *Orientalia Suecana* 40, 187–219.

2003. *The Arabs in Antiquity: Their History from the Assyrians to the Umayyads*. London: Routledge.

Richardson, S., 2012. Early Mesopotamia: The Presumptive State, *Past and Present* 215, 3–49.

Rindos, D., 1984. *The Origins of Agriculture: An Evolutionary Perspective*. Orlando, FL: Academic Press.

Robb, J., 2013. Material Culture, Landscapes of Action, and Emergent Causation, *Current Anthropology* 54(6), 657–83.

Robbins, P., 2001. Fixed Categories in a Portable Landscape: The Causes and Consequences of Land-Cover Categorization, *Environment and Planning A* 33, 161–79.

2003. Beyond Ground Truth: GIS and the Environmental Knowledge of Herders, Professional Foresters, and Other Traditional Communities, *Human Ecology* 31(2), 233–53.

# Bibliography

Robin, C., 1987. Trois Inscriptions Sabeennes Decouvertes pres de Baraqish (Republique Arabe du Yemen), *Proceedings of the Seminar for Arabian Studies* 17, 165–77.

1988. Quelques Observation sur la date de Construction et al Chronologie de la Premiere Digue de Ma'rib, d'apres les Inscriptions, *Proceedings of the Seminar for Arabian Studies* 18, 95–114.

2013. À propos de Ymnt et Ymn: «nord» et «sud», «droite» et «gauche», dans les inscriptions de l'Arabie antique, in *Entre Carthage et l'Arabie Heureuse. Mélanges Offerts À François Bron*, eds. F. Briquel-Chatonnet, C. Fauveaud & I. Gajda. Paris: de Boccard, 119–40.

Robin, C.J. & M. Arbach, 2009. L'inscription de fondation du barrage du Wadi Harir (Yemen), in *Philologisches Und Historisches Zwischen Anatolien Und Sokotra; Analecta Semitica in Memoriam Alexander Sima*. Wiesbaden: Harrassowitz Verlag, 297–306.

Robin, C.J. & H. Dridi, 2004. Deux barrages du Yémen antique, *Comptes rendus des séances de l'Académie des Inscriptions et Belles-Lettres* 148, 67–121.

Rodionov, M., 1997. Mawla Matar and other Awliya': On Social Functions of Religious Places in Western Hadramawt, *Mare Erythraeum* 1, 107–14.

1999. Irrigation in the Western Hadramawt: Khayyil as a Social Role, *Proceedings of the Seminar for Arabian Studies* 29, 119–23.

Root, K.P.E. & T. Papakos, 2010. Flooding Impacts and Modeling Challenges of Tropical Storms in Eastern Yemen, *World Environmental and Water Resources Congress* 1970–79.

Roper, D.C., 1979. The Method and Theory of Site Catchment Analysis: A Review, *Advances in Archaeological Method and Theory* 2, 119–40.

Rosen, A.M. & S. Weiner, 1994. Identifying Ancient Irrigation: a New Method Using Opaline Phytoliths from Emmer Wheat, *Journal of Archaeological Science* 21, 125–32.

Rosen, S.A., 2011. The Desert and the Pastoralist: An Archaeological Perspective on Human-Landscape Interaction in the Negev over the Millennia, *Annals of Arid Zone* 50, 1–15.

Rosenberg, M., 1998. Cheating at Musical Chairs: Territoriality and Sedentism in an Evolutionary Context, *Current Anthropology* 39(5), 653–81.

Rosgen, D.L. 1996. *Applied River Morphology*. Pagosa Springs, CO: Wildland Hydrology.

Rost, S., 2010. Irrigation Management in the Ur III Period: A Reconstruction Based on a Case Study of the Maintenance of the Id-Nina-Se-Du Canal of the Province of Lagas, in *The Empirical Dimension of Ancient Near Eastern Studies*, ed. G.J. Selz.: Lit Verlag Dr. W. Hopf, 211–69.

Rost, S. & A. Hamdani, 2011. Traditional Dam Construction in Modern Iraq: A Possible Analogy for Ancient Mesopotamian Irrigation Practices, *Iraq* 73, 201–20.

Rowley, W.D., 2006. *Reclamation: Managing Water in the West – The Bureau of Reclamation Origins and Growth to 1945, Volume 1*. Washington, D.C.: US Bureau of Reclamation.

Rowley-Conwy, P., 2011. Westward Ho! The Spread of Agriculturalism from Central Europe to the Atlantic, *Current Anthropology* 52(S4), S431–S451.

Russell, K.W., 1988. *After Eden: The Behavioural Ecology of Early Food Production in the Near East and North Africa.* Oxford: British Archaeological Reports.

Ryckmans, J., 1971. Some Recent Views of the Public Institutions of Saba (Ancient South Arabia), *Proceedings of the Seminar for Arabian Studies* 1, 24–26.

Ryzewski, K., 2012. Multiply Situated Strategies? Multi-Sited Ethnography and Archeology, *Journal of Archaeology* 19(2), 241–68.

Sahlins, M., 2004. *Apologies to Thucydides: Understanding History as Culture and Vice Versa.* Chicago: University of Chicago Press.

Said, E.W., 1978. *Orientalism.* New York, NY: Vintage Books.

1993 *Culture and Imperialism.* New York, NY: Vintage Books.

Sauer, C., 1952. *Agricultural Origins and Dispersals.* New York: American Geographical Society.

Scarborough, V.L., 1991. Water Management Adaptations in Nonindustrial Complex Societies: An Archaeological Perspective, *Archaeological Method and Theory* 3(1991), 101–54.

1998. Ecology and Ritual: Water Management and the Maya, *Latin American Antiquity* 9(2), 135–59.

2003. *The Flow of Power: Ancient Water Systems and Landscapes.* Santa Fe, NM: SAR Press.

Scarborough, V.L. & B.L. Isaac (eds.), 1993. *Economic Aspects of Water Management in the Prehispanic New World.* London: JAI Press.

Scarborough, V.L. & L.J. Lucero, 2010. The Non-Hierarchical Development of Complexity in the Semitropics: Water and Cooperation, *Water History* 2, 185–205.

Schaloske, M., 1995. *Antike Technologie – Die Sabaische Wasserwirtschaft von Marib: Untersuchungen Der Sabaischen Bewasserungsanlagen in Marib.* Mainz: Verlag Philipp Von Zabern.

Schiettecatte, J., 2007. Urbanization and Settlement Pattern in Ancient Hadramawt (1st mill. BC), *Bulletin of Archaeology of the Kanazawa University* 28, 11–28.

2010. Why did the Cities of the Jawf Valley Collapse? An Archaeo-Geographical Approach, in *Regards Croisés Sur L'étude Archéologique Des Paysages Anciens: Nouvelles Recherches Dans Le Bassin Méditerranéen, En Asie Centrale et Au Proche et Moyen-Orient*, eds. H. Alarashi, M.-L. Chambrade, S. Gondet, A. Jouvenel, C. Sauvage & H. Ronchere. Lyon: Maison de l'Orient et de la Mediterranee, 149–61.

Schmidt, J., 1988. The Sabean Irrigation Economy of Marib, in *Yemen: 3000 Years of Art and Civilization in Arabia Felix*, ed. D. Werner. Innsbruck: Pinquin-Verlag, 55–63.

Schmidt, J.C., 2010. A Watershed Perspective of Changes in Streamflow, Sediment Supply, and Geomorphology of the Colorado River, *Proceedings of the Colorado River Basin Science and Resource Management Symposium* 51–76.

Schuetter, J.M., P.K. Goel, J.O.Y. McCorriston, J. Park, M.J. Senn & M. Harrower, 2013. Autodetection of Ancient Arabian Tombs in High-Resolution Satellite Imagery, *International Journal of Remote Sensing* 34(19), 6611–35.

Sedov, A. V., 1995. Bi'r Hamad: A Pre-Islamic Settlement in the Western Wadi Hadramawt: Notes on an Archaeological Map of the Hadramawt, *Arabian archaeology and epigraphy* 6(2), 103–15.

# Bibliography

Sedov, A. V., 1996. On the Origin of the Agricultural Settlements in Hadramawt, in *Arabia Antiqua: Early Origins of South Arabian States*, ed. C.J. Robin. Rome: Instituto Italiano per il Medio ed Estrmeo Oriente, 67–86.

1997. Die Archaologishchen Denkmaler Von Raybun im Unteren Wadi Daucan, Hadramawt, *Mare Erythraeum* 1, 31–106.

2005. *Temples of Ancient Hadramawt*. Pisa: L'erma di Bretschneider.

Sedov, A. V. & A. Batayi, 1994. Temples of Ancient Hadramawt, *Proceedings of the Seminar for Arabian Studies* 24, 183–96.

Seland, E.H., 2005. Ancient South Arabia: Trade and Strategies of State Control as Seen in the "Periplus Maris Erythraei," *Proceedings of the Seminar for Arabian Studies* 35, 271–78.

2014. Archaeology of Trade in the Western Indian Ocean, 300 BC – AD 700, *Journal of Archaeological Research* 22, 367–402.

Serjeant, R.B., 1960. Archaeological Discoveries in South Arabia, Bowen, R. and Albright, F.P. (Book Review), *Bulletin of the School of Oriental and African Studies* 23(3), 582–85.

1964. Some Irrigation Systems in the Hadramawt, *Bulletin of the School of African and Oriental Studies* 27, 33–76.

1988. Observations on Irrigation in Southwest Arabia, *Proceedings of the Seminar for Arabian Studies* 18, 145–53.

Service, E., 1962. *Primitive Social Organization: An Evolutionary Perspective*. New York: Random House.

Shahin, M., 1996. *Hydrology and Scarcity of Water Resources in the Arab Region*. Rotterdam: A.A. Balkema.

2007. *Water Resources and Hydrometeorology of the Arab Region*. Dordrecht, The Netherlands: Springer.

Sherratt, A., 1980. Water, Soil and Seasonality in Early Cereal Cultivation, *World Archaeology* 11(3), 313–30.

Shiva, V., 2002. *Water Wars: Privatization, Pollution, and Profit*. Cambridge, MA: South End Press.

Silverstein, J.E., D. Webster, H. Martinez & A. Soto, 2009. Rethinking the Great Earthwork of Tikal: A Hydraulic Hypothesis for the Classic Maya Polity, *Ancient Mesoamerica* 20, 45–58.

Simmons, A., 2007. *The Neolithic Revolution in the Near East: Transforming the Human Landscape*. Tucson, AZ: University of Arizona Press.

Smith, A.T., 2003. *The Political Landscape: Constellations of Authority in Early Complex Polities*. Berkeley, CA: University of California Press.

2011. Archaeologies of Sovereignty, *Annual Reviews of Anthropology* 40, 415–32.

Smith, B., 2001. Low-Level Food Production, *Journal of Archaeological Research* 9, 1–43.

Smith, G.R. (ed.), 2008. *A Traveller in Thirteenth-Century Arabia: Ibn AL-Mujāwir's Tārkh Al-Mustabsir*. London: The Hakluyt Society.

Smith, M.E., 2009. V. Gordon Childe and the Urban Revolution a Historical Perspective on a Revolution in Urban Studies, *Town Planning Review* 80(1), 3–29.

Smith, M.E. (ed.), 2011. *The Comparative Archaeology of Complex Societies*. Cambridge: Cambridge University Press.

Smith, M.E. and P. Peregrine, 2011. Approaches to Comparative Analysis in Archaeology, in *The Comparative Archaeology of Complex Societies*, ed. M.E. Smith. Cambridge: Cambridge University Press, 4–21.

Snead, J.E., 2006. Mirror of the Earth: Water, Landscape, and Meaning in the Precolumbian Southwest, in *Precolumbian Water Management: Ideology, Ritual and Power*, eds. L.J. Lucero & B.W. Fash. Tucson, AZ: University of Arizona Press, 205–20.

Soja, E., 1989. *Post-Modern Geographies: The Reassertion of Space in Critical Social Theory*. London: Verso.

Solomon, S., 2010. *Water: The Epic Struggle for Wealth, Power, and Civilization*. New York: Harper Collins.

Stahl, A.B., 1993. Concepts of Time and Approaches to Analogical Reasoning in Historical Perspective, *American Antiquity* 58(2), 235–60.

Stanish, C.S., 1994. The Hydraulic Hypothesis Revisited: Lake Titicaca Basin Raised Fields in Theoretical Perspective, *Latin American Antiquity* 5(4), 312–32.

Steimer-Herbet, T., F. Braemer & G. Davtian, 2006. Pastoralists' tombs and settlement patterns in Wadi Wash'ah during the Bronze Age (Hadramawt, Yemen), *Proceedings of the Seminar for Arabian Studies* 36, 257–65.

Stein, P., 2010. Irrigation Management in Pre-Islamic South Arabia according to the Epigraphic Evidence, *Proceedings of the Seminar for Arabian Studies* 40, 337–44.

   2013. Palaeography of the Ancient South Arabian script. New Evidence for an Absolute Chronology, *Arabian archaeology and epigraphy* 195, 186–95.

Steward, J.H., 1930. Irrigation without Agriculture, *Papers of the Michigan Academy of Science, Arts, and Letters* 12, 149–156.

   1933. Ethnography of the Owens Valley Paiute, *University of California Publications in American Archaeology and Ethnology* 33(3), 233–350.

   1938. *Basin-Plateau Aboriginal Sociopolitical Groups*. Washington, D.C.: Smithsonian Institution Press.

   1942. The Direct Historical Approach to Archaeology, *American Antiquity* 7, 337–43.

   1949. Cultural Causality and Law: A Trial Formulation of the Development of Early Civilizations, *American Anthropologist* 51, 1–27.

   1955a. *Theory of Culture Change: The Methodology of Multilinear Evolution*. Urbana, IL: University of Illinois Press.

   1955b. Introduction: The Irrigation Civilizations a Symposium on Method and Result in Cross Cultural Regularities, in *Irrigation Civilizations: A Comparative Study*. Washington, D.C.: Pan American Union, 1–5.

   1977. Wittfogel's Irrigation Hypothesis, in *Evolution and Ecology: Essays on Social Transformation*, ed. J.H. Steward. Urbana, IL: University of Illinois Press, 87–99.

Steward, J.H., R.M. Adams & D. Collier, 1955. *Irrigation Civilizations: A Comparative Study*. Washington, D.C.: Pan American Union.

Stockhammer, P.W., 2012. Conceptualizing Cultural Hybridization in Archaeology, in *Conceptualizing Cultural Hybridization, Transcultural Research*, ed. P.W. Stockhammer. Berlin: Springer-Verlag, 43–58.

# Bibliography

Stoffle, R.W. & M.N. Zedeño, 2001. Historical Memory and Ethnographic Perspectives on the Southern Paiute Homeland, *Journal of California and Great Basin Anthropology* 23(2), 229–48.

Stone, G.D., 1996. *Settlement Ecology: The Social and Spatial Organization of Kofyar Agriculture*. Tucson, AZ: University of Arizona Press.

Stringfellow, K., 2013. Owens Valley and the Aqueduct, *Boom: A Journal of California* 3(3): 50–59.

Sulas, F., M. Madella & C. French, 2009. State Formation and Water Resources Management in the Horn of Africa: The Aksumite Kingdom of the Northern Ethiopian Highlands, *World Archaeology* 41(1), 2–15.

Taha, F.A., 1988. *The Yemen Arab Republic: An Export Market Profile*. Washington, D.C.: U.S. Dept. of Agriculture Economic Research Service Trade and Analysis Division.

Tamburrino, A., 2010. Water Technology in Ancient Mesopotamia, in *Ancient Water Technologies*, ed. L.W. Mays. New York: Springer, 29–51.

Tesfai, M. & J. De Graaff, 2000. Participatory Rural Appraisal of Spate Irrigation Systems in Eastern Eritrea, *Agriculture and Human Values* 17, 359–70.

Tesfai, M. & L. Stroosnijder, 2001. The Eritrean Spate Irrigation System, *Agricultural Water Management* 48, 51–60.

Tilly, C.Y., 1994. *A Phenomenology of Landscape: Places, Paths, and Monuments*. Oxford: Berg Publishers.

Tindale, N.B., 1977. Adaptive Significance of the Panara Grass Seed Culture of Australia, in *Stone Tools as Cultural Markers*, ed. R.V.S. Wright. Canberra, Australia: Australian Institute of Aboriginal Studies, 345–50.

Toynbee, A.J., 1934. *A Study of History*. Oxford: Oxford University Press.

Trigger, B., 1968. The Determinants of Settlement Patterns, in *Settlement Archaeology*, ed. K.C. Chang. Palo Alto, CA: National Press, 53–78.

2003. *Understanding Early Civilizations: A Comparative Study*. Cambridge: Cambridge University Press.

Tuan, Y.-F., 1977. *Space and Place: The Perspective of Experience*. Minneapolis, MN: University of Minnesota Press.

Turner, F.J., 1894. The Significance of the Frontier in American History, in *Annual Report of the American Historical Association*. Washington DC: American Historical Association, 197–228.

Turner, B.S., 1994. *Orientalism, Postmodernism and Globalism*. New York: Routledge.

Tvedt, T. (ed.), 2010. *A History of Water*, 3 Volumes. London: I.B. Tauris.

Uerpmann, H.-P., D.T. Potts & M. Uerpmann, 2009. The Holocene (RE-) Occupation of Eastern Arabia, in *Evolution of Human Populations in Arabia*, eds. M.D. Petraglia & J.I. Rose. Dordrecht, Netherlands: Springer, 205–14.

Uerpmann, H., M. Uerpmann, A. Kutterer & S.A. Jasim, 2013. The Neolithic Period in the Central Region of the Emirate of Sharjah (UAE), *Arabian Archaeology and Epigraphy* 108, 102–8.

Uil, H. & F.C. Dufour, 1990. *Water Resources Wadi Adhanah and Marib Area, Water Resources Assessment Yemen Vol 15*. The Netherlands: TNO.

Ulin, D.L., 2013. There It Is. Take It, *Boom: A Journal of California* 3(3), 28–37.

Uphoff, N., 1986. *Getting the Process Right: Improving Irrigation Management with Farmer Organization and Participation*. Ithaca, NY: Cornell University.

Ur, J.A., 2006. Google Earth and Archaeology, *Society for American Archaeology: Archaeological Record* 6(3), 35–38.

2010. Cycles of Civilization in Northern Mesopotamia, 4400–2000 BC, *Journal of Archaeological Research* 18, 387–431.

Ur, J.A., P. Karsgaard & J. Oates, 2007. Early Urban Development in the Near East, *Science* 317, 1188.

Van Beek, G.W., 1956. A Radiocarbon Date for Early South Arabia, *Bulletin of the American Schools of Oriental Research* 143, 6–9.

1969. *Hajar Bin Humeid: Investigations at a Pre-Islamic Site in South Arabia*. Baltimore, MD: Johns Hopkins Press.

1997. Hajar bin Humeid, in *The Oxford Encyclopedia of Archaeology in the Near East*, ed. E.M. Meyers. Oxford: Oxford University Press, 457–58.

van der Gun, J.A.M. & A.A. Ahmed (eds.), 1995. *The Water Resources of Yemen: A Summary Digest of Available Information*. Delft, The Netherlands: TNO Institute of Applied Geoscience.

Varisco, D.M., 1983. Sayl and Ghayl: The Ecology of Water Allocation in Yemen, *Human Ecology* 11, 365–383.

1991. The Future of Terrace Farming in Yemen: A Development Dilemma, *Agriculture and Human Values* 8(1–2), 166–72.

1996. Water Sources and Traditional Irrigation in Yemen, *New Arabian Studies* 3, 238–57.

1997. *Medieval Folk Astronomy and Agriculture in Arabia and the Yemen*. Brookfield, VT: Ashgate.

2007. *Reading Orientalism: Said and the Unsaid*. Seattle, WA: University of Washington Press.

2009. Agriculture in Al-Hamdānī's Yemen: A Survey from Early Islamic Geographical Texts, *Journal of the Economic and Social History of the Orient* 52, 382–412.

Vavilov, N.I., 1951. *The Origin, Variation, Immunity, and Breeding of Cultivated Plants: Selected Writings*. Waltham, MS: Chronica Botanica.

Verhoeven, M., 2005. Ethnoarchaeology, Analogy, and Ancient Society, in *Archaeologies of the Middle East: Critical Perspectives*, eds. S. Pollock & R. Bernbeck. Malden, MA: Blackwell, 251–70.

Vita-Finzi, C. & E.S. Higgs, 1970. Prehistoric Economy in the Mount Carmel Area of Palestine: Site Catchment Analysis, *Proceedings of the Prehistoric Society* 36, 1–42.

Vogel, H., 1987. Terrace Farming in Yemen, *Journal of Soil and Water Conservation* 42(1), 18–21.

Vogt, B., 2004. Towards a New Dating of the Great Dam of Marib: Preliminary Results of the 2002 Fieldwork of the German Institute of Archaeology, *Proceedings of the Seminar for Arabian Studies* 34, 377–88.

Vogt, B. & A. V Sedov, 1998. The Sabir Culture and Coastal Yemen during the Second Millennium BC – the Present State of Discussion, *Proceedings of the Seminar for Arabian Studies* 28, 261–70.

Vogt, B., V. Buffa & U. Brunner, 2002. Ma'layba and the Bronze Age Irrigation in Coastal Yemen, *Archäologische Berichte aus dem Yemen* 9, 15–26.

# Bibliography

Wahl, R.W., 1989. *Markets for Federal Water: Subsidies, Property Rights, and the Bureau of Reclamation*. Washington, D.C.: Resources for the Future.

Wallace, M., G. Jones, M. Charles, R. Fraser, P. Halstead, T.H.E. Heaton & A. Bogaard, 2013. Stable Carbon Isotope Analysis as a Direct Means of Inferring Crop Water Status and Water Management Practices, *World Archaeology* 45(3), 388–409.

Walton, J., 1992. *Western Times and Water Wars*. Berkeley, CA: University of California Press.

Ward, C., 2009. Water Conflict in Yemen: The Case for Strengthening Local Resolution Mechanisms, in *Water in the Arab World: Management Perspectives and Innovations*, eds. N.V. Jagannathan, A.S. Mohamed & A. Kremer. Washington, D.C.: The World Bank, 233–68.

Weisiger, M., 2004. The Origins of Navajo Pastoralism, *Journal of the Southwest* 46(2), 253–82.

Weiss, B.G., 1998. *The Spirit of Islamic Law*. Athens, GA: University of Georgia Press.

Wendorf, F. & R. Schild, 1994. Are the Early Holocene Cattle in the Eastern Sahara Domestic or Wild?, *Evolutionary Anthropology* 3(4), 118–28.

1998. Nabta Playa and its Role in Northeastern African Prehistory, *Journal of Anthropological Archaeology* 17, 97–123.

Wendorf, F., R. Schild & A. Close (eds.), 1989. *The Prehistory of Wadi Kubbaniya, Vols. 1 and 2*. Dallas, TX: Southern Methodist University Press.

Wendrich, W. & G. van der Kooij, 2002. *Moving Matters: Ethnoarchaeology of the Near East*. Leiden: University of Leiden.

Wengrow, D., 2001. Rethinking "Cattle Cults" in Early Egypt: Towards a Prehistoric Perspective on the Narmer Palette, *Cambridge Archaeological Journal* 1, 91–104.

Wengrow, D., M. Dee, S. Foster, A. Stevenson & C.B. Ramsey, 2014. Cultural Convergence in the Neolithic of the Nile Valley: A Prehistoric Perspective on Egypt's Place in Africa, *Antiquity* 88, 95–111.

Western, D. & V. Finch, 1986. Cattle and Pastoralism: Survival and Production in Arid Lands, *Human Ecology* 14(1), 77–94.

Wetterstrom, W., 1993. Foraging and Farming in Egypt: The Transition from Hunting and Gathering to Horticulture in the Nile Valley, in *The Archaeology of Africa: Food, Metals and Towns*, eds. T. Shaw, P. Sinclair, B. Andah & A. Okpoko. London: Routledge, 165–226.

White, D.A. & S.L. Surface-Evans, 2012. *Least Cost Analysis of Social Landscapes: Archaeological Case Studies*. Salt Lake City: The University of Utah Press.

White, R., 1991. *"It's Your Misfortune and None of My Own": A New History of the American West*. Norman, OK: University of Oklahoma Press.

1994. *Frederick Jackson Turner and Buffalo Bill*, in ed. J.R. Grossman. Berkeley, CA: University California Press, 7–66.

1995. *The Organic Machine: The Remaking of the Columbia River*. New York, NY: Hill and Wang.

Widtsoe, J.A., 1911. *Dry-Farming*. New York: The Macmillan Company.

Wilber, C.D., 1881. *The Great Valley and Prairies of Nebraska and the Northwest*. Omaha, NE: Daily Republican Printing Company.

Wilkinson, J.C., 1983. Traditional Concepts of Territory in South East Arabia, *The Geographical Journal* 149(3), 301–15.
1990. Muslim Land and Water Law, *Journal of Islamic Studies* 1(1), 54–72.
Wilkinson, T.J., 1999. Settlement, Soil Erosion and Terraced Agriculture in Highland Yemen: A Preliminary Statement, *Proceedings of the Seminar for Arabian Studies* 29, 183–91.
2003a. *Archaeological Landscapes of the Near East*. Tucson, AZ: The University of Arizona Press.
2003b. The Organization of Settlement in Highland Yemen during the Bronze and Iron Ages, 33 33, 157–68.
2005. Soil Erosion and Valley Fills in the Yemen Highlands and Southern Turkey: Integrating Settlement, Geoarchaeology, and Climate Change, *Geoarchaeology* 20(2), 169–92.
2006. From Highland to Desert: The Organization of Landscape and Irrigation in Southern Arabia, in *Agricultural Strategies*, eds. J. Marcus & C. Stanish. Los Angeles, CA: Cotsen Institute of Archaeology, University of California, 38–70.
2009. Environment and Long-Term Population Trends in Southwest Arabia, in *The Evolution of Human Populations in Arabia*, eds. M.D. Petraglia & J.I. Rose. Dordrecht: Springer Netherlands, 51–66.
2013. Hydraulic Landscapes and Irrigation Systems of Sumer, in *The Sumerian World*, ed. H. Crawford. New York: Routledge, 33–54.
2014. Comparative Landscape Analysis: Contrasting the Middle East and Maya Regions, *Archaeological Papers of the American Anthropological Association* 24(1), 183–200.
Wilkinson, T.J. & L. Rayne, 2010. Hydraulic Landscapes and Imperial Power in the Near East, *Journal of Water History* 2 (2), 115–144.
Wilkinson, T.J., R. Boucharlat, M.W. Ertsen, G. Gillmore, D. Kennet, P. Magee, K. Rezakhani & T. De Schacht, 2012. From Human Niche Construction to Imperial Power: Long-Term Trends in Ancient Iranian Water Systems, *Water History* 4(2), 155–76.
Wilkinson, T.J., G. Philip, J. Bradbury, R. Dunford, D. Donoghue, N. Galiatsatos, D. Lawrence, A. Ricci & S.L. Smith, 2014. Contextualizing Early Urbanization: Settlement Cores, Early States and Agro-pastoral Strategies in the Fertile Crescent During the Fourth and Third Millennia BC, *Journal of World Prehistory* 27, 43–109.
Willcox, G., 2005. The Distribution, Natural Habitats and Availability of Wild Cereals in Relation to Their Domestication in the Near East: Multiple Events, Multiple Centres, *Vegetation History and Archaeobotany* 14(4), 534–41.
Wills, W.H. & W.B. Dorshow, 2012. Agriculture and Community in Chaco Canyon: Revisiting Pueblo Alto, *Journal of Anthropological Archaeology* 31(2), 138–55.
Wilson, J., 1990. *Lawrence of Arabia: The Authorized Biography of T.E. Lawrence*. New York: Atheneum.
Wilson, P., 2012. Waterways, Settlements and Shifting Power in the North-western Nile Delta, *Water History* 4, 95–117.
Wilson, P.N., 2002. Economic Science and the Central Arizona Project: Lessons Learned, *Journal of Contemporary Water Research and Education* 123(1), 30–37.

# Bibliography

Winterhalder, B. & D.J. Kennett, 2009. Four Neglected Concepts with a Role to Play in Explaining the Origins of Agriculture, *Current Anthropology* 50(5), 645–48.

Winterhalder, B. & E.A. Smith, 2000. Analyzing Adaptive Strategies: Human Behavioral Ecology at Twenty-five, *Evolutionary Anthropology* 9(2), 51–72.

Winter-Livneh, R., T. Svoray & I. Gilead, 2010. Settlement Patterns, Social Complexity and Agricultural Strategies during the Chalcolithic Period in the Northern Negev, Israel, *Journal of Archaeological Science* 37, 284–94.

Wissler, C., 1914. The Influence of the Horse in the Development of Plains Culture, *American Anthropologist* 16(1), 1–25.

Witschi, N.S. (ed.), 2011. *A Companion to the Literature and Culture of the American West*. Hoboken, NJ: Wiley & Sons.

Wittfogel, K.A., 1935. The Foundations and Stages of Chinese Economic History, *Zeitschrift fur Sozialforschung* 4(1), 26–60.

1938. Die Theorie der Orientalischen Gesellschaft, *Zeitschrift fur Sozialforschung* 7, 90–122.

1955. Developmental Aspects of Hydraulic Societies, in *Irrigation Civilizations: A Comparative Study*. Washington, D.C.: Pan American Union, 43–53.

1957. *Oriental Despotism: A Comparative Study of Total Power*. New Haven, CT: Yale University Press.

1972. The Hydraulic Approach to Pre-Spanish Mesoamerica, in *The Prehistory of the Tehuacan Valley, Vol. 4, Chronology and Irrigation*, ed. F. Johnson. Austin, TX: University of Texas Press, 59–80.

Wolf, E.R., 1964. *Europe and the People Without History*. Berkeley, CA: University of California Press.

Wong, D., 2009. The Modifiable Areal Unit Problem (MAUP), in *The Sage Handbook of Spatial Analysis*, eds. A.S. Fotheringham & P. Rogerson. London: SAGE, 105–24.

Woodbury, R.B., 1961. A Reappraisal of Hohokam Irrigation, *American Anthropologist* 63(3), 550–60.

Worster, D., 1979. *The Dust Bowl: The Southern Plains in the 1930's*. Oxford: Oxford University Press.

1985. *Rivers of Empire: Water, Aridity, and the Growth of the American West*. Oxford: Oxford University Press.

1992. *Under Western Skies: Nature and History in the American West*. Oxford: Oxford University Press.

2001. *A River Running West: The Life of John Wesley Powell*. Oxford: Oxford University Press.

Wylie, A., 1982. An Analogy by Any Other Name is Just as Analogical: A Commentary on the Gould-Watson Dialogue, *Journal of Anthropological Archaeology* 1, 382–401.

1985. The Reaction against Analogy, *Advances in Archaeological Method and Theory* 8, 63–111.

Yoffee, N., 1993. Too Many Chiefs? (or, Safe Texts for the 90's), in *Archaeological Theory: Who Sets the Agenda?*, eds. N. Yoffee & A. Sherratt. Cambridge: Cambridge University Press, 60–78.

2005. *Myths of the Archaic State: Evolution of the Earliest Cities, States, and Civilizations*. Cambridge: Cambridge University Press.

Yukich, S.T.K., 2013. *Spatial Dimensions of Social Complexity: Environment, Economy, and Settlement in the Jabbul Plain, 3000–550 BC, PhD Dissertation*. Baltimore, MD: Johns Hopkins University.

Yule, P., 2013a. A Late Antique Christian King from Zafar, Southern Arabia. *Antiquity* 87, 1124–1135.

2013b. *Zafar, Capital of Himyar, Rehabilitation of a 'Decadent' Society, Excavations of the Ruprecht-Karls-Universitat Heidelberg 1998–2010 in the Highlands of the Yemen*. Wiesbaden: Deutsche Orient-Gesellschaft.

Zarins, J., 1992. Pastoral Nomadism in Arabia: Ethnoarchaeology and the Archaeological Record – a Case Study, in *Pastoralism in the Levant, Archaeological Materials in Anthropological Perspectives*, eds. O. Bar-Yosef & A. Khazanov. Madison, WI: Prehistory Press, 219–40.

1998. View from the South: The Greater Arabian Peninsula, in *The Prehistoric Archaeology of Jordan*, ed. D.O. Henry: BAR International Series 705, 179–94.

Zavala, B.M., 2012. Terraced Lives: Cerros de Trincheras in the Northwest/Southwest, in *The Oxford Handbook of North American Archaeology*, ed. T. Pauketat. Oxford: Oxford University Press, 585–96.

Zeder, M.A., 2011. The Origins of Agriculture in the Near East, *Current Anthropology* 52(S4), S221–S235.

Zeder, M.A. & B.D. Smith, 2009. A Conversation on Agricultural Origins, *Current Anthropology* 50(5), 681–90.

Zohary, D. & M. Hopf, 2000. *Domesticated Plants of the Old World, Third Edition*. Oxford, UK: Oxford University Press.

Zvelebil, M., 2009. Choice and Necessity: A View from the Old World on the Origins and Dispersal of Agriculture, *Current Anthropology* 50(5), 699–702.

Zwettler, M., 2000. Ma'add in Late-Antique Arabian Epigraphy and Other Pre-Islamic Sources, *Wiener Zeitschrift fur die Kunde des Morgenlandes* 90, 223–309.

# Index

a'adhs (also *mata'ir*, surveyors), 123
Abraha (of Aksum), 129, 147–49
Adams, Robert McCormick, 34, 50, 54, 75, 160
Aden, 117
agriculture
   *ak-ciñ* arroyo mouth, 69
   beginnings of
      core regions, 43, 46, 56, 71
      explanations for, 42
      Yemen, 41–46
   Bronze Age, 116–20
   dry-farming, 65–66, 102
   incipient, 65–72
   Native American, 18
   rainfed, 7, 8, 44, 65, 68, 116, 147, 150, 158
   small-scale, 147
   spring water, 147
   terrace, 69, 71, 98, 102, 117, 147, 148, 158
      *trinchera* (trench), 69, 71
      Yemen and, 71
   water and, 44–46
   ancient transitions to, 156–58
Aksum Empire, 147
Al Qaeda, 162
al-Barīra, 142
al-Binā, 142
Albright, Frank P. and William F., 22
al-Hamdānī, al-Ḥasan ibn Aḥmad, 18, 149, 153
Al-Hazm (capital of Jawf Governate), 139
*al-Iklil* (*The Crown*, al-Hamdani), 18
American Dream, 12, 79
American Foundation for the Study of Man (AFSM) expedition (1950–52), 19, 22

American West (1800–1950), 3, 69, 101–2, 113, 133, 160, 164
   ancient Yemen and, 47–49, 55, 69–72, 156
   incursive expansion and, 23
   stereotypes, 9, 52
*Anthropology as Cultural Critique* (Marcus and Fischer), 32
Apache, Chiricahua, 59
*Apologies to Thucydides. Understanding History as Culture and Vice Versa* (Sahlins), 33
*Arab* (defining), 85
Arabia, southwest
   agricultural origins, 109–11
   irrigation, 97–104
   pastoralism, 86–93
   spatial dimensions of water flow, 93–97
   spatial heterogeneity, 150–52
Archaeological Mission to Jawf-Hadramawt (HDOR), 87
archaeology
   post-colonial, 21
   spatial
      future of, 49–50
      traits of effective explanations (Foeglin), 31
archetypes
   American West, 11–22, 154
   Arabia, 11–22, 154
Arnaud, Joseph, 19, 118
*asabiyyah* (group-feeling), 16
Ash-Shumah (Yemen), 62
Aughey, Jr., Samuel, 51
Awsan Kingdom, 7, 137
Awwam Temple at Ma'rib, 22

badu (nomads), 16
baptism (Christian), 16
Baquhaizel, S. A., 123
Bean, L. J., 59
Beeston, Alfred, 131
Bell, Gertrude, 61
Betts, A., 62
Bhabha, H. K., 9
*Big Country* (1958), 13
Binford, L. R., 31
Bisharien (Beja, Red Sea Hills, Sudan), 64
Bowen, Richard, 19, 22, 140
Brunner, U., 7, 118, 134, 141
Bulbeck, D., 56
Butzer, Karl, 73

California Constitution of 1849, 104
Campbell, A. H., 58
canals, 53, 143
　Alamo (1900), 115
　All-American, 115
　Choga Mami (Iraq), 67
　earthen, 144
　flashflood diversion into, 119
　Hohokam, 74, 76, 124
　Islamic access restrictions, 16, 103
　Mesopotamia, 78
　*saqi*, 123
Çatalhöyük (Turkey), 92
Caton, Steven, 20–21, 23
Caton-Thompson, Gertrude, 19, 87, 144
Central Arizona Project (1968-), 116
Central Valley Project (1933- ), 116
Cerro Juanaqueña, 71
Chalcolithic period, 67
Charbonnier, J., 144, 146
Childe, V. G., 52
*Chinatown* (1974), 13
cinema, American, 13, 20–21
cisterns, 16, 53, 62, 66
　Hadramawt, 131
　rock-cut (*naqab*), 140
　Tawila, near Aden, 18
Clark, William, 13
Clarke, David, 34
climates, 38
Cody, Buffalo Bill, 13
Colorado Doctrine, 104
Colorado River Basin, 164
Colorado River Compact of 1922, 133
*Coming of Age in Samoa* (Mead), 32

*Comparative Archaeology of Complex Societies* (Smith), 31
Crassard, Rémy, 87, 88
*Creation of Inequality, The. How Our Prehistoric Ancestors Set the Stage for Monarchy, Slavery and Empire* (Flannery and Marcus), 49
Crockett, Davy, 13
crop cultivation, 7, 29, 39, 53, 63, 69
　ancient Yemen, 41
　irrigation and, 79, 116, 127
　barley, 70, 98, 100
　beans, 55
　chickpeas, 98
　forager-pastoralism and, 97
　lentils, 70, 98
　maize, 55, 69, 71, 158
　millet, 70
　　broomcorn, 98
　peas, 98
　requirements for, 73
　sorghum, 69
　squash, 55
　wheat, 70, 98, 100
culture
　change, theory of (Stewart), 30, 31
　core, 30
　material, 159
　　Hohokam, 124
　nature and, 99
　Trincheras, 71
　water and, 50, 154
*Culture and Imperialism* (Said), 8

dams, 53
　al-Mabna, 149
　check, 99
　Glen Canyon (1966), 74
　Hoover (1936), 13, 74, 115–16, 133, 151, 153
　Ma'rib, Great Dam at, 18, 41, 48, 81, 113, 118, 127–30, 137, 145, 147–50, 151, 153
　　collapse (575 AD), 2
　St. Francis, 1928 collapse, 1
Darbas, 142
de Châtel, F., 41
De Maigret, A., 126
debitage (Paleolithic Levallois), 87
Desert Land Act of 1877, 114
Dhamar Governate, 117

# Index

Digital Elevation Model (DEM), 37, 95, 106
*Dirt. The Erosion of Civilizations* (Montgomery), 145
dolmen monuments, 157
domestication, 43
  ancient Yemen and, 61, 86
  animal, 6
    provisioning, 62
    water control for, 78
    Yemen, 157
  camels, 82, 126, 132, 159
  caprines, 82, 157
  cattle, 62, 82, 86, 93–97, 98, 157
    sacrifice, 92–93, 157
  crop, 44, 58, 61, 65
  goats, 86
  horses, 60, 82, 157
  maize, 102
  Neolithic, 52
  plants, 86, 97
  sheep, 86
  water, 67
Doolittle, W. E., 68, 102
Doyel, D. E., 151
drought, 111, 150

Earle, T., 151
Eaton, Fred, 80
ecology
  cultural, 30
  human behavioral, 101
  rangeland, 63
*El Dorado* (1966), 13
erosion, 38, 71, 93, 95, 100, 108, 145, 164
ethnography (defined), 30
ethnology, multi-sited, and juxtaposition, 31–33
Evans-Pritchard, Sir Edward, 20
Ezana, King (of Aksum), 129, 147

Fakhry, Ahmed, 19
Fasad peoples, 90
Finlayson, C., 54, 89
*first in time, first in right*, 103, 133
Fischer, Michael, 32
Flannery, Kent, 49, 65, 71, 114
Fogelin, Lars, 31
Francaviglia, V. M., 118
frankincense, 126, 142, 159
Fuller, Dorian, 57

Gardner, Elinor, 19, 144
gathering, 12, 32, 82, 92, 157
  ancient Yemen, 54–59, 85
  meta-structural social logic of, 159
  ritual, 110
Geertz, C., 49
Gentelle, P., 119, 143
Geographic Information System (GIS), 30, 35
geopolitics, 50, 153–54
  commonalities, 22–28
  contemporary conflicts, 22–28
Glaser, Edward, 19
Global Positioning System (GPS), 30, 35
Google Earth, 36
*Grapes of Wrath, The* (Steinbeck), 24
Greeley, Horace, 79

Hackenberg. R. A., 59
hadar (settled-folk), 16
*hadith* (teachings and practices of The Prophet Mohammed), 16
Hadramawt
  Governate, 94
  Kingdom, 7, 137, 142
  region, 122
  region (Yemen), 38, 41, 93
Haefner, H., 7, 134
Hajar am-Dhaybiyya, 142
Hajar ar-Rayhani, 127
Hajar bin Humeid, 127, 140
Hajar Yahirr (Kingdom of Awsan), 119, 134, 141
Hammat al-Qa, 117
Haraway, D. J., 36
Hard, R. J., 71
Harris, David, 56
Hayt al-Suad, 98
Headland, T. N., 56
headworks, 144
Hehmeyer, I., 16
Henton, Elizabeth, 94
herding, 86
heterogeneity, spatial
  contextual, 37
  defined, 112
  key resources, 72
  water, 4, 5, 7, 54, 74, 77, 132, 134, 150–52, 154, 161
  state formation and, 78

*High-Value Target. Countering Al-Qaeda in Yemen* (Hull), 24
Holocene pluvial period, 38
　foraging in, 56
Homestead Act of 1862, 79, 114
homesteading, 13
Hopf. M., 56
Houthi insurgents, 162
Hull, Edmund, 23
Human Behavioral Ecology (Kennett and Winterhalder), 59
Hunt, Robert, 124
hunting, 32, 82, 157
　ancient Yemen, 54–59, 85
Huot, J.-L., 47
Hureidha (Wadi 'Amd), 19, 144
hydraulic hypothesis (Wittfogel), 11, 47, 53, 73, 75–77, 160
　beyond, 83

Ibn al-Mujawir, Yūsuf, 18
Ibn Battuta, Muhammad, 18
Ibn Khaldūn, 'Abd-ar-Rahmān, 16, 61, 85
incense, 40, 145
inscriptions
　construction, 130
　　canals, 41
　　cisterns, 41
　　wells, 41
　date-palm stalk, 159
　foundation, 146
　importance of water and, 40
　irrigation and, 113, 125, 127, 141, 142, 144
　　Ma'rib, 127
　Karib'il Watar bin Damar'ali, 128
　Ma'rib dam, 128–30
　　sluice, 128
　　stelae, 129
　　　boundary, 131
　　　Great Dam at Ma'rib, 147
　　temple, 128
Intertropical Convergence Zone (ITCZ), 95, 105
irrigation, 7
　*aflaj*, 45
　agriculture and, 44–46
　among chiefdoms, kingdoms, and states and, 72–82
　Bronze Age, 116–20
　civilization and, 30, 46
　crop agriculture and, in southern Arabia, 39
　diversion channels, 99
　flash floodwater (*sayl*), 68, 127, 140, 163
　flood-recession, 53
　floodwater, 137, 158
　hill-slope runoff, 67, 102
　ill-conceived, in the American West, 114
　in contemporary California, 150
　in contemporary Yemen, 151
　incipient agriculture and, 64–72
　inferred, 68
　intermediate scale
　　comparative perspective, 120–25
　　defined, 120
　Iron Age, 125–34, 142, 144
　　Kingdom of Himyar and rise of Highland Power, 144–50
　large-scale, 150, 160
　　centrally-managed, 7, 75, 83
　　defining, 76, 120
　　Yemen, 117, 145
　　Mesopotamia, 77
　*naqab*, 140
　organizational requirements for large-scale, 10
　pastoralism and, 60–64
　rainfall and, 148
　*sayl*, 117
　small-scale
　　American West, 102
　　Ancient Yemen, 102, 117, 121, 150
　spate, 53
　spring flow ('*ayn* and *ghayl*), 68
　spring-fed, 69
　surface runoff (*mudarrajât* and *shrûj*), 68, 95
　systems, 47
　underground infiltration galleries (*qanâts* and *aflaj*), 53, 68, 119
*Irrigation without Agriculture* (Stewart), 55
Islamic State (ISIS), 162

Jackson, Andrew, 13
Jackson, John Brinckerhoff, 39
*Jahiliyya* (The Age of Ignorance), 149
Jamme, Albert, 22
Jebel Faya (UAE), 88
Jubabat al-Juruf (Yemen), 70, 98
juxtaposition, contrastive, 23, 50, 154
　defined, 4

# Index

*kabir* (leader), 130
Kahrl, William, 26
Kaleb, King (of Aksum), 129, 147
Karib'il Watar bin Damar'ali, 127, 160
Kersel, M., 162
Kfar HaHoresh (Israel), 92
*khiyyl* (irrigation manager), 123
Kheshiya, 92, 93
Khuzma-as-Shumlya (Khuzmum), 89, 98
Khuzmum Rockshelters (Wadi Sana), 87
*King of the Pecos* (1936), 13
Kingdom of Qatabān, 139
Krajeski, Thomas, 24
Kroeber, A. L., 59

Lake Mead, 164
Lake Powell, 164
landforms and landcover
    class definitions, 91
    classifying, 37
*Law of the Ranger* (1937), 13
*Lawrence of Arabia* (1962), 20–21
Lawton, H. W., 59
Le Houérou, Henri-Noël, 63
Levantine peoples, 110
Lewis, Meriwether, 13
*lijna* (water-users' committees), 123, 165
Lincoln, Abraham, 14, 160
lithics
    Early Holocene, 87, 91
    Paleolithic, 87
Los Angeles-Owens Valley Aqueduct (1913), 1, 80, 112
Lucero, Lisa, 76, 151
Luke, Christina, 162

*Ma'add* (kind of nomadism and warfare), 85
Ma'in Kingdom, 7, 137, 138
Ma'layba, 117
Ma'rib (Kingdom of Saba), 118, 134, 137, 146
Mabry, J. B., 68, 102
Makarewicz, Cheryl, 61
*malik* (king), 113
Manayzah, 91
Marcus, George, 32, 33
Marcus, Joyce, 49
Martin, Louise, 92
*Mawla Matar* (Patron of Rain), 16
McCorriston, J., 63, 86
McGee, W. J., 65
*mdrr* (controller of irrigation), 130

Mead, Margaret, 32
Mesopotamia, 160
*mikveh* traditions (Jewish), 16
Mithen, Steven, 67
MOMS (Modular Optoelectronic Multispectral Scanner) satellite imagery, 7
Montgomery, David, 145
Morris, Ian, 27, 162
Mouton, M., 132
Mujahid Nur al-Din Ali, King, 18
*mukarrib* (honorific title), 113
Mulholland, William, 80

Nabhan, G. P., 69
Navajo (Diné) Indians, 101
Nebes, Norbert, 149
*Necessity for Ruins, The* (Jackson), 39
*Need of Being Versed in Country Things, The* (Jackson), 39
Nuer (southern Sudan), 64
nut-grass (*Cyperus rotundus*, *Cyperus esculentus*), 56

O'Connell, J. F., 58
O'odham (Papago) Indians (Arizona), 59, 69
Oches, Eric, 100
*Oklahoma Frontier* (1938), 13
Oklahoma Land Rush, 84
Oman
    Bronze Age, 119
    Sultanate of, 162
*Once Upon a Time in the West* (1969), 13
Optically Stimulated Luminescence (OSL) dating, 100
*Organic Machine, The. The Remaking of the Columbia River* (White), 53
Oriental Despotism, 10
*Orientalism* (Said), 8
Owen's Valley (California), 55

Paiute Indians (Owen's Valley, California), 55, 57
Paleolake Mundafan (Saudi Arabia), 87
pastoralism
    forager-, 61
    irrigation and, 60–64
    specialized, 61
        irrigation and, 61
Phillips, Wendell, 22
phytoliths, cereal, 68

pixel size, 36
polities
    complex
        American West and, 74
        ancient, 83
        communality and, 117
        emergence of, 126, 131
        Ethiopia, 148
        irrigation and, 77, 93, 125
            ancient Yemen, 74
        Mesopotamia, 77
        pre-Islamic, 149
        rise of, 46–49, 158–61
        Southwest Arabia, 150–52
        spatial heterogeneity and, 134
        water scarcity and, 4, 10
        water-sharing, 132
    defined, 11
    spatial heterogeneity and, 54, 74, 77
Pottery Neolithic (ca. 7000 BC) period, 67
Powell, John Wesley, 74, 165
precipitation, 104, 118
    flooding, 107, 108
    Yemen, 116
Pre-Pottery Neolithic (PPN) period, 88
Pre-Pottery Neolithic A (PPNA) period, 66
Pre-Pottery Neolithic B (PPNB, c. 8700–7000 BC) period, 67, 87
projectile points
    el-Khiam, 88
    Fasad, 87, 89, 110
    Faya, 88
    Helwan, 88
    Rub al-Khali, 90

Qabr Hud, 41
Qal'at Habshiya (Iron Age hillfort), 148
Qarnaw, 134
*Qataban and Sheba. Exploring the Ancient Kingdoms on the Biblical Spice Routes of Arabia* (Phillips), 22
Qatabān Kingdom, 7, 127, 137
*qayl* (a prince or lord), 130
*qdm* (leader, commander, manager or supervisor), 130

*ra'ad* (canal operators), 123
*rain follows the plow*, 51, 82
Ramlat as-Sab'atayn Desert, 7, 40, 116, 126, 132, 135, 151, 159
Raybun (Wadi Daw'an, Iron Age town), 125, 127, 144

Rayne, Louise, 76
Reclamation Act, 115
Reid, L. A., 56
Reisner, M., 153
*Riders of Destiny* (1933), 13
Rindos, David, 56
Robbins, Paul, 37
Robin, C. J., 146
Rodionov, Mikhail, 123
Roots of Agriculture in Southern Arabia (RASA) Project, 86, 98–101
Rub al-Khali (Empty Quarter, Arabia), 116

Saba Kingdom, 7, 138, 144
Sabir, 117
Sahlins, Marshall, 33, 49
Said, Edward, 8
Salalah (Oman), 143
*salat al-istisqa* (prayer for rain), 16
salinity, soil, 146
Salton Sea, 115
samḥ (*Mesembryanthemum forsskalei*) wild grain, 101
Sasanians of Persia, 147
satellite imagery, 30, 35
    Advanced Spaceborne Thermal Emission and Reflection Radiometer (ASTER), 96, 106
    multispectral, 36
    resolution, 36
        radiometric, 36
        spatial, 37
        temporal, 37
scalability, 34
Scarborough, V. L., 151
Schiettecatte, J., 132, 146
Schild, R., 62
segmentary lineage system, 20
Serjeant, R. B., 122
Shabwa (Kingdom of Hadramawt), 119, 127, 134, 142
*sharia* (Islamic law. Literally, path to a watering place), 16
Sherratt, Andrew, 44, 57
Shi'b Kheshiya, 92, 110
Shurahbi'il Ya'fur, 129, 149
Shuttle Radar Topography Mission (SRTM, NASA), 95
*Sifat Jazirat al-Arab*, (*Geography of the Arabian Peninsula*, al-Hamdānī), 18
site catchment analysis, 35

# Index

sluice gates, 144
Smith, B., 56
Snow, Frank H., 51
societies, hydraulic (Wittfogel), 10
Solubba (of Arabia), 62
Southern Dispersal Hypothesis, 54
spatial analysis and theory, 34–37
*Spatial Archaeology* (Clarke), 34
Stahl, Ann, 31
*Stampede* (1949), 13
Steinbeck, John, 24
Steward, Julian, 10, 30, 55, 73
Stockhammer, P. W., 9
Strahler Stream Order, 96
Sumhu'ali Yanuf bin Dhamar'ali, 128
Sumhuram, 143

Tamna', 134, 139
technologies, spatial, 30
Tepe Pardis (Iran), 67
Thomas, Cyrus, 51
Tindale, N. B., 58
tombs, cairn, 39
topography
   American West, 5
   Yemen, 5
Toynbee, Arnold, 150
Trigger, Bruce, 49
Turner, Frederick Jackson, 13, 84

Umm Dabaghiyah (Iraq), 62
*Understanding Early Civilizations. A Comparative Study* (Trigger), 49
United States Reclamation Service (renamed US Bureau of Reclamation, USBR), 115
Uphoff, N., 121

Van Beek, Gus, 22
Varisco, Daniel, 8, 19, 122

wadi
   defined, 64
   outlets, 136
Wadi 'Amd, 19, 144
Wadi 'Atf, 142
Wadi Abu Tulayha (southern Jordan), 67
Wadi al-Kharid, 138
Wadi al-Tayyilah 3, 98
Wadi Bana, 138
Wadi Bayhan (Kingdom of Qataban), 19, 22, 119, 127, 139, 140, 146

Wadi Daw'an Hadramawt, 122, 132, 144, 165
Wadi Dhana, 118
Wadi Dura, 142
Wadi Faynan, 66
Wadi Gufaina, 149
Wadi Hadramawt, 119, 143, 144
Wadi Hammam, 141
Wadi Jawf, 130, 138
Wadi Jirdān, 142
Wadi Kubbaniya (Egypt), 56
Wadi Madhâb, 138
Wadi Marha, 118, 141
Wadi Masila, 143
Wadi Rima, 138
Wadi Sana, 69, 93–97, 99, 148
   spatial dimensions of water flow, 104–9
   watershed, 105–9
Wadi Shumlya, 89
Wadi Surbān, 141
Wadi Surdud, 138
Wadi Tuban, 118, 138
Wadi Zabid, 138
War on Terror, 161–65
*War! What is it Good For?* (Morris), 28
Washington, George, 13
water
   access
      American West, 103
      Islamic law, 16, 21, 103
      riparian rights, 103, 133
   availability
      topography and precipitation and, 134
   availability and periodicity defining environments, 2
   crises, 161–65
   diversion, 67
   flow
      spatial dimensions of Southwest Arabian Kingdoms, 134–44
   histories
      ancient Yemen
         atypical, 52
         comparative perspective, 82–83
      archetypes and, 11–22
      contrastive juxtaposition and, 154–55
      Orientalism and, 8–11
      shaping influences, 38
      spatial analysis and theory, 34–37
      spatial archeology and, 154–55
   human movement and, 54
   importance of, 82

water (*cont.*)
    in ancient contexts, 29, 34, 40
    to Islam, 41
    spatial role of, 4, 150
  as an indispensible resource, 50
  manipulation technologies, 53
  political ideals and, 51
  as thematic, 2, 39
*Water and Power. The Conflict over Los Angeles' Water Supply in the Owen's Valley* (Kahrl), 26
Water Optimization Hypothesis (Finlayson), 54, 89
watersheds, 37
  near wadi outlets, 136
weirs, 144
wells
  cisterns and (*bi'r, birkah, ma'jil, sinâwa*), 68
  diesel pump, 25, 163
  dug, 53, 62, 66
    shallow, 102
  Islamic access restrictions, 16, 103
  submerged, 67
Wendorf, F., 62
Wengrow, D., 63, 131
White, Richard, 13, 53
Wilkinson, Tony, 76, 78, 160
Wittfogel, Karl, 10, 73
Wolf, Eric, 81
*wudu* (Arabic ablution), 16
Wylie, Alison, 31

xenophobia, 161–65

Yalā ad-Durayb, 127
Yemen, ancient (3500 BC - 600 AD), 3, 159
  American West and, 47–49, 55, 69–72, 156
  state-formation factors in, 126
  topography of, 116
Yitha'amar Bayyin, 129

Zafar (capital of Kingdom of Himyar), 145
Zohary, D., 56
Zwettler, M., 85